RUSSIA

KAZAKHSTAN

MONGOLIA

GEORGIA
ARM AZER
TURKEY
SYRIA UZBEK KIRGIZ
LEB TURKMEN TAJIK
ISR OR IRAQ
IRAN AFGH
KUWAIT
BAH
QATAR PAKISTAN NEPAL BHU
SAUDI UAE
ARABIA OMAN INDIA MYANMAR LAOS
ERITREA YEMEN THAILAND VIETNAM
DJIB CAMBODIA
ETHIOPIA
SOMALIA SRI
N KENYA LANKA
BRUNEI
MALAYSIA
SING
TANZANIA
MALAWI
MOZ INDONESIA
MADAGASCAR MAURITIUS
OTHO

CHINA

N.KOREA
S.KOREA JAPAN

HONG
KONG
MACAO TAIWAN

PHILIPPINES

PAPUA
NEW GUINEA

FIJI

AUSTRALIA

NEW ZEALAND

POCKET WORLD IN FIGURES
2006 EDITION

The
Economist

Pocket
World in
Figures
2006 Edition

THE ECONOMIST IN ASSOCIATION WITH
PROFILE BOOKS LTD

Published by Profile Books Ltd,
3A Exmouth House, Pine Street, London EC1R OJH

This edition published by Profile Books in association with
The Economist, 2005

Material researched and compiled by
Andrea Burgess, Marianne Comparet, Ulrika Davies, Mark Doy,
Andrew Gilbert, Conrad Heine, Carol Howard, Stella Jones,
David McKelvey, Keith Potter, Simon Wright

The greatest care has been taken in compiling this book. However
no responsibility can be accepted by the publishers or compile
for the accuracy of the information presented.

Typeset in Officina by MacGuru Ltd
info@macguru.org.uk

Printed in Italy by
Graphicom

A CIP catalogue record for this book is available
from the British Library

ISBN 1 86197 742 5

Contents

CONTENTS

Notes

This 2006 edition of *The Economist Pocket World in Figures*
includes new rankings on such things as births to teenagers,
doing business, foreign investment, maternal mortality, TV
watching, reading, computer/internet use, crime and several
environmental measures. The world rankings consider 182
countries; all those with a population of at least 1m or a GDP
of at least $1bn; they are listed on pages 248–52. The countr
profiles cover 67 major countries. Also included are profiles c
the euro area and the world. The extent and quality of the
statistics available varies from country to country. Every care
has been taken to specify the broad definitions on which the
data are based and to indicate cases where data quality or
technical difficulties are such that interpretation of the
figures is likely to be seriously affected. Nevertheless, figure
from individual countries may differ from standard
international statistical definitions. The term "country" can
also refer to territories or economic entities.

Some country definitions

Macedonia is officially known as the Former Yugoslav Repub
of Macedonia. Data for Cyprus normally refer to Greek Cyprus
only. Data for China do not include Hong Kong or Macau. Fo
countries such as Morocco they exclude disputed areas. Con
refers to the Democratic Republic of Congo, formerly known
Zaire. Congo-Brazzaville refers to the other Congo. Data for
the EU refer to the 15 members as at January 1 2004: Austri
Belgium, Denmark, Finland, France, Germany, Greece,
Ireland, Italy, Luxembourg, Netherlands, Portugal, Spain,
Sweden and the United Kingdom, except where 2003 data is
now available for the 25 members ie, including Cyprus, Czec
Republic, Estonia, Hungary, Latvia, Lithuania, Malta, Polan
Slovakia and Slovenia. The euro area includes all of the 15
except Denmark, Sweden and the United Kingdom.

Statistical basis

The all-important factor in a book of this kind is to be able t
make reliable comparisons between countries. Although th
is never quite possible for the reasons stated above, the be
route, which this book takes, is to compare data for the sam
year or period and to use actual, not estimated, figures
wherever possible. Where a country's data is excessively ou
date, it is excluded, which is the reason there is no country
profile of Iraq in this edition. The research for this edition
The Economist Pocket World in Figures was carried out in 20

using the latest available sources that present data on an
internationally comparable basis. Data, therefore, unless
otherwise indicated, refer to the year ending December 31 2003.

In the country profiles, life expectancy, crude birth, death
and fertility rates are based on 2005–10 averages; human
development indices and energy data are for 2002; marriage
and divorce data refer to the latest year for which figures are
available. Employment, health and education data are for the
latest year between 1999 and 2003.

Other definitions

Data shown in country profiles may not always be consistent
with those shown in the world rankings because the
definitions or years covered can differ. Data may also differ
between two different rankings.

Most countries' national accounts are now compiled on a
GDP basis so, for simplicity, the term GDP has been used
interchangeably with GNP or GNI.

Statistics for principal exports and principal imports are
normally based on customs statistics. These are generally
compiled on different definitions to the visible exports and
imports figures shown in the balance of payments section.

Definitions of the statistics shown are given on the relevant
page or in the glossary on page 246. Figures may not add
exactly to totals, or percentages to 100, because of rounding
or, in the case of GDP, statistical adjustment. Sums of money
have generally been converted to US dollars at the official
exchange rate ruling at the time to which the figures refer.

Energy consumption data are not always reliable,
particularly for the major oil producing countries;
consumption per head data may therefore be higher than in
reality. Energy exports can exceed production and imports
can exceed consumption if transit operations distort trade
data or oil is imported for refining and re-exported.

Abbreviations

	billion (one thousand million)	GNP	Gross national product
	Commonwealth of Independent	GRT	Gross tonnage
	States	ha	Hectare
	European Union	m	million
	kilogram	PPP	Purchasing power parity
	kilometre	trn	trillion (one thousand billion)
	Gross domestic product	...	not available
	Gross national income		

World rankings

Countries: natural facts

Countries: the largest[a]

'000 sq km

1	Russia	17,075		31	Tanzania	945
2	Canada	9,971		32	Nigeria	924
3	China	9,561		33	Venezuela	912
4	United States	9,373		34	Namibia	824
5	Brazil	8,512		35	Pakistan	804
6	Australia	7,682		36	Mozambique	799
7	India	3,287		37	Turkey	779
8	Argentina	2,767		38	Chile	757
9	Kazakhstan	2,717		39	Zambia	753
10	Sudan	2,506		40	Myanmar	677
11	Algeria	2,382		41	Afghanistan	652
12	Congo	2,345		42	Somalia	638
13	Saudi Arabia	2,200		43	Central African Rep	622
14	Greenland	2,176		44	Ukraine	604
15	Mexico	1,973		45	Madagascar	587
16	Indonesia[b]	1,904		46	Kenya	583
17	Libya	1,760		47	Botswana	581
18	Iran	1,648		48	France	544
19	Mongolia	1,565		49	Yemen	528
20	Peru	1,285		50	Thailand	513
21	Chad	1,284		51	Spain	505
22	Niger	1,267		52	Turkmenistan	488
23	Angola	1,247		53	Cameroon	475
24	Mali	1,240		54	Papua New Guinea	463
25	South Africa	1,226		55	Sweden	450
26	Colombia	1,142		56	Morocco	447
27	Ethiopia	1,134			Uzbekistan	447
28	Bolivia	1,099		58	Iraq	438
29	Mauritania	1,031		59	Paraguay	407
30	Egypt	1,000		60	Zimbabwe	391

Mountains: the highest[c]

	Name	Location	Height (m)
1	Everest	Nepal-China	8,848
2	K2 (Godwin Austen)	Pakistan	8,611
3	Kangchenjunga	Nepal-Sikkim	8,586
4	Lhotse	Nepal-China	8,516
5	Makalu	Nepal-China	8,463
6	Cho Oyu	Nepal-China	8,201
7	Dhaulagiri	Nepal	8,167
8	Manaslu	Nepal	8,163
9	Nanga Parbat	Pakistan	8,125
10	Annapurna I	Nepal	8,091
11	Gasherbrum I	Pakistan-China	8,068
12	Broad Peak	Pakistan-China	8,047
13	Xixabangma (Gosainthan)	China	8,046
14	Gasherbrum II	Pakistan-China	8,035

a Includes freshwater. b Excludes East Timor, 14,874 sq km.
c Includes separate peaks which are part of the same massif.

Rivers: *the longest*

	Name	Location	Length (km)
1	Nile	Africa	6,695
2	Amazon	South America	6,516
3	Yangtze	Asia	6,380
4	Mississippi-Missouri system	North America	6,019
5	Ob'-Irtysh	Asia	5,570
6	Yenisey-Angara	Asia	5,550
7	Hwang He (Yellow)	Asia	5,464
8	Congo	Africa	4,667
9	Parana	South America	4,500
10	Mekong	Asia	4,425
11	Amur	Asia	4,416
12	Lena	Asia	4,400
13	Mackenzie	North America	4,250
14	Niger	Africa	4,030
15	Missouri	North America	3,969
16	Mississippi	North America	3,779
17	Murray-Darling	Australia	3,750

Deserts: *the largest*

	Name	Location	Area ('000 sq km)
1	Sahara	Northern Africa	8,600
2	Arabia	SW Asia	2,300
3	Gobi	Mongolia/China	1,166
4	Patagonian	Argentina	673
5	Great Victoria	W and S Australia	647
6	Great Basin	SW United States	492
7	Chihuahuan	N Mexico	450
8	Great Sandy	W Australia	400
9	Sonoran	Mexico/US	310
10	Kyzylkum	Central Asia	300

Lakes: *the largest*

	Name	Location	Area ('000 sq km)
1	Caspian Sea	Central Asia	371
2	Superior	Canada/US	82
3	Victoria	E Africa	69
4	Huron	Canada/US	60
5	Michigan	US	58
6	Aral Sea	Central Asia	34
7	Tanganyika	E Africa	33
8	Great Bear	Canada	31
9	Baikal	Russia	30

Notes: Estimates of the lengths of different rivers vary widely according to the rules adopted concerning the selection of tributaries to be followed, the path to take through a delta, where different hydrological systems begin and end etc. The Nile is normally taken as the world's longest river but some estimates put the Amazon as longer if a southerly path through its delta leading to the River Para is followed. The level of aridity commonly used to delimit desert areas is a mean annual precipitation value equal to 250ml or less.

Population: size and growth

Largest populations, 2003

Millions

1	China	1,304.2	34	Kenya	32.0
2	India	1,065.5	35	Algeria	31.8
3	United States	294.0	36	Canada	31.5
4	Indonesia	219.9	37	Morocco	30.6
5	Brazil	178.5	38	Peru	27.2
6	Pakistan	153.6	39	Uzbekistan	26.1
7	Bangladesh	146.7	40	Uganda	25.8
8	Russia	143.2	41	Venezuela	25.7
9	Japan	127.7	42	Iraq	25.2
10	Nigeria	124.0		Nepal	25.2
11	Mexico	103.5	44	Malaysia	24.4
12	Germany	82.5	45	Saudi Arabia	24.2
13	Vietnam	81.4	46	Afghanistan	23.9
14	Philippines	80.0	47	North Korea	22.7
15	Egypt	71.9	48	Taiwan	22.6
16	Turkey	71.3	49	Romania	22.3
17	Ethiopia	70.7	50	Ghana	20.9
18	Iran	68.9	51	Yemen	20.0
19	Thailand	62.8	52	Australia	19.7
20	France	60.1	53	Sri Lanka	19.1
21	United Kingdom	59.3	54	Mozambique	18.9
22	Italy	57.4	55	Syria	17.8
23	Congo	52.8	56	Madagascar	17.4
24	Myanmar	49.5	57	Côte d'Ivoire	16.6
25	Ukraine	48.5	58	Netherlands	16.1
26	South Korea	47.7	59	Cameroon	16.0
27	South Africa	45.0	60	Chile	15.8
28	Colombia	44.2	61	Kazakhstan	15.4
29	Spain	41.1	62	Cambodia	14.1
30	Poland	38.6	63	Angola	13.6
31	Argentina	38.4	64	Burkina Faso	13.0
32	Tanzania	37.0		Ecuador	13.0
33	Sudan	33.6		Mali	13.0

Largest populations, 2050

Millions

1	India	1,563.0	15	Vietnam	117.
2	China	1,392.0	16	Japan	112.
3	United States	395.0		Russia	112.
4	Pakistan	305.0	18	Iran	102.
5	Indonesia	285.0	19	Turkey	101.
6	Nigeria	258.0	20	Afghanistan	97.
7	Brazil	253.0	21	Kenya	83.
8	Bangladesh	243.0	22	Germany	79.
9	Congo	177.0	23	Thailand	75.
10	Ethiopia	170.0	24	Sudan	67
11	Mexico	139.0		Tanzania	67
12	Philippines	127.0		United Kingdom	67
	Uganda	127.0	27	Colombia	66.
14	Egypt	126.0	28	Iraq	64.

Fastest growing populations, 2000–05
Average annual growth, %

1	United Arab Emirates	6.51	11	Somalia	3.20
2	Qatar	5.86	12	Benin	3.18
3	Afghanistan	4.59	13	Burkina Faso	3.17
4	Eritrea	4.26	14	Yemen	3.13
5	Sierra Leone	4.07	15	Burundi	3.03
6	Kuwait	3.73	16	Congo-Brazzaville	3.02
7	Chad	3.42	17	Guinea-Bissau	3.00
8	Uganda	3.40	18	Mali	2.98
9	Niger	3.39		Mauritania	2.98
10	West Bank and Gaza	3.23	20	Gambia, The	2.85

Slowest growing populations, 2000–05
Average annual growth, %

1	Ukraine	-1.10	11	Moldova	-0.33
2	Georgia	-1.07	12	Kazakhstan	-0.28
3	Bulgaria	-0.69	13	Hungary	-0.25
4	Latvia	-0.57	14	Czech Republic	-0.09
5	Belarus	-0.55	15	Serbia & Montenegro	-0.08
	Estonia	-0.55	16	Poland	-0.06
7	Russia	-0.46	17	Slovakia	0.00
8	Armenia	-0.43		Slovenia	0.00
9	Lithuania	-0.40	19	Germany	0.08
10	Romania	-0.37	20	Lesotho	0.08

Fastest growing populations, 2045–50
Average annual growth, %

1	Uganda	2.39	12	Angola	1.61
2	Niger	2.12	13	Sierra Leone	1.56
3	Burundi	2.10	14	Yemen	1.54
4	Liberia	2.08	15	Guinea	1.45
5	Congo-Brazzaville	2.07	16	Benin	1.44
6	Guinea-Bissau	2.05	17	Somalia	1.42
7	Central African Rep	2.03	18	West Bank and Gaza	1.41
8	Mali	1.84	19	Equatorial Guinea	1.40
9	Afghanistan	1.83	20	Malawi	1.37
10	Burkina Faso	1.75	21	Eritrea	1.36
11	Congo	1.73	22	Mauritania	1.33

Slowest growing populations, 2045–50
Average annual growth, %

1	Ukraine	-1.52	11	Suriname	-0.83
2	Virgin Islands	-1.34	12	Romania	-0.78
3	Georgia	-1.31	13	Armenia	-0.77
4	Cuba	-0.93	14	Poland	-0.70
5	Martinique	-0.92	15	Kazakhstan	-0.69
6	Belarus	-0.91	16	Slovakia	-0.68
7	Lithuania	-0.90		Slovenia	-0.68
8	Latvia	-0.87	18	South Korea	-0.65
9	Andorra	-0.86	19	Croatia	-0.64
10	Moldova	-0.85	20	Czech Republic	-0.62

Population: matters of breeding

Highest fertility rates, 2000–05
Average no. of children per woman

1	Niger	7.91		25	West Bank and Gaza	5.57
2	Afghanistan	7.48		26	Eritrea	5.53
3	Guinea-Bissau	7.10		27	Mozambique	5.51
	Uganda	7.10		28	Madagascar	5.40
5	Mali	6.92		29	Togo	5.37
6	Burundi	6.80		30	Côte d'Ivoire	5.06
	Liberia	6.80		31	Senegal	5.05
8	Angola	6.75		32	Tanzania	5.04
9	Congo	6.70		33	Kenya	5.00
10	Burkina Faso	6.67		34	Central African Rep	4.96
11	Chad	6.65		35	Iraq	4.83
12	Sierra Leone	6.50			Laos	4.83
13	Somalia	6.43		37	Gambia, The	4.75
14	Congo-Brazzaville	6.29		38	Cameroon	4.65
15	Yemen	6.20		39	Guatemala	4.60
16	Malawi	6.10		40	Sudan	4.45
17	Guinea	5.92		41	Bhutan	4.40
18	Equatorial Guinea	5.89		42	Ghana	4.39
19	Benin	5.87		43	Pakistan	4.27
	Ethiopia	5.87		44	Cambodia	4.14
21	Nigeria	5.85		45	Papua New Guinea	4.10
22	Mauritania	5.79		46	Saudi Arabia	4.09
23	Rwanda	5.70		47	Gabon	4.02
24	Zambia	5.65		48	Haiti	3.98

Fertility rates, 2045–50
Average no. of children per woman

Highest				Lowest		
1	Niger	3.64		1	Macau	1.46
2	Burundi	3.48		2	Hong Kong	1.52
3	Uganda	3.36		3	Ukraine	1.67
4	Liberia	3.33		4	Slovakia	1.71
5	Chad	3.31		5	Moldova	1.74
6	Guinea-Bissau	3.24			Slovenia	1.74
7	Afghanistan	3.14		7	Belarus	1.75
8	Mali	3.10		8	Bulgaria	1.76
9	Sierra Leone	3.06			Poland	1.76
10	Congo-Brazzaville	3.01		10	South Korea	1.77
11	Angola	2.98		11	Czech Republic	1.78
	Congo	2.98			Greece	1.78
13	Burkina Faso	2.92			Romania	1.78
14	Equatorial Guinea	2.77		14	Lithuania	1.79
15	Somalia	2.75		15	Cuba	1.80
16	Malawi	2.58		16	Hungary	1.8
17	Guinea	2.52		17	Bosnia	1.8
18	Benin	2.50			Latvia	1.8
	Ethiopia	2.50		19	Singapore	1.8
20	Yemen	2.49				
21	Mauritania	2.44				
22	Zambia	2.43				

Lowest fertility rates, 2000–05

Average no. of children per woman

1	Macau	0.84		Singapore		1.35
2	Hong Kong	0.94	26	Estonia		1.37
3	Ukraine	1.12	27	Austria		1.39
4	Czech Republic	1.17	28	Channel Islands		1.40
5	Slovakia	1.20	29	Switzerland		1.41
6	Slovenia	1.22	30	Portugal		1.47
7	Moldova	1.23	31	Georgia		1.48
	South Korea	1.23	32	Barbados		1.50
9	Belarus	1.24		Malta		1.50
	Bulgaria	1.24	34	Canada		1.51
11	Greece	1.25	35	Macedonia		1.53
12	Latvia	1.26	36	Cuba		1.61
	Poland	1.26		Trinidad & Tobago		1.61
	Romania	1.26	38	Cyprus		1.63
15	Spain	1.27	39	Sweden		1.64
16	Italy	1.28	40	Serbia & Montenegro		1.65
	Lithuania	1.28	41	Belgium		1.66
18	Hungary	1.30		United Kingdom		1.66
19	Bosnia	1.32	43	China		1.70
	Germany	1.32	44	Finland		1.72
21	Armenia	1.33		Netherlands		1.72
	Japan	1.33	46	Luxembourg		1.73
	Russia	1.33	47	Australia		1.75
24	Croatia	1.35		Denmark		1.75

Crude birth rates, 2000–05

Average no. of live births per 1,000 population

Highest			Lowest		
1	Niger	55.2	1	Latvia	7.8
2	Angola	52.3	2	Bulgaria	7.9
3	Somalia	52.1	3	Slovenia	8.3
4	Uganda	50.7	4	Ukraine	8.4
5	Congo	50.2	5	Hong Kong	8.5
6	Liberia	50.0	6	Austria	8.6
7	Guinea-Bissau	49.9		Russia	8.6
	Mali	49.9	8	Estonia	8.7
9	Sierra Leone	49.6		Germany	8.7
10	Chad	48.4		Switzerland	8.7
11	Burkina Faso	47.8	11	Belarus	8.8
12	Afghanistan	47.4		Czech Republic	8.8
13	Yemen	45.0		Hungary	8.8
14	Malawi	44.6		Italy	8.8
15	Burundi	44.2		Lithuania	8.8
	Congo-Brazzaville	44.2	16	Greece	9.1
17	Rwanda	44.0	17	Japan	9.2
18	Equatorial Guinea	43.1		Spain	9.3
19	Guinea	42.9	18	Poland	9.6
20	Ethiopia	42.5	19	Armenia	9.7
21	Zambia	42.2	20	Bosnia	9.7
22	Mauritania	41.8		Macau	9.7
23	Madagascar	41.6		Singapore	10.2

Population: age

Highest median age[a]

Years, 2005

1	Japan	42.9
2	Italy	42.3
3	Germany	42.1
4	Finland	40.9
5	Switzerland	40.8
6	Austria	40.6
	Belgium	40.6
	Bulgaria	40.6
	Croatia	40.6
10	Slovenia	40.2
11	Sweden	40.1
12	Channel Islands	39.7
	Greece	39.7
14	Denmark	39.5
	Latvia	39.5
16	Portugal	39.5
17	France	39.3
	Netherlands	39.3
19	Czech Republic	39.0
	Ukraine	39.0
	United Kingdom	39.0
22	Estonia	38.9
	Hong Kong	38.9
24	Hungary	38.8
25	Canada	38.6
	Spain	38.6
27	Norway	38.2
28	Luxembourg	38.1
	Malta	38.1
30	Bosnia	38.0
31	Belarus	37.8
	Lithuania	37.8
33	Singapore	37.5
34	Russia	37.3
35	Andorra	37.0

Lowest median age[a]

Years, 2005

1	Uganda	14.8
2	Niger	15.5
3	Mali	15.8
4	Burkina Faso	16.2
	Guinea-Bissau	16.2
6	Chad	16.3
	Congo	16.3
	Congo-Brazzaville	16.3
	Liberia	16.3
	Malawi	16.3
11	Yemen	16.5
12	Angola	16.6
13	Afghanistan	16.7
	Zambia	16.7
15	Burundi	17.0
16	West Bank and Gaza	17.1
17	Eritrea	17.4
18	Ethiopia	17.5
	Nigeria	17.5
	Rwanda	17.5
21	Benin	17.6
	Equatorial Guinea	17.6
23	Mozambique	17.7
24	Madagascar	17.8
25	Kenya	17.9
	Somalia	17.9
	Togo	17.9
28	Guinea	18.0
29	Central African Rep	18.1
	Guatemala	18.1
	Swaziland	18.1
32	Senegal	18.2
	Tanzania	18.
34	Mauritania	18.
	Sierra Leone	18.

Highest median age[a]

Years, 2050

1	Macau	54.4
2	South Korea	53.9
3	Martinique	53.0
4	Italy	52.5
5	Japan	52.3
6	Singapore	52.1
7	Slovenia	51.9
	Ukraine	51.9
9	Slovakia	51.8
10	Lithuania	51.7

Lowest median age[a]

Years, 2050

1	Burundi	20.
2	Uganda	20.
3	Liberia	20.
4	Chad	21.
5	Guinea-Bissau	21.
	Niger	21.
7	Equatorial Guinea	21.
8	Congo-Brazzaville	21.
9	Congo	22.
10	Angola	22.

a Age at which there are an equal number of people above and below.

Highest pop. aged 0–14
%, 2005

1	Uganda	50.5
2	Niger	49.0
3	Mali	48.2
4	Guinea-Bissau	47.5
5	Chad	47.3
	Congo	47.3
	Malawi	47.3
8	Burkina Faso	47.2
9	Congo-Brazzaville	47.1
	Liberia	47.1
11	Afghanistan	46.5
	Angola	46.5
13	Yemen	46.4
14	Zambia	45.8
15	West Bank and Gaza	45.5
16	Burundi	45.0
17	Eritrea	44.8
18	Ethiopia	44.5
19	Equatorial Guinea	44.4
20	Nigeria	44.3
21	Benin	44.2
22	Somalia	44.1
23	Madagascar	44.0
	Mozambique	44.0
25	Guinea	43.7
26	Rwanda	43.5
	Togo	43.5
28	Guatemala	43.2
29	Central African Rep	43.0
	Mauritania	43.0
31	Kenya	42.8

Highest pop. aged 60+
%, 2005

1	Japan	26.3
2	Italy	25.6
3	Germany	25.1
4	Sweden	23.4
5	Greece	23.0
6	Austria	22.7
7	Latvia	22.5
8	Belgium	22.4
	Bulgaria	22.4
10	Portugal	22.3
11	Croatia	22.1
12	Switzerland	21.8
13	Estonia	21.6
14	Spain	21.4
15	Finland	21.3
16	United Kingdom	21.2
17	Denmark	21.1
	France	21.1
19	Ukraine	20.9
20	Hungary	20.8
21	Lithuania	20.7
22	Slovenia	20.5
23	Czech Republic	20.0
	Norway	20.0
25	Channel Islands	19.4
26	Romania	19.3
27	Bosnia	19.2
	Netherlands	19.2
29	Malta	18.8
30	Belarus	18.6
31	Serbia & Montenegro	18.5

Highest pop. aged 0–14
%, 2050

1	Burundi	38.5
2	Uganda	37.9
3	Chad	37.0
	Liberia	37.0
5	Niger	36.2
6	Guinea-Bissau	36.1
7	Congo-Brazzaville	35.5
8	Equatorial Guinea	35.0
9	Congo	34.8
10	Angola	33.9
11	Afghanistan	33.1
	Mali	33.1
13	Sierra Leone	32.5
14	Malawi	32.2
15	Burkina Faso	32.1

Highest pop. aged 60+
%, 2050

1	Japan	41.7
2	Italy	41.3
3	Macau	41.2
	South Korea	41.2
5	Martinique	40.3
6	Slovenia	40.2
7	Spain	39.7
8	Czech Republic	39.3
9	Bulgaria	38.8
10	Hong Kong	38.7
	Ukraine	38.7
12	Slovakia	38.6
13	Latvia	38.3
14	Singapore	38.0
15	Lithuania	37.9
	Poland	37.9

Population: sex and teenage births

Most male populations
Number of males per 100 females

1	United Arab Emirates	214
2	Qatar	206
3	Kuwait	150
4	Bahrain	132
5	Oman	128
6	Saudi Arabia	117
7	Greenland	113
8	Jordan	108
9	Afghanistan	107
	Andorra	107
	Brunei	107
	Faroe Islands	107
	Libya	107
14	China	106
	Pakistan	106
	Papua New Guinea	106
17	French Polynesia	105
	Guinea	105
	India	105
	New Caledonia	105
	Niger	105
	Taiwan	105

Most female populations
Number of males per 100 females

1	Latvia	84
2	Estonia	85
	Ukraine	85
4	Armenia	87
	Lesotho	87
	Lithuania	87
	Russia	87
8	Belarus	88
9	Hong Kong	89
	Netherlands Antilles	89
11	Aruba	90
	Georgia	90
	Martinique	90
14	Hungary	91
	Virgin Islands	91
16	Kazakhstan	92
	Moldova	92
	Puerto Rico	92
19	Croatia	93
	Guadeloupe	93
	Macau	93
	Swaziland	93

Births per 1,000 women
Lowest, aged 15-19

1	North Korea	2
2	South Korea	3
3	Japan	4
4	China	5
	Netherlands	5
	Switzerland	5
7	Hong Kong	6
	Italy	6
	Singapore	6
	Spain	6
11	Denmark	7
	Libya	7
	Sweden	7
	Tunisia	7
15	Finland	8
	Slovenia	8
17	Belgium	9
	France	9
19	Greece	10
20	Germany	11
	Norway	11
22	Austria	12
23	Ireland	15

Highest, aged 15-19

1	Niger	233
2	Congo	230
3	Angola	229
4	Liberia	227
5	Somalia	213
6	Sierra Leone	212
7	Uganda	211
8	Guinea-Bissau	197
9	Chad	195
10	Mali	191
11	Guinea	163
	Malawi	163
13	Congo-Brazzaville	146
14	Zambia	14
15	Madagascar	13
16	Burkina Faso	136
17	Nicaragua	13
18	Central African Rep	13
19	Gambia, The	12
20	Cameroon	12
21	Tanzania	12
22	Bangladesh	11
	Nepal	11
24	Côte d'Ivoire	11
25	Eritrea	11

Refugees and asylum seekers[a]

Largest refugee nationalities
'000, 2003

#	Country	Value		#	Country	Value
1	Afghanistan	2,136.0		11	Bosnia	300.0
2	Sudan	606.2		12	Serbia & Montenegro	296.6
3	Burundi	531.6		13	Azerbaijan	253.3
4	Congo	453.4		14	Croatia	230.2
5	West Bank and Gaza	427.8		15	Turkey	185.6
6	Somalia	402.2		16	Myanmar	147.5
7	Iraq	368.4		17	Iran	132.5
8	Vietnam	363.2		18	China	132.4
9	Liberia	353.3		19	Sri Lanka	122.0
10	Angola	323.6		20	Bhutan	104.0

Countries with largest refugee populations
'000, 2003

#	Country	Value		#	Country	Value
1	Pakistan	1,124.3		11	Kenya	237.5
2	Iran	984.9		12	Congo	234.0
3	Germany	960.4		13	Uganda	230.9
4	Tanzania	649.7		14	Zambia	226.7
5	United States	452.6		15	Guinea	184.3
6	China	299.4		16	Algeria	169.0
7	Serbia & Montenegro	291.4		17	India	164.8
8	United Kingdom	276.5		18	Chad	146.4
9	Saudi Arabia	240.8		19	Netherlands	140.9
10	Armenia	239.3		20	Sudan	138.2

Nationality of asylum applications in indust. countries
'000, 2003

#	Country	Value		#	Country	Value
1	Iraq	49.4		11	Colombia	12.4
2	Serbia & Montenegro	32.1		12	Iran	11.6
3	Turkey	29.2		13	Mexico	10.7
4	China	26.3		14	Pakistan	10.1
5	Afghanistan	25.4		15	Algeria	9.8
6	Russia	19.9		16	Sri Lanka	8.8
7	India	14.9		17	Zimbabwe	8.6
8	Nigeria	13.3		18	Georgia	8.4
9	Congo	13.1		19	Armenia	8.2
10	Somalia	12.7		20	Bosnia	8.0

Asylum applications in industrialised countries
'000, 2003

#	Country	Value		#	Country	Value
1	United Kingdom	61.1		10	Norway	16.0
2	United States	60.7		11	Netherlands	13.4
3	France	51.4		12	Czech Republic	11.4
4	Germany	50.5		13	Slovakia	10.3
5	Austria	32.4		14	Greece	8.2
6	Canada	31.9		15	Ireland	7.9
7	Sweden	31.4		16	Poland	6.9
8	Switzerland	21.1		17	Spain	5.7
9	Belgium	16.9		18	Denmark	4.6

a As reported by UNHCR.

City living

Biggest cities[a]
Population m, 2003

1	Tokyo, Japan	35.0	
2	Mexico City, Mexico	18.7	
3	New York[b], USA	18.3	
4	São Paulo, Brazil	17.9	
5	Mumbai, India	17.4	
6	Delhi, India	14.1	
7	Kolkata, India	13.8	
8	Buenos Aires, Argentina	13.0	
9	Shanghai, China	12.8	
10	Jakarta, Indonesia	12.3	
11	Los Angeles[c], USA	12.0	
12	Dhaka, Bangladesh	11.6	
13	Osaka, Japan	11.2	
	Rio de Janeiro, Brazil	11.2	
15	Karachi, Pakistan	11.1	
16	Beijing, China	10.8	
	Cairo, Egypt	10.8	
18	Moscow, Russia	10.5	
19	Manila, Philippines	10.4	
20	Lagos, Nigeria	10.1	
21	Paris, France	9.8	
22	Seoul, South Korea	9.7	
23	Istanbul, Turkey	9.4	
24	Tianjin, China	9.3	
25	Chicago, USA	8.6	
26	Lima, Peru	7.9	
27	London, UK	7.6	
28	Bogotá, Colombia	7.3	
29	Tehran, Iran	7.2	
30	Hong Kong, Hong Kong	7.0	
31	Chennai, India	6.7	
32	Essen, Germany	6.6	
33	Bangkok, Thailand	6.5	
34	Bangalore, India	6.1	
35	Lahore, Pakistan	6.0	
36	Hyderabad, India	5.9	
37	Wuhan, China	5.7	
38	Baghdad, Iraq	5.6	
39	Santiago, Chile	5.5	
40	Kinshasa, Congo	5.3	
	Philadelphia, USA	5.3	
	St Petersburg, Russia	5.3	
43	Miami, USA	5.2	
44	Madrid, Spain	5.1	
	Riyadh, Saudi Arabia	5.1	
46	Belo Horizonte, Brazil	5.0	
47	Ahmadabad, India	4.9	
	Ho Chi Minh City, Vietnam	4.9	
	Shenyang, China	4.9	
	Toronto, Canada	4.9	
51	Chongqing, China	4.8	

Fastest growing cities[d]
Average annual growth, 2000–05, %

1	Beihai, China	11.5	
2	Ghaziabad, India	6.4	
3	Surat, India	6.2	
	Toluca, Mexico	6.2	
5	Faridabad, India	5.4	
6	Kabul, Afghanistan	5.1	
7	Lagos, Nigeria	5.0	
	Las Vegas, USA	5.0	
	Sana'a, Yemen	5.0	
10	Chittagong, Bangladesh	4.9	
11	East Rand, South Africa	4.8	
	Santa Cruz, Bolivia	4.8	
13	Dar es Salaam, Tanzania	4.7	
	Nairobi, Kenya	4.7	
15	Nashik, India	4.6	
16	Suwon, South Korea	4.5	
17	Patna, India	4.4	
18	Bamako, Mali	4.
	Jaipur, India	4.
	Rajkot, India	4.
21	Delhi, India	4.
	Dhaka, Bangladesh	4.
	Valencia, Venezuela	4.
24	Pune, India	4.
25	Riyadh, Saudi Arabia	4.
26	Brasília, Brazil	3.
	Indore, India	3.
	Luanda, Angola	3.
	Lubumbashi, Congo	3.
30	Antananarivo, Madagascar	3.
	Kampala, Uganda	3.
	Tijuana, Mexico	3

a Urban agglomerations of more than 1 million. Data may change from year-to-year based on reassessments of agglomeration boundaries.
b New York–Newark
c Los Angeles–Long Beach–Santa Ana
d Urban agglomerations with a population of at least 1 million in 2003.

Proportion of a country's pop. residing in a single city[a]
%, 2003

1	Hong Kong	100.0
	Singapore	100.0
3	San Juan, Puerto Rico	60.1
4	Beirut, Lebanon	49.1
5	Kuwait City, Kuwait	48.5
6	Tel Aviv, Israel	45.3
7	Montevideo, Uruguay	39.3
8	Tripoli, Libya	36.1
9	Yerevan, Armenia	35.3
10	Santiago, Chile	34.7
11	Buenos Aires, Arg.	34.0
12	Athens, Greece	29.3
13	Lima, Peru	29.1
14	Brazzaville, Congo-Braz.	29.0
15	Auckland, New Zealand	28.8
16	Asunción, Paraguay	27.9
17	Tokyo, Japan	27.4
18	Vienna, Austria	26.8
19	San José, Costa Rica	26.0
20	Dublin, Ireland	25.7
21	Port-au-Prince, Haiti	23.6
22	Amman, Jordan	22.6
23	Baghdad, Iraq	22.3
24	San Salvador, El Sal.	21.9
25	Baku, Azerbaijan	21.7
	Sydney, Australia	21.7
27	Dakar, Senegal	21.5
28	Santo Domingo, Dominican Republic	21.3
29	Riyadh, Saudi Arabia	21.2
30	Tbilisi, Georgia	20.8
31	Helsinki, Finland	20.6

Population living in urban areas

Highest, %, 2003

1	Bermuda	100.0
	Cayman Islands	100.0
	Hong Kong	100.0
	Singapore	100.0
5	Guadeloupe	99.7
6	Macau	98.9
7	Belgium	97.2
8	Puerto Rico	96.7
9	Kuwait	96.3
10	Martinique	95.7
11	Guam	93.7
12	Virgin Islands	93.6
13	Iceland	92.8
14	Uruguay	92.6

Lowest, %, 2003

1	Bhutan	8.5
2	Burundi	9.9
3	Uganda	12.2
4	Papua New Guinea	13.2
5	Nepal	15.0
6	Ethiopia	15.6
7	Malawi	16.3
8	Burkina Faso	17.8
9	Lesotho	17.9
10	Rwanda	18.3
11	Cambodia	18.6
12	Eritrea	19.9
13	Laos	20.7
14	Sri Lanka	21.0
15	Niger	22.2

Quality of life index[e]

Highest, New York=100, Nov. 2004

1	Geneva, Switzerland	106.5
	Zurich, Switzerland	106.5
3	Vancouver, Canada	106.0
	Vienna, Austria	106.0
5	Dusseldorf, Germany	105.5
	Frankfurt, Germany	105.5
	Munich, Germany	105.5
8	Auckland, New Zealand	105.0
	Bern, Switzerland	105.0
	Copenhagen, Denmark	105.0
	Sydney, Australia	105.0

Lowest, New York=100, Nov. 2004

1	Baghdad, Iraq	14.5
2	Bangui, Central Afr. Rep.	29.0
3	Brazzaville, Congo-Braz.	29.5
4	Khartoum, Sudan	31.0
5	Pointe Noire, Congo-Braz.	33.5
6	Ndjamena, Chad	36.5
7	Port Harcourt, Nigeria	37.5
	Sana'a, Yemen	37.5
9	Nouakchott, Mauritania	38.5
10	Ouagadougou, Burk. Faso	39.5
11	Kinshasa, Congo	40.0

e Based on 39 factors ranging from recreation to political stability

The world economy

Biggest economies

GDP, $bn

1	United States	10,948.6	26	Poland	209.6
2	Japan	4,300.9	27	Indonesia	208.3
3	Germany	2,403.2	28	Greece	172.2
4	United Kingdom	1,794.9	29	Finland	161.9
5	France[a]	1,757.6	30	South Africa	159.9
6	Italy	1,468.3	31	Hong Kong	156.7
7	China	1,417.0	32	Ireland	153.7
8	Canada	856.5	33	Portugal	147.9
9	Spain	838.7	34	Thailand	143.0
10	Mexico	626.1	35	Iran	137.1
11	South Korea	605.3	36	Argentina	129.6
12	India	600.6	37	Israel	110.2
13	Australia	522.4	38	Malaysia	103.7
14	Netherlands	511.5	39	Singapore	91.3
15	Brazil	492.3	40	Czech Republic	89.7
16	Russia	432.9	41	Venezuela	85.4
17	Switzerland	320.1	42	Hungary	82.7
18	Belgium	301.9	43	Egypt	82.4
19	Sweden	301.6	44	Pakistan	82.3
20	Taiwan	286.2	45	Philippines	80.6
21	Austria	253.1	46	New Zealand	79.6
22	Turkey	240.4	47	Colombia	78.7
23	Norway	220.9	48	Myanmar[b]	74.5
24	Saudi Arabia	214.7	49	Chile	72.4
25	Denmark	211.9	50	United Arab Emirates[c]	71.0

Biggest economies by purchasing power

GDP PPP, $bn

1	United States	10,923	21	Thailand	471
2	China	6,446	22	Iran	464
3	Japan	3,568	23	Argentina	445
4	India	3,078	24	Poland	435
5	Germany	2,291	25	Philippines	352
6	France	1,654	26	Pakistan	311
7	United Kingdom	1,611	27	Colombia	299
8	Italy	1,563	28	Saudi Arabia	298
9	Brazil	1,376	29	Belgium	294
10	Russia	1,324	30	Egypt	267
11	Canada	970	31	Ukraine	266
12	Mexico	938	32	Bangladesh	244
13	Spain	920	33	Austria	243
14	South Korea	861	34	Sweden	24
15	Indonesia	722	35	Malaysia	230
16	Australia	589	36	Switzerland	22.
17	Taiwan	556	37	Greece	220
18	Turkey	479	38	Vietnam	20
19	Netherlands	476	39	Algeria	19
20	South Africa	474	40	Portugal	18

a Includes overseas departments. b Estimate, purchasing-power parity exchange rate. c
Note: For list of all countries with their GDP see pages 248–252.

Regional GDP

$bn, 2003		% annual growth 1998–2003	
World	36,330	World	3.6
Advanced economies	29,120	Advanced economies	2.4
G7	23,620	G7	2.1
Euro area	8,220	Euro area	1.9
Asia[a]	2,770	Asia[a]	6.6
Latin America	1,760	Latin America	1.4
Eastern Europe[b]	1,411	Eastern Europe[b]	4.9
Middle East	710	Middle East	4.1
Africa	560	Africa	4.6

Regional purchasing power

GDP, % of total		$ per head	
World	100.0	World	8,220
Advanced economies	55.5	Advanced economies	29,510
G7	43.9	G7	31,420
Euro area	15.9	Euro area	26,370
Asia[a]	23.8	Asia[a]	3,820
Latin America	7.6	Latin America	7,470
Eastern Europe[b]	7.0	Eastern Europe[b]	8,120
Middle East	2.8	Middle East	5,890
Africa	3.2	Africa	2,220

Regional population

% of total (6.3bn)		No. of countries[c]	
Advanced economies	15.4	Advanced economies	29
G7	11.4	G7	7
Euro area	5.0	Euro area	12
Asia[a]	52.4	Asia[a]	23
Latin America	8.4	Latin America	33
Eastern Europe[b]	7.5	Eastern Europe[b]	28
Middle East	4.0	Middle East	14
Africa	12.4	Africa	48

Regional international trade

Exports of goods and services, % of tot.		Current account balances, $bn	
Advanced economies	73.4	Advanced economies	-231.9
G7	43.8	G7	-368.9
Euro area	32.0	Euro area	25.8
Asia[a]	10.3	Asia[a]	85.8
Latin America	4.1	Latin America	6.6
Eastern Europe[b]	6.4	Eastern Europe[b]	-0.8
Middle East	3.6	Middle East	33.1
Africa	2.1	Africa	-1.7

a Excludes Hong Kong, Japan, Singapore, South Korea and Taiwan.
b Includes Russia and other CIS, Turkey and Malta.
c IMF definition.

Living standards

Highest GDP per head

$

1	Luxembourg	52,990
2	Norway	49,080
3	Switzerland	44,460
4	Denmark	39,330
5	Ireland	38,430
6	United States	37,240
7	Iceland	36,960
8	Bermuda	35,940
9	Sweden	33,890
10	Japan	33,680
11	Netherlands	31,770
12	Austria	31,410
13	Finland	31,070
14	Cayman Islands[ab]	30,950
15	United Kingdom	30,280
16	France	29,240
17	Belgium	29,170
18	Germany	29,130
19	Qatar[b]	27,990
20	Canada	27,190
21	Australia	26,520
22	Italy	25,580
23	United Arab Emirates[b]	23,650
24	Hong Kong	22,380
25	Virgin Islands	22,320
26	Faroe Islands[ac]	21,600
27	Singapore	21,490
28	New Zealand	20,400
	Spain	20,400
30	Guam[ad]	19,750
31	Greenland[ac]	19,640
32	Aruba[b]	18,940
33	Andorra[a]	18,790
34	Brunei[d]	18,260
35	Macau	17,790
36	Puerto Rico[b]	17,420
37	Israel	17,220
38	Kuwait	16,700
39	Bahamas	16,590
40	Greece	15,650
41	Martinique[a]	15,560
42	Cyprus	14,790
43	Portugal	14,640
44	French Polynesia[d]	14,190
45	Slovenia	14,130
46	South Korea	12,690
47	Taiwan	12,670
48	Malta	12,160
49	New Caledonia[d]	11,920
50	Netherlands Antilles	11,140
51	Bahrain[b]	10,790
52	Barbados	9,690
53	Saudi Arabia	8,870
54	Czech Republic	8,790
55	Hungary	8,360
56	Trinidad & Tobago	8,010
57	Guadeloupe[a]	7,950
58	Oman	7,480
59	Estonia	6,990
60	Croatia	6,540
61	Mexico	6,050
62	Slovakia	6,040
63	Equatorial Guinea	5,900
64	Réunion[a]	5,750
65	Poland	5,430
66	Lithuania	5,360
67	Lebanon	5,040
68	Latvia	4,770
69	Chile	4,590
70	Gabon	4,510

Lowest GDP per head

$

1	Burundi	90
	Ethiopia	90
3	Congo	110
4	Liberia	130
5	Malawi	140
6	Guinea-Bissau	160
	Sierra Leone	160
8	Eritrea	180
9	Rwanda	190
10	Afghanistan	200
11	Mozambique	230
	Nepal	230
	Niger	230
14	Uganda	240
15	Tajikistan	250
16	Gambia, The	280
	Tanzania	280
18	Bhutan	300
	Cambodia	300
	Chad	300

a Estimate.   b 2002   c 2001   d 2000

Highest purchasing power
GDP per head in PPP (USA = 100)

1	Luxembourg	147.0	36	Guam[ad]	52.3
2	Norway	100.4	37	Greenland[ae]	52.0
3	United States	100.0	38	Cyprus	51.9
4	Bermuda	95.2	39	Kuwait	51.6
5	Switzerland	85.4	40	Israel	51.5
6	Denmark	82.3	41	Slovenia	50.6
7	Cayman Islands[a]	82.0	42	Andorra	49.8
8	Ireland	81.9	43	Brunei[ad]	48.1
9	Iceland	81.0	44	South Korea	47.7
10	Canada	79.6	45	Malta	47.1
11	Austria	78.8	46	Portugal	46.9
12	Belgium	76.6	47	Virgin Islands[ab]	45.6
13	Australia	76.2	48	Bahrain[b]	42.9
14	Hong Kong	76.0		Puerto Rico[e]	42.9
15	Netherlands	75.7	50	Bahamas[b]	42.8
16	Japan	75.4	51	Czech Republic	41.3
17	Aruba[ab]	74.2	52	Martinique[a]	41.2
18	United Kingdom	73.4	53	Barbados	39.9
19	France	73.2	54	Hungary	36.7
20	Germany	73.1	55	Slovakia	35.6
21	Finland	72.7	56	Saudi Arabia	35.0
22	Italy	71.1	57	Oman	34.4
23	Sweden	70.8	58	Estonia	33.6
24	Taiwan	65.3	59	Argentina	30.2
25	French Polynesia	65.2		Lithuania	30.2
26	Singapore	64.1	61	Mauritius[d]	29.9
27	Channel Islands[ac]	61.7	62	Poland	29.7
28	Qatar[a]	61.5	63	Netherlands Antilles[a]	29.5
29	New Caledonia[d]	58.8	64	Croatia	28.1
30	Spain	58.7	65	Trinidad & Tobago	27.5
31	Macau[b]	58.1	66	Latvia	27.0
32	Faroe Islands[a]	57.2	67	South Africa	26.8
33	New Zealand	56.6	68	Libya[a]	26.3
34	United Arab Emirates[b]	55.4	69	Chile	26.0
35	Greece	52.7	70	Costa Rica	24.2

Lowest purchasing power
GDP per head in PPP (USA = 100)

1	Sierra Leone	1.4		Madagascar	2.1
2	Malawi	1.6	12	Niger	2.2
	Tanzania	1.6		Yemen	2.2
4	Burundi	1.7	14	Zambia	2.3
	Congo	1.7	15	Liberia[a]	2.4
6	Guinea-Bissau	1.8		Nigeria	2.4
7	Congo-Brazzaville	1.9	17	Mali	2.5
	Ethiopia	1.9	18	Eritrea	2.7
	Myanmar[a]	1.9		Kenya	2.7
10	Afghanistan[a]	2.1			

Note: for definition of purchasing power parity see page 247.
a Estimate. b 2002 c 1999 d 2000 e 2001

The quality of life

Human development index[a]

Highest

1	Norway	95.6
2	Sweden	94.6
3	Australia	94.6
4	Canada	94.3
5	Belgium	94.2
	Netherlands	94.2
7	Iceland	94.1
8	United States	93.9
9	Japan	93.8
10	Ireland	93.6
	Switzerland	93.6
	United Kingdom	93.6
13	Finland	93.5
14	Austria	93.4
15	Luxembourg	93.3
16	Denmark	93.2
	France	93.2
18	New Zealand	92.6
19	Germany	92.5
20	Spain	92.2
21	Italy	92.0
22	Israel	90.8
23	Hong Kong	90.3
24	Greece	90.2
	Singapore	90.2
26	Portugal	89.7
27	Slovenia	89.5
28	Barbados	88.8
	South Korea	88.8
30	Cyprus	88.3
31	Malta	87.5
32	Czech Republic	86.8
33	Brunei	86.7
34	Argentina	85.3
	Estonia	85.3
36	Poland	85.0
37	Hungary	84.8
38	Bahrain	84.3
39	Lithuania	84.2
	Slovakia	84.2
41	Chile	83.9
42	Kuwait	83.8
43	Costa Rica	83.4
44	Qatar	83.3
	Uruguay	83.3
46	Croatia	83.0
47	United Arab Emirates	82.4
48	Latvia	82.3
49	Bahamas	81.5
50	Cuba	80.9
51	Mexico	80.2
52	Trinidad & Tobago	80.1
53	Bulgaria	79.6
54	Russia	79.5
55	Libya	79.4
56	Macedonia	79.3
	Malaysia	79.3
58	Panama	79.1
59	Belarus	79.0
60	Mauritius	78.5

Human development index[a]

Lowest

1	Sierra Leone	27.3
2	Niger	29.2
3	Burkina Faso	30.2
4	Mali	32.6
5	Burundi	33.9
6	Guinea-Bissau	35.0
7	Mozambique	35.4
8	Ethiopia	35.9
9	Central African Rep	36.1
10	Congo	36.5
11	Chad	37.9
12	Angola	38.1
13	Malawi	38.8
14	Zambia	38.9
15	Côte d'Ivoire	39.9
16	Tanzania	40.7
17	Benin	42.1
18	Guinea	42.5

a GDP or GDP per head is often taken as a measure of how developed a country is, but its usefulness is limited as it refers only to economic welfare. In 1990 the UN Development Programme published its first estimate of a Human Development Index, which combined statistics on two other indicators – adult literacy and life expectancy – with income levels to give a better, though still far from perfect, indicator of human development. In 1991 average years of schooling was combined with adult literacy to give a knowledge variable. The HDI is shown here scaled from 0 to 100; countries scoring over 80 are considered to have high human development, those scoring from 50 to 79 medium and those under 50 low.

Economic freedom index[b]

1	Hong Kong	1.35	21	Belgium	2.13
2	Singapore	1.60		Cyprus	2.13
3	Luxembourg	1.63	23	Lithuania	2.18
4	Estonia	1.65	24	El Salvador	2.20
5	Ireland	1.70	25	Bahamas	2.25
	New Zealand	1.70	26	Italy	2.28
7	United Kingdom	1.75	27	Taiwan	2.29
8	Denmark	1.76	28	Latvia	2.31
	Iceland	1.76	29	Malta	2.33
10	Australia	1.79		Norway	2.33
11	Chile	1.81	31	Spain	2.34
12	Switzerland	1.85	32	Barbados	2.35
	United States	1.85	33	Czech Republic	2.36
14	Sweden	1.89		Israel	2.36
15	Finland	1.90	35	Hungary	2.40
16	Canada	1.91	36	Slovakia	2.43
17	Netherlands	1.95	37	Botswana	2.44
18	Germany	2.00		Portugal	2.44
19	Austria	2.09	39	Japan	2.46
20	Bahrain	2.10	40	Trinidad & Tobago	2.49

Gender-related development index[c]

1	Norway	95.5	21	Italy	91.4
2	Sweden	94.6	22	Israel	90.6
3	Australia	94.5	23	Hong Kong	89.8
4	Canada	94.1	24	Greece	89.4
5	Belgium	93.8		Portugal	89.4
	Iceland	93.8	26	Slovenia	89.2
	Netherlands	93.8	27	Barbados	88.4
8	United States	93.6		Singapore	88.4
9	United Kingdom	93.4	29	South Korea	88.2
10	Finland	93.3	30	Cyprus	87.5
11	Japan	93.2	31	Malta	86.6
	Switzerland	93.2	32	Czech Republic	86.5
13	Denmark	93.1	33	Estonia	85.2
14	France	92.9	34	Poland	84.8
	Ireland	92.9	35	Hungary	84.7
16	Luxembourg	92.6	36	Argentina	84.1
17	Austria	92.4		Lithuania	84.1
	New Zealand	92.4	38	Slovakia	84.0
19	Germany	92.1	39	Bahrain	83.2
20	Spain	91.6	40	Chile	83.0

b Ranks countries on the basis of ten indicators of how government intervention can restrict the economic relations between individuals. The economic indicators, published by the Heritage Foundation, are trade policy, taxation, monetary policy, the banking system, foreign-investment rules, property rights, the amount of economic output consumed by the government, regulation policy, the size of the black market and the extent of wage and price controls. A country can score between 1 and 5 in each category, 1 being the most free and 5 being the least free.
c Combines similar data to the HDI (and also published by the UNDP) to give an indicator of the disparities in human development between men and women in individual countries. The lower the index, the greater the disparity.

Economic growth

Highest economic growth, 1993–2003

Average annual % increase in real GDP

1	Equatorial Guinea	25.9	26	Bangladesh	5.0
2	Bosnia[a]	18.5	27	Botswana	4.9
3	Liberia	13.7		Mauritius	4.9
4	China	8.9		Poland	4.9
5	Myanmar[b]	8.3	30	Nicaragua	4.8
6	Ireland	7.9		Senegal	4.8
	Mozambique	7.9		United Arab Emirates[c]	4.8
8	Armenia	7.4	33	Latvia	4.7
	Vietnam	7.4		Turkmenistan	4.7
10	Bhutan	7.1	35	Chile	4.6
11	Angola	6.8		Taiwan	4.6
	Cambodia	6.8		Tunisia	4.6
13	Uganda	6.7	38	Egypt	4.5
14	Albania	6.4	39	Burkina Faso	4.4
15	India	6.2		Croatia	4.4
	Laos	6.2		Eritrea	4.4
17	Sudan	5.7		Estonia	4.4
18	Mali	5.5		Luxembourg	4.4
	Yemen	5.5		Nepal	4.4
20	South Korea	5.4		Sri Lanka	4.4
21	Benin	5.2		Tanzania	4.4
	Dominican Republic	5.2	47	Costa Rica	4.3
	Malaysia	5.2		Ghana	4.3
	Singapore	5.2		Puerto Rico[b]	4.3
25	Chad	5.1		Slovakia	4.3

Lowest economic growth, 1993–2003

Average annual % change in real GDP

1	Moldova	-3.1		Switzerland	1.1
2	West Bank and Gaza[a]	-2.8	20	Bulgaria	1.3
3	Ukraine	-2.6		Japan	1.3
4	Congo	-1.8	22	Germany	1.4
5	Sierra Leone	-1.2		Paraguay	1.4
	Venezuela	-1.2	24	New Caledonia	1.5
7	Burundi	-1.1		Zambia	1.5
8	Guinea-Bissau	-0.2	26	Central African Rep	1.6
	Haiti	-0.2		Kuwait	1.6
10	Uruguay	0.3		Serbia & Montenegro[d]	1.6
11	Zimbabwe[c]	0.5	29	Italy	1.7
12	Russia	0.7	30	Saudi Arabia	1.8
13	Argentina	0.8		Macau[c]	1.8
	Jamaica	0.8	32	Congo-Brazzaville	1.9
	Papua New Guinea	0.8		Côte d'Ivoire	1.9
	Tajikistan	0.8		Kenya	1.9
17	Kirgizstan	0.9	35	Barbados	2.0
18	Macedonia	1.1		Romania	2.0

a 1994–2003   b 1993–2001   c 1993–2002   d 1995–2003

Highest economic growth, 1983–93
Average annual % increase in real GDP

1	China	10.5	Swaziland	6.8
2	Thailand	8.7	13 Bhutan	6.5
3	Botswana	8.6	14 Hong Kong	6.4
4	Taiwan	8.3	15 Mauritius	6.2
5	South Korea	8.2	New Caledonia	6.2
6	Macau	7.7	17 Luxembourg	6.1
7	Chile	7.6	18 Cyprus	5.9
8	Singapore	7.4	19 Lesotho	5.6
9	Indonesia	7.0	Pakistan	5.6
10	Malaysia	6.9	Vietnam[a]	5.6
11	Oman	6.8	22 Turkey	5.4

Lowest economic growth, 1983–93
Average annual % increase in real GDP

1	Liberia	-18.8	12 Sierra Leone	-1.4
2	Iraq[b]	-17.0	13 Angola	-1.1
3	Georgia	-12.5	Haiti	-1.1
4	Latvia	-4.7	Hungary	-1.1
5	Moldova	-4.1	16 Cameroon	-0.7
6	Estonia	-3.4	17 Suriname	-0.6
7	Congo-Brazzaville	-2.8	18 Bulgaria	-0.4
8	Albania	-2.7	19 Niger	-0.1
9	Romania	-2.5	20 Rwanda	0.2
10	Nicaragua	-2.3	Togo	0.2
11	Trinidad & Tobago	-2.2		

Highest services growth, 1993–2003[c]
Average annual % increase in real terms

1	Georgia	17.9	9 Bhutan	7.0
2	Armenia	11.1	Ethiopia	7.0
3	Equatorial Guinea	9.4	Nicaragua	7.0
4	China	8.3	12 Tajikistan	6.9
5	India	8.0	13 Botswana	6.8
6	Uganda	7.7	14 Laos	6.7
7	Albania	7.3	Vietnam	6.7
8	Iran	7.2		

Lowest services growth, 1993–2003[c]
Average annual % increase in real terms

1	Congo	-7.1	8 Bulgaria	0.1
2	Central African Rep	-5.9	Rwanda	0.1
3	Ukraine	-3.3	10 Paraguay	0.2
4	Sierra Leone	-1.0	11 Kirgizstan	0.4
5	Burundi	-0.4	12 Russia	0.9
6	West Bank and Gaza	-0.2	Uruguay	0.9
7	Venezuela	-0.1	14 Zimbabwe	1.0

---

a 1984–93   b 1983–91   c Or nearest available years.
Note: Rankings of highest industrial growth 1993–2003 can be found on page 44 and highest agricultural growth on page 47.

Trading places

Biggest exporters

% of total world exports (visible & invisible)

1	Euro area	17.48	23	Hong Kong	1.06
2	United States	12.72	24	Denmark	1.04
3	Germany	9.55	25	Saudi Arabia	0.99
4	United Kingdom	6.42	26	Australia	0.98
5	Japan	6.02		Norway	0.98
6	France	5.32	28	Thailand	0.94
7	China	4.85	29	Luxembourg	0.85
8	Italy	4.04	30	Brazil	0.84
9	Canada	3.67	31	India	0.80
10	Netherlands	3.54	32	Poland	0.72
11	Belgium	2.77	33	Turkey	0.70
12	Spain	2.53	34	Finland	0.68
13	South Korea	2.30	35	Indonesia	0.67
14	Switzerland	2.07	36	United Arab Emirates	0.64
15	Mexico	1.75	37	Czech Republic	0.57
16	Taiwan	1.74	38	Hungary	0.51
17	Russia	1.58	39	Portugal	0.49
18	Ireland	1.55	40	South Africa	0.46
19	Sweden	1.51	41	Philippines	0.45
20	Austria	1.44	42	Israel	0.43
21	Singapore	1.19	43	Greece	0.37
22	Malaysia	1.18		Iran	0.37

Most trade dependent

Trade as % of GDP[a]

1	Aruba	117.9
2	Liberia	89.3
3	Malaysia	88.8
4	Singapore	78.4
5	Bahrain	76.6
6	United Arab Emirates	72.2
7	Slovakia	68.5
8	Equatorial Guinea	66.1
9	Belgium	65.8
10	Lesotho	65.7
11	Puerto Rico	65.5
12	Tajikistan	62.2
13	Hungary	62.0
14	Belarus	61.2
15	Estonia	59.4
16	Malta	58.8
17	Vietnam	57.5
18	Moldova	56.9
19	Czech Republic	55.7
20	Cambodia	54.9
21	Papua New Guinea	54.5

Least trade dependent

Trade as % of GDP[a]

1	Myanmar	3.0
2	Somalia	4.4
3	North Korea	5.3
4	United States	9.0
5	Cuba	9.1
6	Japan	9.2
	Rwanda	9.2
8	Guam	9.3
9	Central African Rep	10.2
10	India	10.5
11	Zimbabwe	11.6
12	Brazil	12.3
13	Egypt	13.5
14	Euro area	13.6
15	Hong Kong	13.9
16	Burkina Faso	14.0
17	Burundi	14.1
18	Sudan	14.3
	Uganda	14.
20	Pakistan	14.
21	Greece	14.

Notes: The figures are drawn from balance of payment statistics and, therefore, have differing technical definitions from trade statistics taken from customs or similar sources. The invisible trade figures do not show some countries due to unavailable data. For Hong Kong and Singapore, domestic exports and retained imports only are used.

Biggest visible traders
% of world visible exports

1	Euro area	16.34	24	Thailand	1.08
2	Germany	10.46	25	Brazil	1.02
3	United States	9.95	26	Australia	0.98
4	Japan	6.24	27	Norway	0.96
5	China	6.09	28	Denmark	0.90
6	France	5.03	29	Indonesia	0.88
7	United Kingdom	4.28	30	Poland	0.85
8	Italy	4.07	31	United Arab Emirates	0.84
9	Canada	3.97	32	India	0.78
10	Netherlands	3.51	33	Puerto Rico	0.77
11	Belgium	2.82	34	Finland	0.73
12	South Korea	2.75	35	Turkey	0.71
13	Mexico	2.29	36	Czech Republic	0.68
14	Spain	2.22	37	Hungary	0.60
15	Taiwan	1.99	38	South Africa	0.54
16	Russia	1.89	39	Iran	0.50
17	Switzerland	1.60	40	Philippines	0.48
18	Malaysia	1.46	41	Portugal	0.46
19	Sweden	1.42	42	Israel	0.42
20	Saudi Arabia	1.30	43	Argentina	0.41
21	Austria	1.24	44	Venezuela	0.38
	Ireland	1.24	45	Algeria	0.34
23	Singapore	1.11	46	Ukraine	0.33

Biggest invisible traders
% of world invisible exports

1	Euro area	19.25	24	Australia	0.95
2	United States	18.30	25	Russia	0.83
3	United Kingdom	10.85	26	Greece	0.80
4	Germany	7.14		India[b]	0.80
5	France	5.76	28	Turkey	0.65
6	Japan	5.28	29	Thailand	0.58
7	Italy	3.81	30	Finland	0.56
8	Netherlands	3.46	31	Portugal	0.53
9	Spain	3.10	32	Malaysia	0.52
10	Switzerland	3.00	33	Mexico	0.50
11	Canada	2.86	34	Israel	0.44
12	Hong Kong	2.74	35	Brazil	0.42
13	Belgium	2.55	36	Poland	0.41
14	Luxembourg	2.35	37	Egypt	0.36
15	Ireland	2.15	38	Philippines	0.35
16	China	1.92	39	Czech Republic	0.32
17	Austria	1.81	40	Hungary	0.29
18	Sweden	1.64		South Africa	0.29
19	Singapore	1.35	42	Croatia	0.28
20	Denmark	1.31	43	Saudi Arabia	0.27
21	South Korea	1.22	44	New Zealand	0.24
22	Taiwan	1.10	45	Argentina	0.22
23	Norway	0.98	46	Indonesia	0.19

a Average of imports plus exports of goods as % of GDP.   b 2002

Balance of payments: current account

Largest surpluses
$m

1	Japan	136,220	26	India	6,495
2	Germany	54,870	27	Qatar	5,754
3	China	45,875	28	Algeria[a]	5,669
4	Switzerland	43,618	29	France	4,380
5	Russia	35,410	30	Brazil	4,016
6	Taiwan	29,202	31	Brunei	3,813
7	Norway	28,326	32	Egypt	3,743
8	Singapore	28,183	33	Libya	3,641
9	Saudi Arabia	28,085	34	Pakistan	3,573
10	Euro area	25,450	35	Philippines	3,347
11	Sweden	22,844	36	Macau	3,061
12	Canada	17,268	37	Ukraine	2,891
13	Hong Kong	16,981	38	Luxembourg	2,217
14	Netherlands	16,403	39	Iran	2,063
15	Malaysia	13,381	40	Morocco	1,552
16	Belgium	12,775	41	Oman	1,446
17	South Korea	12,321	42	Trinidad & Tobago	1,351
18	Venezuela	11,448	43	Jordan	963
19	Thailand	7,953	44	Uzbekistan	882
20	Argentina	7,838	45	Dominican Republic	867
21	Kuwait	7,567	46	Syria	752
22	Indonesia	7,252	47	Botswana	462
23	Denmark	6,963	48	Turkmenistan	444
24	Finland	6,829	49	Côte d'Ivoire	353
25	United Arab Emirates	6,800	50	Gabon[a]	281

Largest deficits
$m

1	United States	-530,660	21	Azerbaijan	-2,021
2	United Kingdom	-30,470	22	Bulgaria	-1,676
3	Australia	-30,377	23	South Africa	-1,615
4	Spain	-23,676	24	Austria	-1,363
5	Italy	-20,556	25	Lithuania	-1,278
6	Greece	-11,225	26	Estonia	-1,199
7	Mexico	-8,952	27	Colombia	-1,191
8	Portugal	-8,437	28	Peru	-1,061
9	Turkey	-7,905	29	Guatemala	-1,051
10	Hungary	-7,455	30	Chad[a]	-1,036
11	Czech Republic	-5,661	31	West Bank and Gaza[b]	-1,023
12	Nigeria[a]	-5,115	32	Tanzania	-971
13	Poland	-4,603	33	Costa Rica	-967
14	Lebanon	-3,382	34	Sudan	-955
15	New Zealand	-3,357	35	Latvia	-917
16	Romania	-3,311	36	Nicaragua	-780
17	Serbia & Montenegro	-2,121	37	Equatorial Guinea[c]	-762
18	Ireland	-2,105	38	Jamaica	-761
19	Croatia	-2,092	39	El Salvador	-734
20	Bosnia	-2,038	40	Tunisia	-730

a 2002   b 2000   c 2001

Largest surpluses as % of GDP
%

1	Brunei	58.7		26	Argentina	6.0
2	Macau	38.7		27	Ukraine	5.8
3	Qatar	32.9		28	Thailand	5.6
4	Singapore	30.9		29	Bermuda	5.5
5	Libya	19.0		30	Dominican Republic	5.2
6	Kuwait	18.1		31	Gabon[a]	4.6
7	Switzerland	13.6		32	Egypt	4.5
8	Venezuela	13.4		33	Pakistan	4.3
9	Saudi Arabia	13.1		34	Belgium	4.2
10	Malaysia	12.9			Finland	4.2
	Trinidad & Tobago	12.9			Philippines	4.2
12	Norway	12.8		37	Indonesia	3.5
13	Hong Kong	10.8			Morocco	3.5
14	Taiwan	10.2			Syria	3.5
15	Jordan	9.8		40	Denmark	3.3
16	United Arab Emirates	9.6			Ghana	3.3
17	Uzbekistan	8.9		42	China	3.2
18	Algeria[a]	8.5			Japan	3.2
19	Luxembourg	8.4			Netherlands	3.2
20	Russia	8.2		45	Côte d'Ivoire	2.6
21	Sweden	7.6		46	Paraguay	2.4
22	Turkmenistan	7.2		47	Germany	2.3
23	Oman	6.7			Mauritius	2.3
24	Namibia	6.3		49	Canada	2.0
25	Botswana	6.1			South Korea	2.0

Largest deficits as % of GDP
%

1	Chad[a]	-39.7		21	Tanzania	-9.4
2	West Bank and Gaza[b]	-29.6		22	Jamaica	-9.3
3	Bosnia	-29.2		23	Hungary	-9.0
4	Azerbaijan	-28.3		24	Nigeria[a]	-8.8
5	Equatorial Guinea[c]	-26.1		25	Bulgaria	-8.4
6	Nicaragua	-19.1		26	Latvia	-8.3
7	Lebanon	-17.8		27	Mongolia[a]	-8.2
8	Eritrea	-17.1		28	Bahamas	-8.0
9	Suriname	-13.8			Madagascar	-8.0
10	Estonia	-13.2			Togo[a]	-8.0
11	Mozambique	-11.9		31	Liberia	-7.7
12	Malawi	-11.8		32	Aruba	-7.5
13	Rwanda	-11.7		33	Croatia	-7.3
14	Fiji	-11.4		34	Lithuania	-7.0
15	Sierra Leone	-11.1		35	Armenia	-6.8
16	Burkina Faso	-10.7		36	Moldova	-6.7
17	Lesotho[a]	-10.4			Senegal	-6.7
18	Serbia & Montenegro	-10.2		38	Albania	-6.6
19	Georgia	-9.6		39	Greece	-6.5
20	Zambia[c]	-9.5		40	Barbados	-6.4

a 2002   b 2000   c 2001

Inflation

Highest inflation, 2004
Consumer price inflation, %

1	Zimbabwe[a]	140.1	31	Ukraine	9.0
2	Angola	43.5	32	Turkey	8.6
3	Myanmar[b]	36.6	33	Kirgizstan	8.5
4	Congo[a]	32.0	34	Honduras	8.1
5	Dominican Republic[b]	27.5	35	Burundi	7.9
6	Suriname[b]	23.0	36	Vietnam	7.8
7	Haiti	22.8	37	Slovakia	7.6
8	Zambia[a]	22.2		Sri Lanka	7.6
9	Venezuela	21.8	39	Guatemala	7.5
10	Belarus	18.1	40	Pakistan	7.4
11	Ethiopia[b]	17.8	41	Swaziland[b]	7.3
12	Iran[b]	16.5	42	Botswana	7.0
13	Laos[b]	15.5	43	Armenia	6.9
14	Nigeria	15.0		Rwanda[b]	6.9
15	Papua New Guinea[b]	14.7	45	Hungary	6.8
16	Paraguay[b]	14.2	46	Kazakhstan	6.7
	Sierra Leone	14.2		Lesotho[b]	6.7
18	Madagascar	13.8	48	Brazil	6.6
19	Jamaica	13.6	49	Bulgaria	6.4
20	Mozambique[b]	13.4	50	Indonesia	6.2
21	Ghana	12.6		Latvia	6.2
22	Moldova	12.5	52	Colombia	5.9
23	Costa Rica	12.3		Philippines	5.9
24	Romania	11.9		Sudan[c]	5.9
25	Kenya	11.6	55	Bangladesh[b]	5.7
26	Egypt	11.3	56	Georgia[a]	5.6
27	Russia	10.9	57	Mauritania[b]	5.2
28	Yemen[b]	10.8		Nicaragua[b]	5.2
29	Malawi[b]	9.6	59	Mongolia[b]	5.1
30	Uruguay	9.2	60	Gambia, The[a]	4.1

Highest inflation, 1999–2004
Average annual consumer price inflation, %

1	Congo[d]	234.1	16	Laos[e]	14.
2	Angola	129.6	17	Iran[e]	14.
3	Zimbabwe[d]	87.7	18	Nigeria	13.
4	Belarus	56.4	19	Moldova	13.
5	Turkey	36.4	20	Mozambique[e]	13.
6	Suriname[e]	33.1	21	Papua New Guinea[e]	12.
7	Ecuador	27.5	22	Dominican Republic[e]	12.
8	Myanmar[e]	26.9	23	Ukraine	10.
9	Romania	25.4	24	Costa Rica	10.
10	Zambia[d]	23.2	25	Paraguay[e]	10.
11	Ghana	22.2		Uruguay	10.
12	Venezuela	20.6	27	Burundi	9.
13	Haiti	19.5	28	Yemen[e]	9.
14	Malawi[e]	18.9	29	Madagascar	9.
15	Russia	16.4		Swaziland[e]	9.

a 2002   b 2003   c 2001   d 1999–2002   e 1999–2003

Lowest inflation, 2004
Consumer price inflation, %

1	Libya[a]	-9.8		Morocco[b]	1.2
2	Guinea-Bissau[b]	-3.5		Netherlands	1.2
3	Chad[b]	-1.9	29	Panama[b]	1.4
4	Mali[b]	-1.4	30	South Africa	1.4
5	Togo[b]	-1.0	31	Benin[b]	1.5
6	Burkina Faso	-0.4		Malaysia	1.5
	Hong Kong	-0.4	33	Barbados[b]	1.6
	Israel	-0.4		Bhutan[b]	1.6
	Macedonia	-0.4	35	Germany	1.7
	Oman	-0.4		Singapore	1.7
11	Japan	0.0	37	Canada	1.8
	Senegal[b]	0.0	38	Netherlands Antilles[b]	2.0
13	Finland	0.2	39	Austria	2.1
14	Niger	0.3		Belgium	2.1
15	Saudi Arabia	0.4		Euro area	2.1
	Sweden	0.4		France	2.1
17	Gabon[c]	0.5	43	Ireland	2.2
	Norway	0.5		Italy	2.2
19	Switzerland	0.8		Luxembourg	2.2
20	Syria[a]	1.0	46	Albania	2.3
21	Chile	1.1		Australia	2.3
	Kuwait	1.1		Cyprus	2.3
23	Bahrain[a]	1.2		Jordan[b]	2.3
	China[b]	1.2		New Zealand	2.3
	Denmark	1.2		Qatar[b]	2.3
	Lithuania	1.2	52	Portugal	2.4

Lowest inflation, 1999–2004
Average annual consumer price inflation, %

1	Libya[d]	-7.2		Qatar[e]	1.4
2	Hong Kong	-2.3	18	Germany	1.5
3	Oman[e]	-0.8		Malaysia	1.5
4	Japan	-0.5		Senegal[e]	1.5
5	Saudi Arabia	-0.2	21	Belize[e]	1.6
6	Syria[d]	0.0		Israel	1.6
7	Bahrain[d]	0.3		Morocco[e]	1.6
	China[e]	0.3		Niger	1.6
9	Lithuania	0.5		Sweden	1.6
	Taiwan	0.5	26	Barbados[e]	1.7
11	Singapore	0.8		Burkina Faso	1.7
12	Switzerland	0.9		Cameroon[d]	1.7
13	Panama[e]	1.0		Finland	1.7
14	Congo-Brazzaville	1.1		Jordan[e]	1.7
15	Cambodia	1.4		Thailand	1.7
	Kuwait	1.4	32	France	1.9

a 2002 b 2003 c 2000 d 1999–2002 e 1999–2003
Notes: Inflation is measured as the % change in the consumer price index. The five-year figures shown are based on the changes in the average level of the index during the relevant years

Debt

Highest foreign debt[a]

$m, 2003

1	Brazil	235,431	25	Peru	29,857
2	China	193,567	26	South Africa	27,807
3	Russia	175,257	27	Croatia	23,452
4	Argentina	166,207	28	Algeria	23,386
5	Turkey	145,662	29	Kazakhstan	22,835
6	Mexico	140,004	30	United Arab Emirates	22,218
7	Indonesia	134,389	31	Syria	21,566
8	South Korea	132,558	32	Singapore	22,218
9	India	113,467	33	Romania	21,280
10	Poland	95,219	34	Morocco	18,795
11	Israel	70,974	35	Bangladesh	18,778
12	Philippines	62,663	36	Lebanon	18,598
13	Taiwan	60,796	37	Slovakia	18,379
14	Hong Kong	59,237	38	Sudan	17,496
15	Thailand	51,793	39	Ecuador	16,864
16	Malaysia	49,074	40	Ukraine	16,309
17	Hungary	45,785	41	Vietnam	15,871
18	Chile	43,231	42	Tunisia	15,502
19	Pakistan	36,345	43	Serbia & Montenegro	14,885
20	Nigeria	34,963	44	Bulgaria	13,289
21	Venezuela	34,851	45	Slovenia	12,530
22	Czech Republic	34,630	46	Côte d'Ivoire	12,187
23	Colombia	32,979	47	Uruguay	11,764
24	Egypt	31,383	48	Iran	11,601

Highest foreign debt

As % of exports of goods and services, average, 2001–03

1	Burundi	3,051	21	Nicaragua	436
2	Liberia	1,522	22	Mozambique	430
3	Sierra Leone	1,152	23	Chad	427
4	Central African Rep	1,061	24	Guinea	408
5	Rwanda	974		Uganda	408
6	Congo	923	26	Gambia, The	379
7	Guinea-Bissau	891	27	Benin	347
8	Malawi	660	28	Cameroon	335
9	Ethiopia	621	29	Uruguay	334
10	Laos	611	30	Bolivia	308
11	Sudan	561	31	Brazil	299
12	Eritrea	543	32	Ghana	285
13	Niger	542	33	Kirgizstan	282
14	Zambia	529		Mali	282
15	Burkina Faso	497	35	Peru	27
16	Argentina	473	36	Zimbabwe	27
17	Madagascar	466	37	Bhutan	27
18	Mauritania	459	38	Serbia & Montenegro	26
19	Lebanon	458	39	Congo-Brazzaville	26
20	Tanzania	457	40	Syria	26

a Foreign debt is debt owed to non-residents and repayable in foreign currency; the figures shown include liabilities of government, public and private sectors. Developed countries have been excluded.

Highest foreign debt burden

Foreign debt as % of GDP, average, 2001–03

1	Liberia	603	23	Guinea	106
2	Guinea-Bissau	369	24	Madagascar	105
3	Congo-Brazzaville	242	25	Angola	104
4	Congo	222		Argentina	104
5	Mauritania	218		Lebanon	104
6	Sierra Leone	216	28	Croatia	102
7	Burundi	210	29	Estonia	100
8	Malawi	181		Moldova	100
9	Nicaragua	178	31	Mali	97
10	Zambia	172	32	Cameroon	96
11	Gambia, The	170		Tajikistan	96
12	Laos	155	34	Kazakhstan	94
13	Mozambique	139		Serbia & Montenegro	94
14	Ghana	128	36	Latvia	93
15	Mongolia	127		Niger	93
16	Central African Rep	125	38	Rwanda	91
	Kirgizstan	125	39	Jordan	90
18	Sudan	123	40	Gabon	87
19	Togo	116		Honduras	87
20	Ethiopia	112		Papua New Guinea	87
	Syria	112	43	Uruguay	86
22	Côte d'Ivoire	107	44	Senegal	84

Highest debt service ratios[b]

%, average, 2001–03

1	Lithuania	84	23	Bolivia	23
2	Lebanon	80		Philippines	23
3	Brazil	72	25	India	22
4	Burundi	68		Latvia	22
5	Colombia	46		Mexico	22
6	Turkey	45	28	Estonia	21
7	Kazakhstan	42		Romania	21
8	Argentina	40	30	Algeria	19
9	Mongolia	37		Kirgizstan	19
10	Chile	34		Pakistan	19
	Hungary	34	33	Guinea-Bissau	18
12	Zambia	32		Jamaica	18
13	Ecuador	31		Sierra Leone	18
14	Poland	30		Slovakia	18
	Venezuela	30	37	Angola	17
16	Sri Lanka	29		Ghana	17
17	Indonesia	27		Jordan	17
	Morocco	27		Kenya	17
19	Croatia	26		Serbia & Montenegro	17
20	Uruguay	25		Thailand	17
21	Peru	24	43	Cameroon	16
	Uzbekistan	24			

Debt service is the sum of interest and principal repayments (amortisation) due on outstanding foreign debt. The debt service ratio is debt service expressed as a percentage of the country's exports of goods and services.

Aid

Largest bilateral and multilateral donors[a]

$m

1	United States	16,320	14	Denmark	1,748
2	Japan	8,880	15	Switzerland	1,299
3	France	7,253	16	Australia	1,219
4	Germany	6,784	17	Finland	558
5	United Kingdom	6,282	18	Austria	505
6	Netherlands	3,981	19	Ireland	504
7	Italy	2,433	20	South Korea	366
8	Sweden	2,400	21	Greece	362
9	Saudi Arabia	2,391	22	Portugal	320
10	Norway	2,042	23	Luxembourg	194
11	Canada	2,031	24	United Arab Emirates	188
12	Spain	1,961	25	New Zealand	165
13	Belgium	1,853	26	Kuwait	133

Largest recipients of bilateral and multilateral aid

$m

1	Congo	5,381	33	Mali	528
2	Iraq	2,265	34	Morocco	523
3	Vietnam	1,769	35	French Polynesia	519
4	Indonesia	1,743	36	Cambodia	508
5	Tanzania	1,669	37	Peru	500
6	Afghanistan	1,533	38	Angola	499
7	Ethiopia	1,504	39	Malawi	498
8	Bangladesh	1,393	40	Kenya	483
9	China	1,325	41	Nepal	467
10	Serbia & Montenegro	1,317	42	New Caledonia	454
11	Russia	1,255	43	Niger	453
12	Jordan	1,234	44	Burkina Faso	451
13	Poland	1,191	45	Senegal	450
14	Pakistan	1,068	46	Israel	440
15	Mozambique	1,033	47	Bulgaria	414
16	West Bank and Gaza	972	48	Honduras	389
17	Uganda	959	49	Lithuania	372
18	India	942	50	Albania	342
19	Bolivia	930	51	Rwanda	332
20	Ghana	907	52	Ukraine	323
21	Egypt	894	53	Nigeria	318
22	Cameroon	884	54	Eritrea	307
23	Nicaragua	833	55	Tunisia	304
24	Colombia	802	56	Laos	29
25	Philippines	737	57	Azerbaijan	29
26	Sri Lanka	672		Sierra Leone	29
27	South Africa	625	59	Brazil	29
28	Sudan	621	60	Benin	29
29	Romania	601	61	Kazakhstan	26
30	Zambia	560	62	Czech Republic	26
31	Bosnia	539	63	Côte d'Ivoire	25
	Madagascar	539	64	Hungary	24

Largest bilateral and multilateral donors[a]
% of GDP

1	Saudi Arabia	1.11	14	Germany	0.28
2	Norway	0.92	15	United Arab Emirates	0.26
3	Denmark	0.84	16	Australia	0.25
4	Luxembourg	0.81	17	Canada	0.24
5	Netherlands	0.80	18	New Zealand	0.23
6	Sweden	0.79		Spain	0.23
7	Belgium	0.60	20	Portugal	0.22
8	France	0.41	21	Greece	0.21
9	Ireland	0.39	22	Austria	0.20
	Switzerland	0.39		Japan	0.20
11	Finland	0.35	24	Iceland	0.17
12	United Kingdom	0.34		Italy	0.17
13	Kuwait	0.32	26	United States	0.15

Largest recipients of bilateral and multilateral aid
$ per head

1	French Polynesia	2,161		Zambia	55
2	New Caledonia	2,064	33	Bahrain	54
3	West Bank and Gaza	301		Laos	54
4	Jordan	239	35	Bulgaria	53
5	Serbia & Montenegro	161	36	Lebanon	51
6	Netherlands Antilles	158	37	Latvia	49
7	Nicaragua	156	38	Belize	48
8	Bosnia	131	39	Tanzania	47
9	Macedonia	114	40	Ghana	46
10	Albania	109		Malawi	46
11	Lithuania	107		Mali	46
12	Bolivia	106	43	Benin	45
13	Congo	104		Senegal	45
14	Mongolia	101	45	Equatorial Guinea	44
15	Guinea-Bissau	100		Lesotho	44
16	Iraq	94	47	Gambia, The	43
17	Mauritania	92	48	Georgia	42
18	Bhutan	91	49	Papua New Guinea	41
19	Armenia	81		Rwanda	41
20	Macau	75	51	Kirgizstan	40
21	Barbados	74		Niger	40
22	Namibia	73	53	Cambodia	39
23	Eritrea	71		Uganda	39
24	Israel	67	55	Angola	38
25	Estonia	62		Burkina Faso	38
	Fiji	62	57	Azerbaijan	36
27	Honduras	57	58	Sri Lanka	35
	Sierra Leone	57	59	Madagascar	33
29	Cameroon	56	60	Burundi	32
	Mozambique	56		Liberia	32
31	Afghanistan	55			

China also provides aid, but does not disclose amounts.

Industry and services

Largest industrial output

$bn

1	United States	2,256	26	Poland	56
2	Japan	1,120	27	Denmark	53
3	China	746	28	Malaysia	50
4	Germany	693	29	Finland	49
5	United Kingdom	475	30	Iran	48
6	France	432	31	South Africa	45
7	Italy	427	32	Ireland	44
8	Canada	256		Portugal	44
9	Spain	240		Turkey	44
10	South Korea	209	35	Argentina	42
11	Brazil	196	36	Venezuela	40
12	Mexico	150	37	Greece	39
13	India	142	38	Czech Republic	35
14	Australia	138	39	Algeria	34
15	Russia	132	40	Singapore	30
16	Netherlands	127	41	Egypt	26
17	Saudi Arabia	120		Philippines	26
18	Indonesia	91	43	Hungary	25
19	Taiwan	87	44	Colombia	22
20	Sweden	85		New Zealand	22
21	Norway	79	46	Chile	21
22	Belgium	75	47	Romania	19
23	Switzerland	73	48	Hong Kong	18
24	Austria	61	49	Ukraine	17
25	Thailand	59	50	Peru	16

Highest growth in industrial output

Average annual real % growth, 1993–2003[a]

1	Equatorial Guinea	44.8	10	Albania	9.2
2	Mozambique	17.2	11	Eritrea	9.1
3	Cambodia	15.6	12	Angola	8.6
4	Vietnam	11.1	13	Mali	8.2
5	Chad	10.9	14	Armenia	7.3
	China	10.9	15	Bangladesh	7.1
7	Uganda	10.6	16	Togo	7.0
8	Laos	10.4	17	Malaysia	6.8
9	Bhutan	9.7	18	Syria	6.7

Lowest growth in industrial output

Average annual real % growth, 1993–2003[a]

1	West Bank and Gaza	-8.8	11	Zambia	-1.1
2	Moldova	-8.0	12	Russia	-0.9
3	Tajikistan	-4.7	13	Lebanon	-0.4
4	Kirgizstan	-2.8	14	Iran	-0.2
5	Ukraine	-2.6		Jamaica	-0.2
6	Congo	-2.5		Uzbekistan	-0.
7	Papua New Guinea	-1.8	17	Bulgaria	-0.
	Sierra Leone	-1.8	18	Venezuela	0.
9	Zimbabwe	-1.6	19	Japan	0.
10	Uruguay	-1.3			

Largest manufacturing output
$bn

1	United States	1,398	21	Austria	47
2	Japan	894	22	Belgium	40
3	China	614	23	Poland	33
4	Germany	407	24	Ireland	32
5	United Kingdom	291		Malaysia	32
6	Italy	216	26	Puerto Rico	30
7	France	213	27	Argentina	29
8	Canada	151	28	South Africa	28
9	South Korea	142	29	Finland	27
10	Brazil	115		Turkey	27
11	Mexico	103	31	Denmark	24
	Russia	103		Portugal	24
13	Spain	96		Singapore	24
14	India	84	34	Saudi Arabia	22
15	Taiwan	74	35	Norway	18
16	Australia	60		Philippines	18
17	Sweden	56	37	Iran	16
18	Netherlands	55		Romania	16
19	Indonesia	51		Venezuela	16
20	Thailand	49	40	Egypt	15

Largest services output
$bn

1	United States	8,633	26	Greece	123
2	Japan	3,118	27	Poland	121
3	Germany	1,672	28	Finland	107
4	United Kingdom	1,306	29	Portugal	95
5	France	1,284		South Africa	95
6	Italy	1,015	31	Saudi Arabia	85
7	Canada	610	32	Indonesia	83
8	Spain	572	33	Ireland	76
9	China	455	34	Thailand	71
10	Mexico	395	35	Iran	69
11	South Korea	377	36	Argentina	65
12	Netherlands	375	37	Singapore	56
13	Australia	353	38	Hungary	55
14	India	285	39	New Zealand	53
15	Brazil	260	40	Czech Republic	47
16	Russia	235	41	Malaysia	43
17	Belgium	226		Philippines	43
18	Sweden	205	43	Venezuela	40
19	Taiwan	193	44	Colombia	39
20	Switzerland[b]	173	45	Egypt	38
21	Denmark	154	46	Peru	35
22	Hong Kong	139	47	Chile	34
23	Austria	136		Pakistan	34
	Norway	136	49	Romania	28
25	Turkey	130	50	Bangladesh	26

Or nearest available years.
[b] 2002

Agriculture

Most economically dependent on agriculture

% of GDP from agriculture

1	Guinea-Bissau	69	24	Cambodia	34
2	Central African Rep	61	25	Bhutan	33
3	Congo[a]	58	26	Uganda	32
4	Myanmar	57	27	Burkina Faso	31
5	Sierra Leone	53		Guyana[a]	31
6	Afghanistan[a]	52	29	Gambia, The	30
7	Burundi	49	30	Madagascar	29
	Laos	49	31	Haiti[a]	28
9	Chad	46		Mongolia	28
10	Tanzania	45	33	Paraguay	27
11	Cameroon	44	34	Côte d'Ivoire	26
12	Ethiopia	42		Mozambique	26
	Rwanda	42		Nigeria	26
14	Nepal	41		Papua New Guinea	26
	Togo	41	38	Albania	25
16	Niger	40		Guinea	25
17	Kirgizstan	39		Turkmenistan[b]	25
	Sudan[a]	39	41	Armenia	24
19	Malawi	38	42	Moldova	23
	Mali	38		Pakistan	23
21	Benin	36		Syria	23
	Ghana	36		Tajikistan	23
23	Uzbekistan	35		Zambia	23

Least economically dependent on agriculture

% of GDP from agriculture

1	Hong Kong	0.1	24	France	2.7
	Singapore	0.1		Italy	2.7
3	Kuwait[b]	0.5	26	Australia	2.9
4	Luxembourg	0.6	27	Poland	3.1
5	Puerto Rico[b]	0.7		Slovenia	3.1
6	Bahrain	0.8	29	South Korea	3.2
7	United Kingdom	1.0	30	Hungary	3.3
	United States	1.0		Spain	3.3
9	Germany	1.1	32	Czech Republic	3.5
10	Switzerland[c]	1.2		Finland	3.5
	Trinidad & Tobago	1.2	34	Slovakia	3.7
12	Belgium	1.3	35	South Africa	3.8
	Japan	1.3	36	Mexico	4.1
14	Norway	1.5	37	Estonia	4.1
15	Sweden	1.8		Ireland	4.1
	Taiwan	1.8		Latvia	4.1
17	Oman	1.9		Saudi Arabia	4.1
18	Denmark	2.1		Venezuela	4.1
19	Canada	2.2	42	French Polynesia[c]	4.1
	Jordan	2.2	43	New Zealand	4.1
21	Austria	2.4	44	Jamaica	5.1
	Botswana	2.4		Russia	5.1
	Netherlands	2.4	46	Portugal	5

a 2002   b 2001   c 2000

Highest growth
Average annual real % growth, 1993–2003[a]

1	Angola	10.5	10	Morocco	5.6
2	Sudan	8.6	11	Laos	5.2
3	Bulgaria	6.5		Yemen	5.2
	Equatorial Guinea	6.5	13	Chad	4.8
5	Cameroon	6.3	14	Guinea	4.7
6	Rwanda	6.2		Malawi	4.7
7	Benin	5.9	16	Gambia	4.6
8	Peru	5.8	17	Ecuador	4.4
9	Mozambique	5.7		Iran	4.4

Lowest growth
Average annual real % growth, 1993–2003[a]

1	West Bank and Gaza	-7.1	9	Belarus	-2.8
2	Moldova	-5.5	10	Iceland	-1.8
3	Hong Kong	-5.2		Japan	-1.8
4	Kazakhstan	-4.7	12	Jordan	-1.7
5	Haiti	-4.3	13	Jamaica	-1.6
6	Luxembourg	-3.1	14	Colombia	-1.4
7	Singapore	-3.0	15	United Kingdom	-1.1
	Ukraine	-3.0	16	Portugal	-1.0

Biggest producers
'000 tonnes

Cereals

1	China	376,123	6	Indonesia	62,989
2	United States	348,897	7	France	54,914
3	India	232,785	8	Canada	50,168
4	Brazil	66,895	9	Bangladesh	40,667
5	Russia	65,464	10	Germany	39,358

Meat

1	China	70,899	6	India	5,941
2	United States	38,911	7	Spain	5,474
3	Brazil	18,388	8	Russia	4,934
4	Germany	6,601	9	Mexico	4,908
5	France	6,394	10	Canada	4,248

Fruit

1	China	76,893	6	Italy	15,727
2	India	46,911	7	Mexico	14,743
3	Brazil	34,298	8	Iran	12,697
4	United States	28,953	9	Indonesia	12,277
5	Spain	17,497	10	Philippines	11,804

Vegetables

1	China	401,538	5	Russia	15,250
2	India	79,671	6	Italy	15,155
3	United States	37,043	7	Egypt	14,873
4	Turkey	25,672	8	Spain	12,052

a Or nearest available years.

Commodities

Wheat

Top 10 producers
'000 tonnes

1	EU25	106,200
2	China	86,500
3	India	65,100
4	United States	63,800
5	Russia	34,100
6	Australia	25,700
7	Canada	23,600
8	Pakistan	19,200
9	Turkey	18,500
10	Argentina	14,500

Top 10 consumers
'000 tonnes

1	China	107,500
2	EU25	107,300
3	India	70,200
4	Russia	34,800
5	United States	32,500
6	Pakistan	19,500
7	Turkey	17,800
8	Egypt	13,600
9	Iran	13,400
10	Brazil	10,200

Rice[a]

Top 10 producers
'000 tonnes

1	China	112,462
2	India	87,000
3	Indonesia	35,024
4	Bangladesh	26,152
5	Vietnam	22,082
6	Thailand	18,011
7	Myanmar	10,730
8	Philippines	9,000
9	Brazil	8,708
10	Japan	7,091

Top 10 consumers
'000 tonnes

1	China	135,000
2	India	84,350
3	Indonesia	36,000
4	Bangladesh	26,400
5	Vietnam	18,200
6	Philippines	10,250
7	Myanmar	10,200
8	Thailand	9,470
9	Brazil	8,500
10	Japan	8,357

Sugar[b]

Top 10 producers
'000 tonnes

1	Brazil	26,000
2	India	21,700
3	EU15	16,600
4	China	11,400
5	United States	8,000
6	Thailand	7,700
7	Mexico	5,400
8	Australia	5,300
9	Pakistan	4,100
10	Colombia	2,600

Top 10 consumers
'000 tonnes

1	India	18,600
2	EU15	14,100
3	China	11,100
4	Brazil	10,200
5	United States	8,800
6	Russia	6,900
7	Mexico	5,300
8	Pakistan	3,900
9	Indonesia	3,800
10	Egypt	2,500

Coarse grains[c]

Top 5 producers
'000 tonnes

1	United States	275,700
2	China	125,900
3	EU25	123,400
4	Brazil	44,800
5	Russia	31,800

Top 5 consumers
'000 tonnes

1	United States	225,800
2	China	134,500
3	EU25	133,600
4	Brazil	42,600
5	Mexico	36,900

Tea

Top 10 producers '000 tonnes		*Top 10 consumers* '000 tonnes	
1 India	857	1 India	693
2 China	768	2 China	510
3 Sri Lanka	303	3 Russia	168
4 Kenya	294	4 Turkey	153
5 Indonesia	168	5 Japan	133
6 Turkey	155	6 United Kingdom	125
7 Japan	87	7 Pakistan	118
8 Vietnam	83	8 United States	94
9 Argentina	60	9 Iran	84
10 Iran	58	10 Iraq	80

Coffee

Top 10 producers '000 tonnes		*Top 10 consumers* '000 tonnes	
1 Brazil	1,729	1 United States	1,230
2 Vietnam	890	2 Brazil	825
3 Colombia	660	3 Germany	548
4 Indonesia	388	4 Japan	406
5 Mexico	273	5 Italy	330
6 India	270	6 France	326
7 Ethiopia	232	7 Spain	170
8 Guatemala	217	8 United Kingdom	131
9 Honduras	178	9 Indonesia	120
10 Côte d'Ivoire	160	10 Netherlands	110

Cocoa

Top 10 producers '000 tonnes		*Top 10 consumers* '000 tonnes	
1 Côte d'Ivoire	1,352	1 United States	689
2 Ghana	497	2 Germany	280
3 Indonesia	410	3 France	218
4 Nigeria	173	4 United Kingdom	215
5 Brazil	163	5 Russia	167
6 Cameroon	160	6 Japan	155
7 Ecuador	86	7 Italy	102
8 Dominican Republic	45	8 Brazil	98
9 Papua New Guinea	43	9 Spain	78
10 Colombia	38	10 Mexico	65

a Milled.
b Raw.
c Includes: maize (corn), barley, sorghum, rye, oats and millet.

Copper

Top 10 producers[a]
'000 tonnes

1	Chile	4,904
2	United States	1,120
3	Indonesia	1,003
4	Peru	843
5	Australia	830
6	Russia	665
7	China	604
8	Canada	557
9	Poland	503
10	Kazakhstan	485

Top 10 consumers[b]
'000 tonnes

1	China	3,084
2	United States	2,290
3	Japan	1,202
4	Germany	1,010
5	South Korea	901
6	Italy	665
7	Taiwan	619
8	France	551
9	Russia	422
10	Mexico	410

Lead

Top 10 producers[a]
'000 tonnes

1	China	955
2	Australia	688
3	United States	435
4	Peru	308
5	Mexico	135
6	Canada	81
7	Poland	55
8	Sweden	51
9	Ireland	50
10	South Africa	40

Top 10 consumers[b]
'000 tonnes

1	United States	1,494
2	China	1,286
3	Germany	384
4	South Korea	344
5	Japan	311
6	United Kingdom	308
7	Mexico	307
8	Italy	258
9	Spain	210
10	France	189

Zinc

Top 10 producers[a]
'000 tonnes

1	China	2,029
2	Australia	1,480
3	Peru	1,369
4	Canada	788
5	United States	767
6	Mexico	427
7	Ireland	419
8	Kazakhstan	393
9	India	280
10	Sweden	186

Top 10 consumers[c]
'000 tonnes

1	China	2,318
2	United States	1,129
3	Japan	619
4	Germany	558
5	South Korea	438
6	Italy	355
7	India	346
8	Belgium	333
9	Taiwan	330
10	France	273

Tin

Top 5 producers[a]
'000 tonnes

1	China	101.8
2	Indonesia	64.0
3	Peru	40.2
4	Bolivia	16.4
5	Brazil	12.2

Top 5 consumers[b]
'000 tonnes

1	China	71.7
2	United States	44.4
3	Japan	28.8
4	Germany	20.7
5	South Korea	17.

Nickel

Top 10 producers[a]
'000 tonnes

1	Russia	300.7		
2	Australia	191.6		
3	Canada	163.2		
4	New Caledonia	111.9		
5	Indonesia	103.5		
6	Cuba	74.0		
7	China	61.1		
8	Colombia	47.9		
9	South Africa	40.8		
10	Brazil	30.5		

Top 10 consumers[b]
'000 tonnes

1	Japan	181.7
2	China	132.8
3	United States	126.0
4	South Korea	112.5
5	Taiwan	102.6
6	Germany	94.3
7	Finland	89.7
8	Italy	70.5
9	Spain	48.4
10	France	45.6

Aluminium

Top 10 producers[d]
'000 tonnes

1	China	5,547
2	Russia	3,478
3	Canada	2,792
4	United States	2,705
5	Australia	1,857
6	Brazil	1,381
7	Norway	1,192
8	India	799
9	South Africa	733
10	Germany	661

Top 10 consumers[e]
'000 tonnes

1	United States	5,667
2	China	5,178
3	Japan	2,023
4	Germany	1,916
5	South Korea	982
6	Italy	956
7	Russia	803
8	India	798
9	France	754
10	Canada	697

Precious metals

Gold [a]
Top 10 producers
tonnes

1	South Africa	373.3
2	Australia	282.0
3	United States	276.1
4	China	194.4
5	Russia	176.9
6	Peru	173.0
7	Indonesia	164.4
8	Canada	141.5
9	Uzbekistan	82.0
10	Ghana	71.5

Silver [a]
Top 10 producers
tonnes

1	Peru	2,921
2	Mexico	2,551
3	China	2,000
4	Australia	1,868
5	Chile	1,313
6	Canada	1,309
7	Poland	1,237
8	United States	1,236
9	Kazakhstan	816
10	Bolivia	464

Platinum
Top 3 producers
tonnes

1	South Africa	144.0
2	Russia	32.7
3	North America	9.2

Palladium
Top 3 producers
tonnes

1	Russia	91.8
2	South Africa	72.2
3	North America	29.4

a Mine production.   b Refined consumption.   c Slab consumption.
d Primary refined production.   e Primary refined consumption.

Rubber (natural and synthetic)

Top 10 producers
'000 tonnes

1	Thailand	3,001
2	United States	2,192
3	Indonesia	1,830
4	China	1,752
5	Japan	1,577
6	Russia	1,070
7	Malaysia	1,004
8	Germany	888
9	India	793
10	France	717

Top 10 consumers
'000 tonnes

1	China	3,640
2	United States	3,005
3	Japan	1,895
4	India	920
5	Germany	866
6	France	793
7	South Korea	678
8	Russia	651
9	Brazil	606
10	Taiwan	544

Raw wool

Top 10 producers[a]
'000 tonnes

1	Australia	337
2	New Zealand	165
3	China	150
4	Argentina	40
5	India	38
6	United Kingdom	34
7	Uruguay	29
8	South Africa	27
	Turkey	27
10	Iran	24

Top 10 consumers[a]
'000 tonnes

1	China	306
2	India	111
3	Italy	110
4	Turkey	79
5	United Kingdom	38
6	Japan	32
7	Iran	29
8	South Korea	27
9	Russia	26
10	New Zealand	24

Cotton

Top 10 producers
'000 tonnes

1	China	4,871
2	United States	3,975
3	India	3,009
4	Pakistan	1,734
5	Brazil	1,309
6	Turkey	910
7	Uzbekistan	893
8	Greece	386
9	Australia	320
10	Syria	263

Top 10 consumers
'000 tonnes

1	China	7,000
2	India	2,950
3	Pakistan	2,100
4	United States	1,413
5	Turkey	1,350
6	Brazil	825
7	Indonesia	470
8	Mexico	439
9	Thailand	411
10	Bangladesh	341

Major oil seeds[b]

Top 5 producers
'000 tonnes

1	United States	76,131
2	Brazil	52,417
3	China	47,032
4	Argentina	35,371
5	India	25,328

Top 5 consumers
'000 tonnes

1	China	65,361
2	United States	52,391
3	Brazil	34,441
4	EU25	32,371
5	Argentina	29,541

Oil[c]

Top 15 producers '000 barrels per day		Top 15 consumers '000 barrels per day	
1 Saudi Arabia[d]	9,817	1 United States	20,071
2 Russia	8,543	2 China	5,982
3 United States	7,454	3 Japan	5,451
4 Iran[d]	3,852	4 Germany	2,664
5 Mexico	3,789	5 Russia	2,503
6 China	3,396	6 India	2,426
7 Norway	3,260	7 South Korea	2,303
8 Venezuela[d]	2,987	8 Canada	2,149
9 Canada	2,986	9 France	1,991
10 United Arab Emirates[d]	2,520	10 Italy	1,927
11 United Kingdom	2,245	11 Mexico	1,864
12 Kuwait[d]	2,238	12 Brazil	1,817
13 Nigeria[d]	2,185	13 United Kingdom	1,666
14 Algeria[d]	1,857	14 Spain	1,559
15 Brazil	1,552	15 Saudi Arabia[d]	1,437

Natural gas

Top 10 producers Billion cubic metres		Top 10 consumers Billion cubic metres	
1 Russia	578.6	1 United States	629.8
2 United States	549.5	2 Russia	405.8
3 Canada	180.5	3 United Kingdom	95.3
4 United Kingdom	102.7	4 Canada	87.4
5 Algeria	82.8	5 Germany	85.5
6 Iran	79.0	6 Iran	80.4
7 Norway	73.4	7 Japan	76.5
8 Indonesia	72.6	8 Italy	71.7
9 Saudi Arabia	61.0	9 Ukraine	67.5
10 Netherlands	58.3	10 Saudi Arabia	61.0

Coal

Top 10 producers Million tonnes oil equivalent		Top 10 consumers Million tonnes oil equivalent	
1 China	842.6	1 China	799.7
2 United States	551.3	2 United States	573.9
3 Australia	188.7	3 India	185.3
4 India	172.2	4 Japan	112.2
5 South Africa	134.6	5 Russia	111.3
6 Russia	124.9	6 South Africa	88.9
7 Poland	70.8	7 Germany	87.1
8 Indonesia	70.5	8 Poland	58.8
9 Germany	54.1	9 South Korea	51.1
10 Kazakhstan	43.2	10 Australia	50.2

a Clean basis.
b Soybeans, sunflower seed, cottonseed, groundnuts and rapeseed.
c Includes crude oil, shale oil, oil sands and natural gas liquids.
d Opec members.

Energy

Largest producers
Million tonnnes oil equivalent, 2002

1	United States	1,666.1	16	Algeria	150.3
2	China	1,220.8	17	South Africa	146.5
3	Russia	1,034.5	18	United Arab Emirates	142.1
4	Saudi Arabia	462.8	19	Germany	134.8
5	India	438.8	20	France	134.4
6	Canada	385.4	21	Kuwait	106.0
7	United Kingdom	257.5	22	Iraq	105.4
8	Australia	255.2	23	Japan	98.1
9	Indonesia	240.9	24	Kazakhstan	95.8
10	Iran	240.5	25	Argentina	81.7
11	Norway	232.2	26	Malaysia	80.2
12	Mexico	229.9	27	Poland	79.6
13	Venezuela	210.2	28	Colombia	72.3
14	Nigeria	192.7	29	Ukraine	71.5
15	Brazil	161.7	30	Libya	69.5

Largest consumers
Million tonnnes oil equivalent, 2002

1	United States	2,290.4	16	Spain	131.6
2	China	1,228.6	17	Ukraine	130.7
3	Russia	617.8	18	Saudi Arabia	126.4
4	India	538.3	19	South Africa	113.5
5	Japan	516.9	20	Australia	112.7
6	Germany	346.4	21	Nigeria	95.7
7	France	265.9	22	Poland	89.2
8	Canada	250.0	23	Thailand	83.3
9	United Kingdom	226.5	24	Netherlands	77.9
10	South Korea	203.5	25	Turkey	75.4
11	Brazil	190.7	26	Pakistan	65.8
12	Italy	172.7	27	Belgium	56.9
13	Mexico	157.3	28	Argentina	56.3
14	Indonesia	156.1	29	Venezuela	54.0
15	Iran	134.0	30	Egypt	52.4

Energy efficiency[a]

Most efficient		Least efficient	
GDP per unit of energy use, 2002		*GDP per unit of energy use, 2002*	
1 Peru	10.7	1 Uzbekistan	0.
2 Hong Kong	10.6	2 Nigeria	1.
3 Bangladesh	10.5	Trinidad & Tobago	1.
4 Namibia	10.2	Zambia	1.
5 Morocco	10.1	5 Tanzania	1.
6 Uruguay	10.0	Turkmenistan	1.
7 Colombia	9.8	7 Kuwait	1.
8 Costa Rica	9.4	8 Kazakhstan	1.
9 Ireland	9.1	Tajikistan	1.
10 Italy	8.5	10 Ukraine	1.
11 Denmark	8.1	11 Russia	1.

a PPP$, per kg of oil equivalent.   b 2000

Net energy importers
% of commercial energy use, 2002

Highest		
1	Hong Kong	100
	Singapore	100
3	Cyprusᵇ	98
	Luxembourgᵇ	98
	Moldova	98
6	Israel	97
7	Lebanon	96
8	Jordan	95
	Morocco	95
10	Ireland	90
11	Jamaica	88

Lowest		
1	Congo-Brazzaville	-1330
2	Norway	-776
3	Bruneiᵇ	-866
	Gabon	-698
5	Angola	-485
6	Oman	-478
7	Yemen	-441
8	Algeria	-387
9	Kuwait	-378
10	United Arab Emirates	-294
11	Venezuela	-289

Largest consumption per head
Kg of oil equivalent, 2002

1	Qatarᵇ	26,773
2	Icelandᵇ	12,246
3	Bahrainᵇ	9,858
4	United Arab Emirates	9,609
5	Kuwait	9,503
6	Luxembourgᵇ	8,409
7	Canada	7,973
8	United States	7,943
9	Trinidad & Tobago	7,121
10	Finland	6,852
11	Singapore	6,078

12	Norway	5,843
13	Saudi Arabia	5,775
14	Australia	5,732
15	Sweden	5,718
16	Belgium	5,505
17	Netherlands	4,827
18	New Zealand	4,573
19	France	4,470
20	Russia	4,288
21	South Korea	4,272
22	Oman	4,265

Sources of electricity
% of total, 2002

Oil		
1	Senegal	100.0
	Yemen	100.0
3	Iraq	98.8
4	Jamaica	97.2
5	Benin	96.8

Gas		
1	Turkmenistan	100.0
2	Trinidad & Tobago	99.5
3	Algeria	97.6
4	Belarus	94.2
5	United Arab Emirates	92.1

Hydropower		
1	Paraguay	100.0
2	Nepal	99.8
3	Congo	99.7
	Congo-Brazzaville	99.7
	Mozambique	99.7

Nuclear power		
1	Lithuania	81.8
2	France	78.7
3	Belgium	58.5
4	Slovakia	55.7
5	Bulgaria	48.0

Coal		
1	Poland	94.5
2	South Africa	93.1
3	Estonia	90.9
4	Austria	78.3
5	China	77.5

Workers of the world

Highest % of population in labour force

1	Cayman Islands	68.9		21	Russia	50.1
2	Bermuda	59.4			United Kingdom	50.1
3	China	57.8		23	Macau	49.9
4	Switzerland	57.2		24	Ethiopia	49.7
5	Thailand	55.1		25	Cyprus	49.6
6	Iceland	54.0		26	Austria	49.2
7	Canada	53.8		27	Estonia	48.7
	Denmark	53.8			Germany	48.7
9	Norway	52.7			South Korea	48.7
10	Netherlands	52.6		30	Slovakia	48.6
11	Portugal	52.4		31	Latvia	48.3
	Singapore	52.4		32	Slovenia	48.1
13	Japan	52.2		33	Brazil	47.9
14	Hong Kong	51.7		34	Ghana	47.8
15	Australia	50.6		35	Belgium	47.6
	Sweden	50.6		36	Lithuania	47.5
	United States	50.6		37	Bahrain	47.4
18	Czech Republic	50.3		38	Bangladesh	47.3
	New Zealand	50.3			Peru	47.3
20	Finland	50.2		40	Colombia	47.2

Most male workforce
Highest % men in workforce

1	Algeria	87.8
2	West Bank and Gaza	86.5
3	Pakistan	83.9
4	Oman	82.4
5	Syria	78.5
6	Bahrain	78.3
7	Egypt	78.1
8	Guatemala	77.4
9	Tunisia	74.3
10	Morocco	72.9
11	Turkey	72.3
12	Nicaragua	69.2
13	Malta	68.7
14	Sri Lanka	67.2
15	Chile	65.7
	Mexico	65.7
17	Malaysia	65.3
	Mauritius	65.3
19	Costa Rica	64.6
20	Honduras	64.3
21	Suriname	63.1
22	Panama	62.9
23	Bangladesh	62.2
24	Indonesia	61.8
25	Italy	60.9
	Trinidad & Tobago	60.9

Most female workforce
Highest % women in workforce

1	Belarus	53.4
2	Benin	53.1
3	Tanzania	51.0
4	Moldova	50.4
5	Malawi	50.2
6	Armenia	49.7
7	Cayman Islands	49.7
8	Ghana	49.6
	Mongolia	49.6
10	Madagascar	49.5
11	Bahamas	49.4
12	Lithuania	49.3
13	Kazakhstan	49.1
14	Estonia	49.0
15	Ukraine	48.9
16	Latvia	48.6
	Russia	48.6
18	Bermuda	48.5
19	Zimbabwe	48.2
20	Papua New Guinea	47.9
21	Azerbaijan	47.8
22	Finland	47.7
23	Georgia	47.7
24	Norway	47.7
25	Iceland	46.1

Lowest % of population in labour force

1	Oman	20.3	21	Malta	39.9
2	West Bank and Gaza	20.4	22	Croatia	40.4
3	Algeria	27.0		Mexico	40.4
4	Pakistan	29.6	24	El Salvador	40.8
5	Egypt	30.0		Moldova	40.8
6	Puerto Rico	30.4	26	Malaysia	41.3
7	Syria	31.9	27	Zimbabwe	41.5
8	Congo-Brazzaville	32.3	28	Jamaica	41.6
9	Armenia	32.6	29	Sri Lanka	41.7
10	Suriname	34.6	30	Greece	42.1
11	Botswana	35.0		Hungary	42.1
	Guatemala	35.0		Israel	42.1
	Tunisia	35.0	33	Italy	42.2
	Turkey	35.0	34	Albania	42.4
15	Nicaragua	36.5	35	Argentina	42.7
16	Morocco	37.4	36	Costa Rica	43.0
17	Honduras	38.5		Macedonia	43.0
18	Chile	38.7	38	Panama	43.1
19	Mongolia	38.8	39	Luxembourg	43.2
20	Georgia	39.4	40	Philippines	43.3

Highest rate of unemployment

% of labour force[a]

1	Macedonia	36.7	21	Colombia	14.2
2	Namibia	33.8	22	Burundi	14.0
3	South Africa	29.7		Netherlands Antilles	14.0
4	Algeria	27.3		Suriname	14.0
5	Guadeloupe	25.7	25	Panama	13.6
6	West Bank and Gaza	25.6	26	Jordan	13.2
7	Martinique	22.3	27	Kirgizstan	12.5
8	Botswana	19.6	28	Lithuania	12.4
	Poland	19.6	29	Iran	12.3
10	Bulgaria	17.6	30	Nicaragua	12.2
11	Slovakia	17.5	31	Puerto Rico	12.0
12	Uruguay	16.9	32	Morocco	11.9
13	Venezuela	15.8	33	Syria	11.7
14	Argentina	15.6	34	Ecuador	11.5
	Dominican Republic	15.6		Georgia	11.5
16	Albania	15.2		Yemen	11.5
	Serbia & Montenegro	15.2	37	Spain	11.3
18	Jamaica	15.0	38	Barbados	11.0
19	Croatia	14.3		Egypt	11.0
	Tunisia	14.3	40	Bahamas	10.8

---

a ILO definition.
Note: Data refer to the latest year available, 1999–2003.

The business world

Global competitiveness

	Overall	Government	Infrastructure
1	United States	Hong Kong	United States
2	Hong Kong	Singapore	Switzerland
3	Singapore	Finland	Japan
4	Iceland	Denmark	Finland
5	Canada	Australia	Denmark
6	Finland	Iceland	Singapore
7	Denmark	Switzerland	Sweden
8	Switzerland	New Zealand	Canada
9	Australia	Canada	Norway
10	Luxembourg	Ireland	Germany
11	Taiwan	Chile	Iceland
12	Ireland	Luxembourg	Netherlands
13	Netherlands	Estonia	Australia
14	Sweden	Thailand	Belgium
15	Norway	Norway	France
16	New Zealand	United States	Taiwan
17	Austria	Slovakia	Israel
18	Chile	Taiwan	Hong Kong
19	Japan	Austria	Austria
20	United Kingdom	China	South Korea
21	Germany	Sweden	Luxembourg
22	Belgium	Netherlands	United Kingdom
23	Israel	Malaysia	New Zealand
24	Estonia	United Kingdom	Hungary
25	Thailand	Jordan	Czech Republic
26	Malaysia	Israel	Ireland
27	South Korea	Spain	Spain
28	France	South Korea	Malaysia
29	China	South Africa	Portugal
30	Czech Republic	Germany	Italy
31	Hungary	Hungary	Greece
32	Spain	India	Slovenia
33	India	Japan	Estonia
34	Slovakia	Portugal	Jordan
35	Jordan	Belgium	Slovakia
36	Portugal	Colombia	China
37	South Africa	Czech Republic	Chile
38	Colombia	France	Russia
39	Turkey	Russia	Thailand
40	Philippines	Philippines	Argentina
41	Greece	Mexico	Colombia
42	Brazil	Slovenia	Poland
43	Slovenia	Turkey	Turkey
44	Italy	Greece	Brazil

Notes: Rankings reflect assessments for the ability of a country to achieve sustained high rates of GDP growth per head. Column 1 is based on 259 criteria covering: the openness of an economy, the role of the government, the development of financial markets, the quality of infrastructure, technology, business management and judicial and political institutions and labour-market flexibility. Column 2 looks at the extent to which government policies are conducive to competitiveness. Column 3 is based on the extent to which a country is integrated into regional trade blocks.

The business environment

		2005–09 score	2000–2004 score	2000–2004 ranking
1	Denmark	8.74	8.46	6
2	Canada	8.70	8.55	1
3	Hong Kong	8.57	8.49	5
	Singapore	8.57	8.50	4
	United States	8.57	8.51	2
6	Netherlands	8.56	8.51	3
7	Finland	8.55	8.37	9
	United Kingdom	8.55	8.45	7
9	Switzerland	8.51	8.41	8
10	Ireland	8.44	8.24	10
11	Sweden	8.35	8.09	12
12	Belgium	8.31	7.89	15
13	France	8.29	7.93	13
14	Germany	8.23	7.89	14
15	Australia	8.21	7.80	16
16	New Zealand	8.19	8.11	11
17	Norway	8.16	7.52	19
18	Taiwan	8.10	7.38	20
19	Chile	8.02	7.54	18
20	Austria	7.97	7.69	17
21	Spain	7.91	7.33	21
22	Israel	7.71	6.78	23
23	Portugal	7.57	6.76	25
24	Czech Republic	7.45	6.72	29
25	Hungary	7.36	6.74	27
26	Italy	7.35	6.77	24
	South Korea	7.35	6.70	30
28	Japan	7.34	6.75	26
29	Poland	7.30	6.59	32
30	Slovakia	7.28	6.19	33
31	Malaysia	7.24	6.85	22
32	Thailand	7.07	6.73	28
33	Mexico	6.99	6.68	31
34	Greece	6.88	6.15	34
35	South Africa	6.81	5.55	38
36	Bulgaria	6.60	5.50	40
37	Brazil	6.57	6.00	35
38	Romania	6.53	5.18	46
39	Turkey	6.46	5.46	42
40	Philippines	6.45	5.78	36
41	China	6.35	5.24	45
42	Saudi Arabia	6.34	5.54	39
43	India	6.23	5.11	48
44	Sri Lanka	6.10	5.05	50
45	Indonesia	6.06	5.46	43
46	Russia	6.05	5.12	47

Note: Scores reflect the opportunities for, and hindrances to, the conduct of business, measured by countries' rankings in ten categories including market potential, tax and labour-market policies, infrastructure, skills and the political environment. Scores reflect average and forecast average over given date range.

Business creativity and research

Innovation index[a]

1	United States	6.41	23	Slovenia	3.44
2	Taiwan	6.06	24	Spain	3.37
3	Finland	5.74	25	Russia	3.36
4	Japan	5.56	26	Estonia	3.34
5	Sweden	5.37	27	Latvia	3.29
6	Israel	4.94	28	Greece	3.28
7	South Korea	4.62	29	Italy	3.14
	Switzerland	4.62	30	Lithuania	3.11
9	Denmark	4.41	31	Poland	3.07
10	Germany	4.39	32	Portugal	2.99
11	Canada	4.36	33	Hong Kong	2.92
12	Norway	4.24	34	Argentina	2.85
13	Singapore	4.06	35	Hungary	2.79
14	United Kingdom	4.05	36	Chile	2.77
15	Netherlands	4.04	37	Thailand	2.71
16	Austria	4.00	38	Egypt	2.70
17	Australia	3.99	39	Ukraine	2.69
18	New Zealand	3.98	40	Luxembourg	2.66
19	Belgium	3.95	41	Malaysia	2.65
20	France	3.81	42	Panama	2.61
21	Iceland	3.73	43	Czech Republic	2.58
22	Ireland	3.47	44	Slovakia	2.55

Information and communications technology index[b]

1	Iceland	6.36	23	Estonia	5.42
2	Denmark	6.26	24	Ireland	5.39
3	Sweden	6.23	25	Malta	5.37
4	Singapore	6.16	26	Slovenia	5.29
5	Finland	6.11	27	Belgium	5.24
	Norway	6.11	28	Czech Republic	5.14
7	United States	6.07	29	Cyprus	5.08
8	Hong Kong	6.06	30	Spain	5.07
9	Taiwan	6.03	31	Portugal	5.04
10	Netherlands	5.93	32	Italy	5.01
11	Luxembourg	5.90	33	United Arab Emirates	4.89
12	Switzerland	5.89	34	Hungary	4.79
13	Australia	5.87	35	Malaysia	4.69
14	United Kingdom	5.80	36	Latvia	4.63
15	Japan	5.79	37	Greece	4.62
16	Germany	5.77	38	Chile	4.61
17	Canada	5.75		Lithuania	4.61
18	South Korea	5.74	40	Slovakia	4.59
19	Austria	5.70	41	Bahrain	4.51
20	Israel	5.57	42	Croatia	4.49
21	New Zealand	5.54	43	Mauritius	4.38
22	France	5.49	44	Poland	4.26

a The innovation index is a measure of human resources skills, market incentive structures and interaction between business and scientific sectors.
b The information and communications technology (ICT) index is a measure of ICT usage and includes per capita measures of telephone lines, internet usage, personal computers and mobile phone users.

Total expenditure on R&D
% of GDP, 2002

1	Israel	4.66		23	Czech Republic	1.30
2	Sweden[a]	4.27		24	Russia	1.29
3	Finland	3.44		25	China	1.26
4	Japan	3.12		26	New Zealand[a]	1.18
5	Iceland	3.10		27	Ireland[a]	1.14
6	United States	2.64		28	Italy[a]	1.11
7	Switzerland[b]	2.57		29	Brazil[b]	1.04
8	Germany	2.54		30	Hungary	1.02
9	South Korea	2.53		31	Spain[a]	0.95
10	Denmark	2.52		32	Portugal	0.93
11	Taiwan	2.29		33	India[a]	0.77
12	Singapore	2.21		34	South Africa[a]	0.76
13	France	2.18		35	Estonia	0.75
14	Belgium[a]	2.17		36	Malaysia	0.71
15	Austria	1.94		37	Greece[a]	0.65
16	Netherlands[a]	1.88		38	Turkey[b]	0.64
17	Canada	1.87		39	Poland	0.59
	United Kingdom	1.87		40	Slovakia	0.58
19	Luxembourg[b]	1.75		41	Hong Kong[a]	0.56
20	Norway	1.67		42	Chile	0.50
21	Australia[b]	1.58		43	Venezuela[a]	0.45
22	Slovenia	1.46		44	Mexico	0.41

Patents

No. of patents granted to residents
Total, 2001

1	Japan	118,535
2	United States	85,528
3	South Korea	29,363
4	Taiwan	24,700
5	Germany	18,318
6	Russia	14,528
7	France	10,938
8	China	4,989
9	United Kingdom	4,203
10	Italy	4,030
11	Netherlands	2,912
12	Spain	1,785
13	Sweden	1,695
14	Switzerland	1,553
15	Australia	1,270
16	Austria	1,250
17	Canada	1,225
18	South Africa[c]	957
19	Poland	937
20	Belgium	886

No. of patents in force
Per 100,000 inhabitants, 2001

1	Luxembourg	5,804
2	Switzerland	1,166
3	Sweden[b]	1,097
4	Ireland	957
5	Japan	848
6	Belgium	814
7	Netherlands	761
8	Taiwan	748
9	Singapore	704
10	Denmark	657
11	France[b]	631
12	Canada	590
13	United Kingdom	543
14	South Korea	516
15	United States	487
16	Australia	482
17	Germany	452
18	Finland[d]	394
19	Norway[e]	354
20	Spain	252

a 2001   b 2000   c 1997   d 1998   e 1996

Business costs and FDI

Office rents

Occupation cost[o], $ per square metre, January 2005

1	London (West End), UK	2,062	14	Milan, Italy	685
2	London (City), UK	1,354	15	Frankfurt, Germany	676
3	Tokyo (Inner Central), Japan	1,339	16	Geneva, Switzerland	646
4	Tokyo (Outer Central), Japan	1,286	17	Hong Kong	634
			18	Seoul, South Korea	630
5	Paris, France	1,038	19	Munich, Germany	605
6	Birmingham, UK	844	20	Stockholm, Sweden	599
7	Manchester, UK	807	21	Madrid, Spain	596
8	Dublin, Ireland	805	22	Brussels, Belgium	583
9	Edinburgh, UK	766	23	Mumbai, India	568
10	Moscow, Russia	753	24	New York (Midtown, Manhattan), US	565
11	Glasgow, UK	708	25	Athens, Greece	557
	Luxembourg City, Luxembourg	708	26	Sydney, Australia	540
			27	Rome, Italy	539
13	Zurich, Switzerland	707	28	Amsterdam, Netherlands	481

Employment costs

Pay, social security and other benefits, $ per hr. worked for a production worke

1	Denmark	36.59	11	France	23.86
2	Norway	34.40	12	Australia	23.54
3	Germany	33.30	13	United States	22.91
4	Belgium	31.36	14	Ireland	21.88
5	Finland	30.92	15	Japan	21.59
6	Switzerland	30.53	16	Canada	21.28
7	Netherlands	30.17	17	Italy	20.78
8	Sweden	28.47	18	Spain	17.15
9	Austria	28.42	19	New Zealand	13.14
10	United Kingdom	24.01	20	Singapore	7.82

Foreign direct investment[b]

Inflow, $m

1	Luxembourg	87,557	19	Austria	6,855
2	China	53,505	20	Canada	6,580
3	France	46,981	21	Japan	6,324
4	United States	29,772	22	Cayman Islands	4,600
5	Belgium	29,484	23	India	4,269
6	Spain	25,625	24	Poland	4,225
7	Ireland	25,497	25	South Korea	3,753
8	Netherlands	19,674	26	Israel	3,745
9	Italy	16,421	27	Sweden	3,293
10	United Kingdom	14,515	28	Azerbaijan	3,285
11	Hong Kong	13,561	29	Chile	2,982
12	Germany	12,866	30	Finland	2,766
13	Switzerland	12,161	31	Denmark	2,607
14	Singapore	11,409	32	Czech Republic	2,583
15	Mexico	10,783	33	Venezuela	2,531
16	Brazil	10,144	34	Malaysia	2,473
17	Bermuda	8,500	35	Hungary	2,470
18	Australia	7,900	36	Norway	2,372

Business burdens and corruption

Number of days taken to register a new company

Highest			Lowest		
1	Haiti	203	1	Australia	2
2	Laos	198	2	Canada	3
3	Congo	155	3	Denmark	4
4	Mozambique	153	4	United States	5
5	Brazil	152	5	Puerto Rico	7
6	Indonesia	151	6	France	8
7	Angola	146		Singapore	8
8	Burkina Faso	135	8	Turkey	9
9	Azerbaijan	123	9	Hong Kong	11
10	Venezuela	116		Morocco	11
11	El Salvador	115		Netherlands	11
12	Botswana	108	12	New Zealand	12
	Spain	108	13	Italy	13
14	Peru	98	14	Central African Rep	14
15	Zimbabwe	96		Finland	14
16	Cambodia	94		Tunisia	14

Corruption perceptions index[c]

2004, 10 = least corrupt

Lowest			Highest		
1	Finland	9.7	1	Bangladesh	1.5
2	New Zealand	9.6		Haiti	1.5
3	Denmark	9.5	3	Nigeria	1.6
	Iceland	9.5	4	Chad	1.7
5	Singapore	9.3		Myanmar	1.7
6	Sweden	9.2	6	Azerbaijan	1.9
7	Switzerland	9.1		Paraguay	1.9
8	Norway	8.9	8	Angola	2.0
9	Australia	8.8		Congo	2.0
10	Netherlands	8.7		Côte d'Ivoire	2.0
11	United Kingdom	8.6		Georgia	2.0
12	Canada	8.5		Indonesia	2.0
13	Austria	8.4		Tajikistan	2.0
	Luxembourg	8.4		Turkmenistan	2.0
15	Germany	8.2			

Business software piracy

% of software that is pirated

1	China	92	9	Pakistan	83
	Vietnam	92		Paraguay	83
3	Ukraine	91	11	Tunisia	82
4	Indonesia	88	12	Kenya	80
5	Russia	87		Thailand	80
	Zimbabwe	87	14	El Salvador	79
7	Algeria	84		Nicaragua	79
	Nigeria	84	16	Bolivia	78

a Total rent, taxes and operating expenses.
b Investment in companies in a foreign country.
c This index ranks countries based on how much corruption is perceived by business
people, academics and risk analysts to exist among politicians and public officials.

Businesses and banks

Largest businesses
By sales, $bn

1	Wal-Mart Stores	United States	263.0
2	BP	United Kingdom	232.6
3	Exxon Mobil	United States	222.9
4	Royal Dutch/Shell Group	United Kingdom/Netherlands	201.7
5	General Motors	United States	195.3
6	Ford Motor	United States	164.5
7	DaimlerChrysler	United States	156.6
8	Toyota Motor	Japan	153.1
9	General Electric	United States	134.2
10	Total Fina Elf	France	118.4
11	Allianz	Germany	114.9
12	ChevronTexaco	United States	112.9
13	AXA	France	111.9
14	ConocoPhillips	United States	99.5
15	Volkswagen	Germany	98.6
16	Nippon Telegraph & Telephone	Japan	98.
17	ING Group	Netherlands	95.9
18	Citigroup	United States	94.
19	IBM	United States	89.
20	American Intl. Group	United States	81.
21	Siemens	Germany	80.
22	Carrefour	France	79.
23	Hitachi	Japan	76.
24	Hewlett-Packard	United States	73.
25	Honda Motor	Japan	72.
26	McKesson	United States	69.
27	U.S. Postal Service	United States	68.
28	Verizon Communications	United States	67.
29	Assicurazioni Generali	Italy	66.
30	Sony	Japan	66.
31	Matsushita Electric Industrial	Japan	66.
32	Nissan Motor	Japan	65.
33	Nestlé	Switzerland	65.
34	Home Depot	United States	64.
35	Berkshire Hathaway	United States	63.
36	Nippon Life Insurance	Japan	63.
37	Royal Ahold	Netherlands	63.
38	Deutsche Telecom	Germany	63.
39	Peugeot	France	61.
40	Altria Group	United States	60.
	Metro-Goldwyn-Mayer	United States	60.
42	Aviva	United Kingdom	59.
43	ENI	Italy	59.
44	Munich Re Group	Germany	59.

Notes: Industrial and service corporations. Figures refer to the year ended December 31, 2003, except for Japanese companies, where figures refer to year ended March 31 2004. They include sales of consolidated subsidiaries but exclude excise taxes, thus differing, in some instances, from figures published by the companies themselves.

Largest banks
By capital, $m

1	Citigroup	United States	66,871
2	Crédit Agricole Groupe	France	55,435
3	HSBC Holdings	United Kingdom	54,863
4	Bank of America Corp	United States	44,050
5	J.P. Morgan Chase	United States	43,167
6	Mizuho Financial Group	Japan	37,786
7	Mitsubishi Tokyo Financial Group	Japan	37,003
8	Royal Bank of Scotland	United Kingdom	34,623
9	Sumitomo Mitsui Financial Group	Japan	34,244
10	BNP Paribas	France	32,458
11	HBOS	United Kingdom	29,349
12	Deutsche Bank	Germany	27,302
13	Barclays Bank	United Kingdom	26,761
14	Wells Fargo & Co.	United States	25,074
15	Rabobank Nederland	Netherlands	24,830
16	Bank One Corp	United States	24,499
17	ING Bank	Netherlands	24,089
18	UBS	Switzerland	24,064
19	Wachovia Corporation	United States	23,863
20	ABN-Amro Bank	Netherlands	23,037
21	China Construction Bank	China	22,507
22	Santander Central Hispano	Spain	21,408
23	Société Générale	France	21,396
24	UFJ Holding	Japan	20,855
25	Industrial and Commercial Bank of China	China	20,600
26	Lloyds TSB Group	United Kingdom	20,030
27	Crédit Mutuel	France	19,319
28	MetLife	United States	18,980
29	Bank of China	China	18,579
30	Groupe Caisse d'Epargne	France	18,347
31	Banco Bilbao Vizcaya Argentaria	Spain	18,176
32	HypoVereinsbank	Germany	18,142
33	Credit Suisse Group	Switzerland	18,105
34	Banca Intesa	Italy	18,050
35	FleetBoston Financial Corp	United States	16,484
36	Agricultural Bank of China	China	16,435
37	Fortis Bank	Belgium	16,114
38	Groupe Banques Populaires	France	15,429
39	US Bancorp	United States	14,623
40	Washington Mutual	United States	14,408
41	UniCredit	Italy	13,995
42	Norinchukin Bank	Japan	13,781
43	Dexia	Belgium	13,272
44	National Australia Bank	Australia	13,173
45	Commerzbank	Germany	12,954
46	Sanpaolo IMI	Italy	12,677

Notes: Capital is essentially equity and reserves.
Figures for Japanese banks refer to the year ended March 31, 2004. Figures for all other countries refer to the year ended December 31, 2003.

Stockmarkets

Largest market capitalisation

$m, end 2003

1	United States	14,266,266	27	Mexico	122,532
2	Japan	3,040,665	28	Thailand	118,705
3	United Kingdom	2,412,434	29	Greece	106,845
4	France	1,355,643	30	Norway	94,679
5	Germany	1,079,026	31	Chile	86,291
6	Canada	893,950	32	Ireland	85,070
7	Spain	726,243	33	Israel	75,719
8	Switzerland	725,659	34	Turkey	68,379
9	Hong Kong	714,597	35	Portugal	58,285
10	China	681,204	36	Indonesia	54,659
11	Italy	614,842	37	Austria	54,528
12	Australia	585,475	38	Argentina	38,927
13	Netherlands	488,647	39	Luxembourg	37,333
14	Taiwan	379,023	40	Poland	37,165
15	South Korea	329,616	41	Iran	34,444
16	Sweden	287,500	42	New Zealand	33,052
17	India	279,093	43	Egypt	27,073
18	South Africa	267,745	44	Philippines	23,565
19	Brazil	234,560	45	Kuwait[a]	20,772
20	Russia	230,786	46	Czech Republic	17,663
21	Belgium	173,612	47	Hungary	16,729
22	Finland	170,283	48	Pakistan	16,579
23	Malaysia	168,376	49	Peru	16,051
24	Saudi Arabia	157,302	50	Colombia	14,25
25	Singapore	145,117	51	Morocco	13,15
26	Denmark	127,997	52	Jordan	10,96

Highest growth in market capitalisation, $ terms

% increase, 1998–2003

1	Macedonia	4,425	21	Botswana	19
2	Russia	1,020		China	19
3	West Bank and Gaza	957		Tanzania[e]	19
4	Moldova	914	24	Slovenia	19
5	Fiji	760	25	Slovakia	18
6	Georgia[b]	746	26	South Korea	17
7	Kirgizstan[c]	675	27	Trinidad & Tobago	17
8	Ukraine	655	28	India	16
9	Estonia	630	29	Indonesia	14
10	Armenia[d]	460	30	Malta	13
11	Romania	450	31	Iran	13
12	Jamaica	297	32	El Salvador	1
13	Zimbabwe	280	33	Bolivia	1
14	Saudi Arabia	270	34	Hong Kong	1
15	Thailand	240	35	Kenya	1
16	Nigeria	229	36	Turkey	1
17	Lithuania	227	37	Norway	1
18	Pakistan	206		Swaziland	1
19	Iceland	199	39	Bermuda	
	Latvia	199	40	Croatia	

Highest growth in value traded

$ terms, % increase, 1998–2003

1	Serbia & Montenegro	4,023	23	Denmark	132
2	Iceland	4,007	24	Croatia	130
3	Bulgaria	1,542	25	Australia	129
4	Kazakhstan	1,492	26	Trinidad & Tobago	128
5	Saudi Arabia	1,060	27	United Arab Emirates[g]	126
6	Russia	672	28	Barbados	121
7	Pakistan	637	29	Kirgizstan[c]	120
8	Zimbabwe	623	30	India	92
9	Jamaica	507	31	Malaysia	86
10	Nigeria	436	32	United Kingdom	84
11	Nepal[e]	400	33	Czech Republic	83
12	South Korea	369	34	South Africa	76
13	Thailand	347	35	Singapore	73
14	Jordan	299	36	Latvia	71
15	Iran	281	37	France	68
16	Israel	269	38	China	67
17	Macedonia	175	39	Norway	64
18	Sri Lanka	174	40	Hong Kong	61
19	Finland	171	41	Germany	51
	Tanzania[f]	171	42	Chile	48
21	Kenya	165	43	Turkey	46
22	Japan	140	44	Canada	42

Highest growth in number of listed companies

% increase, 1998–2003

1	Uzbekistan[c]	11,850	24	Croatia	32
2	Macedonia	4,500	25	Japan	29
3	Serbia & Montenegro	1,610	26	Switzerland	25
4	Spain	559	27	Malaysia	22
5	Slovenia	379		Zambia[e]	22
6	Cyprus	181	29	Australia	21
7	Canada	159		Tunisia	21
8	Tanzania[e]	150		Zimbabwe	21
9	Bolivia	129	32	New Zealand	20
10	Kazakhstan	128	33	Ghana	19
11	Armenia[d]	103		Ukraine	19
12	Malta	86	33	Bangladesh	19
13	Fiji	67	36	Indonesia	16
14	Taiwan	53		Qatar[h]	16
15	China	52	38	Malawi[b]	14
16	Hong Kong	49	39	Egypt	12
17	Singapore	48		Italy	12
18	South Korea	45		Kuwait[h]	12
19	Trinidad & Tobago	40	42	Bahrain	11
20	Greece	39		United Kingdom	11
21	Botswana	36	44	Finland	10
22	Iran	35	45	Côte d'Ivoire	9
	West Bank and Gaza	35	46	Lebanon	8

a 2000   b 2000–2003   c 1999–2003   d 2001–2003   e 1998–2002
f 1999–2002   g 2000–2001   h 1998–2000

Transport: roads and cars

Longest road networks

Km, 2002 or latest

1	United States	6,378,254	21	Sweden	213,237
2	India	3,319,644	22	Bangladesh	207,486
3	China	1,765,222	23	Philippines	202,124
4	Brazil	1,724,929	24	Austria	200,000
5	Canada	1,408,800	25	Romania	198,755
6	Japan	1,171,647	26	Nigeria	194,394
7	France	893,100	27	Ukraine	169,679
8	Australia	811,603	28	Iran	167,157
9	Spain	664,852	29	Hungary	159,568
10	Russia	537,289	30	Congo	157,000
11	Italy	479,688	31	Saudi Arabia	152,044
12	United Kingdom	371,913	32	Belgium	149,028
13	Poland	364,697	33	Czech Republic	127,204
14	Turkey	354,421	34	Greece	117,000
15	Indonesia	342,700	35	Netherlands	116,500
16	Mexico	329,532	36	Colombia	112,988
17	South Africa	275,971	37	Algeria	104,000
18	Pakistan	257,683	38	Venezuela	96,155
19	Germany	230,735	39	Ireland	95,736
20	Argentina	215,471	40	Vietnam	93,300

Densest road networks

Km of road per km^2 land area, 2002 or latest

1	Macau	20.1	21	United Kingdom	1.5
2	Malta	7.0	22	Bangladesh	1.4
3	Bahrain	5.0		Ireland	1.4
4	Belgium	4.9	24	Cyprus	1.3
	Singapore	4.9		Spain	1.3
6	Barbados	3.7	26	Estonia	1.2
7	Japan	3.1		Lithuania	1.2
8	Netherlands	2.8		Poland	1.2
9	Puerto Rico	2.6	29	India	1.1
10	Austria	2.4		Mauritius	1.1
11	Luxembourg	2.0		Slovenia	1.
12	Denmark	1.7		Taiwan	1.
	Hong Kong	1.7	33	Greece	0.
	Hungary	1.7		Latvia	0.
	Jamaica	1.7		Slovakia	0.
	Switzerland	1.7		South Korea	0.
17	Czech Republic	1.6	37	Israel	0.
	France	1.6		Portugal	0
	Italy	1.6		Romania	0
	Trinidad & Tobago	1.6	40	Lebanon	0.

Most crowded road networks
Number of vehicles per km of road network, 2002 or latest

1	Hong Kong	286.7	26	Barbados	55.8
2	Qatar	283.6		Sri Lanka	55.8
3	United Arab Emirates	231.6	28	Croatia	48.7
4	Germany	194.5	29	Slovenia	47.4
5	Lebanon	190.6	30	Russia	47.3
6	Macau	172.1	31	Mexico	47.0
7	Singapore	167.0	32	Tunisia	45.5
8	South Korea	160.1	33	Guatemala	44.8
9	Kuwait	155.7	34	Puerto Rico	44.5
10	Taiwan	150.1	35	Jordan	40.1
11	Israel	111.0	36	France	39.4
12	Malta	110.3	37	Ukraine	38.1
13	Thailand	108.6	38	Greece	36.6
14	Malaysia	88.6	39	Serbia	36.2
15	Italy	73.3	40	El Salvador	36.1
16	Brunei	73.2		United States	36.1
17	Bahrain	71.4	42	Belgium	35.9
18	Bulgaria	69.1	43	Cyprus	35.1
	Portugal	69.1	44	Slovakia	35.0
20	Mauritius	68.9	45	Macedonia	34.9
21	Japan	63.2	46	Spain	33.3
22	Uruguay	63.1	47	Poland	32.5
23	United Kingdom	62.3	48	Finland	31.9
24	Netherlands	57.9	49	Denmark	31.7
25	Luxembourg	56.5	50	Czech Republic	31.4

Most used road networks
'000 vehicle-km per year per km of road network, 2002 or latest

1	Indonesia	8,134	16	Luxembourg	737
2	Hong Kong	5,888	17	United States	700
3	Taiwan	2,780	18	Greece	678
4	Germany	2,555	19	Japan	675
5	Israel	2,206	20	Denmark	644
6	Bahrain	1,545	21	Chile	631
7	Portugal	1,397	22	Finland	620
8	Sri Lanka	1,342	23	France	610
9	Malta	1,264	24	Croatia	586
10	United Kingdom	1,243	25	Cambodia	563
11	Belgium	1,062	26	Macedonia	489
12	Tunisia	1,012	27	Slovenia	481
13	Netherlands	944	28	China	476
14	Pakistan	910	29	El Salvador	423
15	South Korea	773	30	Ecuador	406

Highest car ownership
Number of cars per 1,000 people, 2002 or latest

1	Lebanon		732
2	New Zealand		613
3	Brunei		576
	Luxembourg		576
5	Iceland		561
6	Canada		559
7	Italy		542
8	Germany		516
9	Switzerland		507
10	Malta		505
11	Austria		494
12	France		491
13	Australia		488
14	United States		481
15	Belgium		464
16	Sweden		452
17	Slovenia		438
18	Japan		428
19	Portugal		426
20	Finland		419
21	Norway		417
22	Spain		408
23	Cyprus		404
24	Netherlands		384
	United Kingdom		384
26	Denmark		360
27	Kuwait		359
28	Czech Republic		356
29	Ireland		349
30	Lithuania		346
31	Cambodia		312
32	Bahrain		307
33	Estonia		296
34	Bulgaria		287
35	Croatia		280
36	Latvia		266
37	Hungary		259
	Poland		259
39	Greece		254
40	Slovakia		247
41	Israel		230
	Puerto Rico		230
43	Qatar		219
44	Taiwan		212
45	South Korea		20.
46	Bahamas		16.
47	Belarus		15.
48	Libya		15.
	Uruguay		15.
50	Malaysia		14.

Lowest car ownership
Number of cars per 1,000 people, 2002 or latest

1	Somalia		0.1
	Tajikistan		0.1
3	Central African Rep		0.3
	Mozambique		0.3
5	Bangladesh		0.5
6	Myanmar		0.6
7	Tanzania		0.8
8	Ethiopia		1.0
	Guatemala		1.0
10	Afghanistan		1.4
	Rwanda		1.4
12	Eritrea		1.5
13	Uganda		1.8
14	Guinea		2.0
15	Malawi		2.3
16	Liberia		2.
17	Burundi		2.
18	Mali		2.
19	Chad		3.
20	Laos		3.
21	Burkina Faso		3
22	Niger		3.
23	Sierra Leone		3
24	Madagascar		4
25	Haiti		4
26	Ghana		4
27	Guinea-Bissau		5
	Lesotho		5
29	India		6
30	China		6

Most accidents

Number of people injured per 100m vehicle-km, 2002 or latest

1	Malawi	2,730		United Kingdom	94
2	Rwanda	1,764	27	Bolivia	90
3	South Korea	510	28	Saudi Arabia	89
4	Costa Rica	406	29	Philippines	86
5	Kenya	363	30	Germany	81
6	India	333		Macedonia	81
7	Honduras	317	32	Spain	76
8	Egypt	222	33	United States	74
9	Sri Lanka	205	34	Ghana	72
10	Portugal	194	35	Malaysia	66
11	Turkey	182		Mexico	66
12	Hong Kong	176	37	Hungary	61
	Morocco	176		Iceland	61
14	Ethiopia	162	39	Yemen	59
15	Japan	149	40	Senegal	56
16	Kirgizstan	134	41	Bahrain	54
17	Colombia	126	42	Iran	53
18	Latvia	125		Oman	53
19	Italy	122	44	Switzerland	49
20	Canada	121	45	Estonia	42
21	Czech Republic	113		Malta	42
22	Belgium	108	47	Nicaragua	40
23	Israel	101		Thailand	40
24	South Africa	100	49	Slovakia	39
25	Slovenia	94	50	New Zealand	37

Most deaths

Number of people killed per 100m vehicle-km, 2002 or latest

1	Malawi	1,117		Saudi Arabia	11
2	Namibia	340		Yemen	11
3	India	65	19	Bolivia	10
4	Ethiopia	53		Mexico	10
5	Egypt	44	21	Malaysia	9
6	Latvia	25	22	Albania	8
7	Kirgizstan	24	23	South Africa	7
8	Sri Lanka	23		Suriname	7
9	Colombia	17		Sweden	7
	South Korea	17	26	Portugal	6
11	Honduras	16		Romania	6
12	Morocco	14		Turkey	6
	Philippines	14	29	Czech Republic	5
14	Thailand	13		Ecuador	5
15	Ghana	12		Iran	5
16	Costa Rica	11		Nicaragua	5

Transport: planes and trains

Most air travel
Million passenger-km[a] per year

1	United States	1,142,984	16	Malaysia	48,392
2	Japan	230,822	17	Brazil	47,100
3	United Kingdom	177,881	18	Thailand	38,131
4	China	134,644	19	Belgium	30,023
5	Germany	122,225	20	Switzerland	29,376
6	France	92,604	21	South Africa	29,016
7	Hong Kong	77,948	22	Mexico	28,592
8	Australia	76,744	23	Saudi Arabia	28,139
9	Canada	70,896	24	United Arab Emirates	26,935
10	Singapore	70,168	25	India	24,206
11	South Korea	69,814	26	New Zealand	23,632
12	Russia	58,017	27	Argentina	19,533
13	Netherlands	57,272	28	Turkey	18,810
14	Italy	51,117	29	Austria	18,678
15	Spain	50,735	30	Indonesia	18,625

Busiest airports

Total passengers, m

1	Atlanta, Hartsfield	83.6
2	Chicago, O'Hare	75.5
3	London, Heathrow	67.3
4	Tokyo, Haneda	62.3
5	Los Angeles, Intl.	60.7
6	Dallas, Ft. Worth	59.4
7	Frankfurt, Main	51.1
8	Paris, Charles de Gaulle	50.9
9	Amsterdam, Schipol	42.5
10	Denver, Intl.	42.4
11	Las Vegas, McCarran Intl.	41.4
12	Phoenix, Skyharbor Intl.	39.5

Total cargo, m tonnes

1	Memphis, Intl.	3.55
2	Hong Kong, Intl.	3.13
3	Anchorage, Intl.	2.37
4	Tokyo, Narita	2.37
5	Seoul, Inchon	2.13
6	Los Angeles, Intl.	1.90
7	Frankfurt, Main	1.84
8	Singapore, Changi	1.80
9	Miami, Intl.	1.78
10	Louisville, Standiford Fd.	1.74
11	Taipei, CKS	1.70
12	NY, John F. Kennedy	1.68

Average daily aircraft movements, take-offs and landings

1	Chicago, O'Hare	2,719	11	Cincinnati, Intl.	1,41
2	Atlanta, Hartsfield	2,643	12	Houston, George Bush Intercont.	1,41
3	Dallas, Ft. Worth	2,197	13	Philadelphia, Intl.	1,33
4	Los Angeles, Intl.	1,794	14	Frankfurt, Main	1,30
5	Denver, Intl.	1,530	15	London, Heathrow	1,30
6	Phoenix, Skyharbor Intl.	1,498	16	Washington, Dulles Intl.	1,28
7	Las Vegas, McCarran Intl.	1,492	17	Charlotte/Douglas, Intl.	1,28
8	Minneapolis, St Paul	1,481	18	Los Angeles, Van Nuys	1,22
9	Paris, Charles de Gaulle	1,465	19	Newark	1,18
10	Detroit, Metro	1,424	20	Amsterdam, Schipol	1,14

a Air passenger–km data refer to the distance travelled by each aircraft of national origin.

Longest railway networks
'000 km

1	United States	233.8	21	Sweden	9.9
2	Russia	85.5	22	Australia	9.5
3	Canada	73.2		Czech Republic	9.5
4	India	63.1	24	Turkey	8.7
5	China	60.5	25	Hungary	8.0
6	Germany	36.1	26	Pakistan	7.8
7	Argentina	34.2	27	Iran	6.2
8	France	29.3	28	Finland	5.9
9	Mexico	26.5	29	Austria	5.8
10	South Africa	22.7	30	Belarus	5.5
11	Brazil	22.1	31	Egypt	5.2
	Ukraine	22.1	32	Cuba	4.8
13	Senegal	21.0	33	Sudan	4.6
14	Poland	19.9	34	Congo-Brazzaville	4.5
15	Japan	18.5		North Korea	4.5
16	United Kingdom	17.1	36	Bulgaria	4.3
17	Italy	16.3		Philippines	4.3
18	Spain	14.4	38	Indonesia	4.2
19	Kazakhstan	13.8	39	Norway	4.1
20	Romania	11.4		Uzbekistan	4.1

Most rail passengers
Km per person per year

1	Japan	1,891	11	Italy	811
2	Switzerland	1,751	12	Belgium	795
3	Belarus	1,344	13	Hungary	740
4	France	1,203	14	Sweden	736
5	Ukraine	1,100	15	Kazakhstan	721
6	Russia	1,080	16	United Kingdom	695
7	Austria	1,008	17	Finland	642
8	Denmark	999	18	Czech Republic	636
9	Netherlands	855	19	South Korea	596
10	Germany	842	20	Egypt	566

Most rail freight
Million tonnes-km per year

1	United States	2,264,982	11	Poland	47,394
2	Russia	1,664,300	12	France	46,835
3	China	1,647,558	13	Australia	41,314
4	India	353,194	14	Belarus	38,402
5	Canada	311,371	15	Japan	22,600
6	Ukraine	225,287	16	Italy	20,753
7	Kazakhstan	148,370	17	United Kingdom	19,561
8	Senegal	105,725	18	Uzbekistan	18,428
9	South Africa	105,719	19	Iran	18,048
10	Germany	73,973	20	Austria	17,863

Transport: shipping

Merchant fleets
By country of registration, gross tonnage, million

1	Panama	131.5	11	Japan	13.2
2	Liberia	53.9	12	United Kingdom	11.1
3	Bahamas	35.4	13	Italy	11.0
4	Greece	32.0	14	United States	10.7
5	Singapore	26.3	15	Russia	8.6
6	Hong Kong	26.1	16	Germany	8.2
7	Malta	22.4	17	South Korea	7.8
8	Cyprus	21.3	18	India	7.5
9	China	20.4	19	Denmark	7.3
10	Norway	15.4	20	Bermuda	6.1

Merchant fleets
By country of ownership, gross tonnage, million

1	Greece	90.4	11	Denmark	13.2
2	Japan	80.6	12	Singapore	12.9
3	Germany	42.9	13	Russia	12.2
4	United States	36.9	14	Italy	11.2
5	China	36.2	15	Switzerland	9.2
6	Norway	32.4	16	India	7.6
7	Hong Kong	26.2	17	Malaysia	7.3
8	South Korea	18.0	18	Saudi Arabia	6.1
9	Taiwan	15.6	19	France	5.7
10	United Kingdom	14.6	20	Turkey	5.6

Crude oil capacity
By country of registration, gross tonnage, '000

1	Panama	23,269	11	Cyprus	2,51
2	Liberia	19,474	12	Japan	2,14
3	Greece	14,881	13	France	1,93
4	Bahamas	11,955	14	Belgium	1,89
5	Singapore	9,606	15	China	1,48
6	Hong Kong	5,201	16	Kuwait	1,44
7	Malta	4,855	17	United States	1,39
8	Norway	3,767	18	Malaysia	1,27
9	India	3,603	19	Italy	98
10	Iran	3,061	20	Saudi Arabia	81

Fish catching capacity
By country of registration, gross tonnage, '000

1	Russia	1,960	11	Iceland	17
2	United States	738	12	United Kingdom	16
3	Japan	435	13	China	14
4	Spain	401	14	Panama	14
5	South Korea	396	15	Ukraine	13
6	Norway	378	16	Honduras	1
7	Argentina	219	17	Canada	13
8	Chile	195	18	Denmark	1
9	Netherlands	190	19	Philippines	1
10	Peru	179	20	France	1

Tourism

Most tourist arrivals
Number of arrivals, '000

1	France	75,048	21	Sweden	7,627
2	Spain	51,830	22	Croatia	7,409
3	United States	41,212	23	Saudi Arabia	7,332
4	Italy	39,604	24	Belgium	6,690
5	China	32,970	25	South Africa	6,640
6	United Kingdom	24,715	26	Switzerland	6,530
7	Austria	19,078	27	Ireland	6,369
8	Mexico	18,665	28	Macau	6,309
9	Germany	18,392	29	United Arab Emirates	5,871
10	Canada	17,534	30	Egypt	5,746
11	Hungary	15,706	31	Singapore	5,705
12	Hong Kong	15,537	32	Japan	5,212
13	Greece	13,969	33	Czech Republic	5,076
14	Poland	13,720	34	South Korea	4,753
15	Turkey	13,341	35	Morocco	4,552
16	Portugal	11,707	36	Indonesia	4,467
17	Malaysia	10,577	37	Australia	4,354
18	Thailand	10,082	38	Brazil	4,091
19	Netherlands	9,181	39	Dominican Republic	3,282
20	Russia	8,015	40	Norway	3,269

Biggest tourist spenders
$m

1	Germany	59,711	11	Austria	11,397
2	United States	56,825	12	Canada	11,144
3	United Kingdom	46,839	13	Hong Kong	11,143
4	Japan	26,147	14	Spain	8,207
5	France	23,734	15	South Korea	8,008
6	Italy	21,101	16	Denmark	7,904
7	China	16,853	17	Norway	7,566
8	Netherlands	14,919	18	Sweden	7,502
9	Russia	13,242	19	Switzerland	7,178
10	Belgium	12,426	20	Taiwan	6,205

Largest tourist receipts
$m

1	United States	64,509	11	Greece	10,701
2	Spain	41,770	12	Canada	10,579
3	France	37,038	13	Australia	10,313
4	Italy	31,222	14	Mexico	9,457
5	Germany	22,984	15	Switzerland	9,325
6	United Kingdom	22,753	16	Netherlands	9,249
7	China	17,406	17	Japan	8,848
8	Hungary	15,537	18	Belgium	8,130
9	Austria	14,068	19	Thailand	7,901
10	Turkey	13,203	20	Hong Kong	7,657

Education

Highest primary enrolment
Number enrolled as % of relevant age group

1	Brazil	148	Ukraine	117
2	Malawi	146	17 China	116
3	Uganda	136	Portugal	116
4	Gabon	134	19 Aruba	115
5	Cambodia	132	Laos	115
6	Dominican Republic	126	21 Bolivia	114
	Equatorial Guinea	126	Libya	114
	Suriname	126	Russia	114
9	Lesotho	124	24 Israel	113
	Togo	124	25 El Salvador	112
11	Nepal	122	Paraguay	112
12	Argentina	120	Philippines	112
	Peru	120	Sri Lanka	112
14	Ecuador	117	Syria	112
	Rwanda	117	Tunisia	112

Lowest primary enrolment
Number enrolled as % of relevant age group

1	Afghanistan	23	Pakistan	73
2	Niger	40	Papua New Guinea	73
3	Burkina Faso	44	17 Angola	74
4	Congo-Brazzaville	50	18 Senegal	75
5	Mali	57	19 Guinea	77
6	Sudan	59	20 Gambia, The	79
7	Eritrea	61	Zambia	79
8	Ethiopia	64	22 Côte d'Ivoire	80
9	Central African Rep	66	23 Ghana	81
10	Saudi Arabia	67	Yemen	81
11	Guinea-Bissau	70	25 Oman	82
	Tanzania	70	26 Moldova	84
13	Burundi	71	27 Congo	84
14	Chad	73	Mauritania	84

Highest tertiary enrolment[a]
Number enrolled as % of relevant age group

1	Finland	86	11 Macau	6
2	South Korea	85	Slovenia	6
3	United States	81	13 Estonia	6
4	Sweden	76	Lithuania	6
5	Australia	74	United Kingdom	6
	New Zealand	74	16 Denmark	6
	Norway	74	17 Bermuda	6
8	Russia	70	18 Belarus	6
9	Latvia	69	Belgium	6
10	Greece	68	Poland	6

Notes: Latest available year 1999–2003. The gross enrolment ratios shown are the actual number enrolled as a percentage of the number of children in the official primary age group. They may exceed 100 when children outside the primary age group are receiving primary education either because they have not moved on to secondary education or because they have started primary education early.

Least literate
% adult literacy rate, latest year 2000–04

1	Burkina Faso	12.8	16	Yemen	49.0
2	Mali	19.0	17	Morocco	50.7
3	Niger	19.9	18	Haiti	51.9
4	Chad	25.5	19	Togo	53.0
5	Sierra Leone	29.6	20	Ghana	54.1
6	Benin	39.8	21	Egypt	55.6
7	Senegal	41.0	22	Liberia	55.9
8	Bangladesh	41.1	23	Burundi	58.9
9	Mauritania	41.2	24	Sudan	59.0
10	Ethiopia	41.5	25	India	61.3
	Pakistan	41.5	26	Rwanda	64.0
12	Mozambique	46.5	27	Malawi	64.1
13	Côte d'Ivoire	48.1	28	Congo-Brazzaville	65.3
14	Central African Rep	48.6	29	Nigeria	66.8
	Nepal	48.6	30	Angola	66.9

Highest education spending
% of GDP

1	Lesotho	10.0		Mongolia	6.5
	Yemen	10.0	15	Finland	6.3
3	Cuba	9.0		Jamaica	6.3
4	Denmark	8.4	17	Kenya	6.2
5	Saudi Arabia	8.3	18	Iceland	6.1
6	Malaysia	7.9	19	Belarus	6.0
	Namibia	7.9		Bolivia	6.0
8	Sweden	7.6		Lithuania	6.0
9	Israel	7.3	22	Belgium	5.9
10	Norway	7.2		Estonia	5.9
11	New Zealand	6.9		Latvia	5.9
12	Tunisia	6.8		Portugal	5.9
13	Barbados	6.5			

Lowest education spending
% of GDP

1	Equatorial Guinea	0.5		Chad	2.0
2	Ecuador	1.0	14	Botswana	2.1
3	Indonesia	1.3		China	2.1
	Myanmar	1.3		Guinea-Bissau	2.1
	Sri Lanka	1.3	17	Tanzania	2.2
6	Guatemala	1.7	18	Bangladesh	2.3
7	Pakistan	1.8		Niger	2.3
8	Central African Rep	1.9		Papua New Guinea	2.3
	Guinea	1.9	21	Dominican Republic	2.4
	United Arab Emirates	1.9		Mozambique	2.4
	Zambia	1.9		Tajikistan	2.4
12	Cambodia	2.0			

a Tertiary education includes all levels of post-secondary education including courses
leading to awards not equivalent to a university degree, courses leading to a first
university degree and postgraduate courses.

Life expectancy

Highest life expectancy
Years, 2005–10

1	Andorra[a]	83.5		Guadeloupe	79.2
2	Japan	82.8	27	Aruba[a]	79.1
3	Hong Kong	82.2		Luxembourg	79.1
4	Iceland	81.4		Malta	79.1
5	Switzerland	81.1		United Arab Emirates	79.1
6	Australia	81.0	31	Channel Islands	79.0
7	Sweden	80.8		Netherlands	79.0
8	Canada	80.7		United Kingdom	79.0
	Macau	80.7	34	Costa Rica	78.8
10	Israel	80.6	35	Greece	78.7
11	Italy	80.6	36	Chile	78.6
12	Norway	80.2		Cuba	78.6
13	Spain	80.1	38	Ireland	78.5
14	Cayman Islands[a]	80.0	39	South Korea	78.2
	France	80.0	40	Portugal	77.9
16	New Zealand	79.8		United States	77.5
17	Austria	79.7	42	Bermuda[a]	77.8
18	Belgium	79.6		Denmark	77.8
19	Martinique	79.4	44	Kuwait	77.
	Singapore	79.4	45	Taiwan	77.
21	Finland	79.3	46	Slovenia	77.
	Germany	79.3	47	Brunei	77.
23	Virgin Islands	79.3	48	Netherlands Antilles	76.
24	Cyprus	79.2	49	Puerto Rico	76.
	Faroe Islands[a]	79.2	50	Barbados	76.

Highest male life expectancy
Years, 2005–10

1	Andorra[a]	80.6	9	Canada	78.
2	Iceland	79.5		Switzerland	78.
3	Hong Kong	79.3	11	Norway	77
4	Japan	79.1	12	New Zealand	77
5	Macau	78.6	13	Singapore	77
	Sweden	78.6	14	Italy	77
7	Australia	78.5	15	United Arab Emirates	77
8	Israel	78.4	16	Cayman Islands[a]	77

Highest female life expectancy
Years, 2005–10

1	Andorra[a]	86.6		Virgin Islands	83
2	Japan	86.4	11	Canada	83
3	Hong Kong	85.1	12	Sweden	83
4	Spain	83.8	13	Aruba[a]	82
	Switzerland	83.8		Belgium	82
6	Italy	83.6		Faroe Islands[a]	82
7	France	83.5		Macau	82
8	Australia	83.4	17	Cayman Islands[a]	82
9	Iceland	83.2		Israel	82

a 2005 estimate.

Lowest life expectancy

Years, 2005–10

1	Swaziland	29.9	26	Ethiopia	48.5
2	Botswana	33.9	27	Somalia	48.8
3	Lesotho	34.3	28	Burkina Faso	49.3
4	Zimbabwe	37.3		Mali	49.3
5	Zambia	39.1	30	Kenya	50.3
6	Central African Rep	39.5	31	Uganda	52.1
7	Malawi	41.1	32	Gabon	53.3
8	Equatorial Guinea	41.5	33	Congo-Brazzaville	53.5
9	Mozambique	41.8		Haiti	53.5
10	Angola	41.9	35	Guinea	54.4
	Sierra Leone	41.9	36	Mauritania	54.5
12	Liberia	42.5	37	Togo	55.8
13	South Africa	44.1	38	Benin	55.9
14	Nigeria	44.2	39	Eritrea	56.0
15	Chad	44.3	40	Madagascar	56.2
16	Rwanda	44.6	41	Laos	56.5
17	Congo	44.7	42	Sudan	56.9
18	Niger	45.4	43	Papua New Guinea	57.1
19	Guinea-Bissau	45.5		Senegal	57.1
20	Burundi	45.6	45	Gambia, The	57.7
21	Namibia	45.9	46	Cambodia	58.0
22	Côte d'Ivoire	46.2	47	Ghana	58.1
23	Cameroon	46.3	48	Iraq	61.0
24	Tanzania	46.6	49	Myanmar	61.8
25	Afghanistan	47.7	50	Yemen	62.7

Lowest male life expectancy

Years, 2005–10

1	Swaziland	30.8	11	Mozambique	41.7
2	Lesotho	34.2	12	Liberia	41.9
3	Botswana	35.0	13	Rwanda	43.1
4	Zimbabwe	38.2	14	Chad	43.3
5	Central African Rep	39.0	15	Congo	43.6
6	Zambia	39.6	16	Nigeria	44.1
7	Angola	40.5	17	South Africa	44.2
	Sierra Leone	40.5	18	Guinea-Bissau	44.3
9	Equatorial Guinea	41.4	19	Burundi	44.5
10	Malawi	41.6	20	Niger	45.4

Lowest female life expectancy

Years, 2005–10

1	Swaziland	29.2	10	Liberia	43.1
2	Botswana	32.7	11	Sierra Leone	43.3
3	Lesotho	34.3	12	Angola	43.4
4	Zimbabwe	36.3	13	South Africa	43.8
5	Zambia	38.6	14	Nigeria	44.3
6	Central African Rep	40.0	15	Namibia	45.1
7	Malawi	40.6	16	Chad	45.4
8	Equatorial Guinea	41.6		Niger	45.4
	Mozambique	41.9	18	Congo	45.8

Death rates and infant mortality

Highest death rates
Number of deaths per 1,000 population, 2005–10

1	Swaziland	31.2	49	Laos	11.3
2	Botswana	28.4		Togo	11.3
3	Lesotho	26.4	51	Madagascar	11.2
4	Zimbabwe	23.0		Serbia & Montenegro	11.2
5	Sierra Leone	22.5	53	Czech Republic	11.1
6	Central African Rep	21.8	54	Kazakhstan	11.0
7	Zambia	21.2	55	Portugal	10.9
8	Angola	21.1		Sudan	10.9
9	Equatorial Guinea	20.9	57	Gambia, The	10.8
10	South Africa	20.6		Moldova	10.8
11	Liberia	20.3	59	Germany	10.7
12	Malawi	19.9		North Korea	10.7
	Mozambique	19.9		Senegal	10.7
14	Chad	19.5	62	Denmark	10.6
	Niger	19.5		Italy	10.6
16	Congo	19.2	64	Greece	10.5
17	Guinea-Bissau	19.0	65	Slovenia	10.4
18	Nigeria	18.4	66	Ghana	10.3
19	Afghanistan	18.0	67	Belgium	10.2
20	Burundi	17.9		United Kingdom	10.2
	Rwanda	17.9	69	Cambodia	10.1
22	Ukraine	16.9		Eritrea	10.1
23	Cameroon	16.8		Poland	10.1
24	Côte d'Ivoire	16.7		Sweden	10.1
25	Mali	16.4	73	Bosnia	9.1
	Namibia	16.4	74	Austria	9.1
27	Tanzania	16.3		Finland	9.1
28	Somalia	16.1		Slovakia	9.1
29	Russia	16.0	77	Armenia	9.
30	Burkina Faso	15.8		France	9.
31	Ethiopia	15.4		Papua New Guinea	9.
32	Belarus	15.0	80	Channel Islands	9.
33	Bulgaria	14.5	81	Myanmar	9.
34	Kenya	13.8		Norway	9.
35	Estonia	13.6	83	Netherlands	9.
	Latvia	13.6		Spain	9
37	Uganda	13.5	85	Uruguay	9.
38	Gabon	13.0	86	Macedonia	8
39	Guinea	12.9	87	Japan	8
	Hungary	12.9		Switzerland	8
41	Mauritania	12.8	89	Faroe Islands[a]	8
42	Haiti	12.7	90	Trinidad and Tobago	8
43	Romania	12.6	91	Iraq	8
44	Congo-Brazzaville	12.2		Malta	8
	Lithuania	12.2		United States	8
46	Croatia	12.1	94	India	8
47	Georgia	11.8		Puerto Rico	8
48	Benin	11.6			

Note: Both death and, in particular, infant mortality rates can be underestimated in certain countries where not all deaths are officially recorded. a 2005 estimate.

Highest infant mortality
Number of deaths per 1,000 live births, 2005–10

1	Sierra Leone	159.8	21	Central African Rep	93.2
2	Niger	145.4	22	Ethiopia	90.9
3	Afghanistan	141.9	23	Cameroon	90.7
4	Angola	141.6	24	Mozambique	90.6
5	Liberia	132.0	25	Zambia	88.4
6	Mali	125.8	26	Mauritania	88.1
7	Burkina Faso	115.6	27	Togo	87.5
8	Côte d'Ivoire	113.8	28	Cambodia	87.3
9	Somalia	113.1	29	Tajikistan	85.2
10	Congo	112.5	30	Iraq	81.5
11	Rwanda	112.3	31	Laos	79.6
12	Chad	111.5	32	Senegal	77.2
13	Guinea-Bissau	111.0	33	Uganda	76.6
14	Nigeria	108.1	34	Turkmenistan	74.7
15	Tanzania	104.0	35	Azerbaijan	72.2
16	Malawi	102.6	36	Madagascar	71.2
17	Burundi	98.9	37	Pakistan	70.5
18	Benin	97.6	38	Congo-Brazzaville	68.0
19	Guinea	96.7		Gambia, The	68.0
20	Equatorial Guinea	94.5	40	Myanmar	66.4

Lowest death rates
No. deaths per 1,000 pop., 2005–10

1	United Arab Emirates	1.3
2	Kuwait	1.9
3	Brunei	2.8
	Oman	2.8
5	Qatar	2.9
6	Bahrain	3.4
	Syria	3.4
8	Saudi Arabia	3.7
	West Bank and Gaza	3.7
10	Jordan	4.0
11	Costa Rica	4.1
	Libya	4.1
13	Mexico	4.5
14	Malaysia	4.7
	Nicaragua	4.7
16	Cayman Islands[a]	4.8
	Macau	4.8
	Paraguay	4.8
	Philippines	4.8
20	Algeria	4.9
21	French Polynesia	5.0
	Guam	5.0
	New Caledonia	5.0
	Panama	5.0
	Venezuela	5.0

Lowest infant mortality
No. deaths per 1,000 live births, 2005–10

1	Singapore	3.0
2	Iceland	3.1
	Japan	3.1
4	Sweden	3.2
5	Norway	3.3
6	South Korea	3.6
7	Finland	3.7
	Hong Kong	3.7
9	Andorra[a]	4.1
	Belgium	4.1
11	France	4.3
	Germany	4.3
	Switzerland	4.3
14	Austria	4.4
	Netherlands	4.4
	Spain	4.4
17	Australia	4.6
18	Denmark	4.7
19	Canada	4.8
	Israel	4.8
21	Cuba	4.9
22	Italy	5.0
	Luxembourg	5.0
	New Zealand	5.0
	United Kingdom	5.0

a 2005 estimate.

Death and disease

Breast cancer
Deaths per 100,000 pop., 2000

1	Denmark	26.5
2	Iceland	24.9
3	Belgium	24.5
4	United Kingdom	24.2
5	Hungary	24.0
6	Switzerland	23.5
7	Germany	23.4
8	Netherlands	23.3
9	Malta	23.2
10	Austria	21.7
11	Italy	20.7
12	Luxembourg	20.1
13	Uruguay	19.9
14	France	19.4
15	Czech Republic	19.3
16	New Zealand	18.5
17	Canada	18.1
	Norway	18.1
	Slovenia	18.1
20	Croatia	17.7

Lung cancer
Deaths per 100,000 pop., 2000

1	Hungary	79.0
2	Belgium	67.5
3	Denmark	66.2
4	United Kingdom	63.3
5	Croatia	58.3
6	Italy	57.0
7	Netherlands	56.9
8	United States	56.7
9	Canada	56.6
10	Czech Republic	53.6
11	Greece	53.6
12	Hong Kong	52.9
13	Poland	51.5
14	Luxembourg	51.1
15	Estonia	49.8
16	Germany	48.5
17	Slovenia	48.1
18	Russia	44.6
19	Spain	44.3
20	Japan	42.4

Maternal mortality rate
Deaths per 100,000 live births, estimates

1	Sierra Leone	2,000
2	Afghanistan	1,900
3	Malawi	1,800
4	Angola	1,700
5	Niger	1,600
6	Tanzania	1,500
7	Rwanda	1,400
8	Mali	1,200
9	Central African Rep	1,100
	Chad	1,100
	Guinea-Bissau	1,100
	Somalia	1,100
	Zimbabwe	1,100
14	Burkina Faso	1,000
	Burundi	1,000
	Kenya	1,000
	Mauritania	1,000
	Mozambique	1,000
19	Congo	990
20	Equatorial Guinea	880
	Uganda	880
22	Benin	850
	Ethiopia	850
24	Nigeria	800

Tuberculosis
Prevalence per 100,000 pop., 2005

1	Swaziland	1,083
2	Lesotho	733
3	Namibia	722
4	Zimbabwe	659
5	Zambia	656
6	Botswana	633
7	Kenya	610
8	South Africa	536
9	Cambodia	508
10	Mozambique	457
11	Malawi	442
12	Sierra Leone	427
13	Somalia	411
	Uganda	411
15	Côte d'Ivoire	396
16	Congo-Brazzaville	380
17	Rwanda	374
18	Tanzania	371
19	Congo	369
20	Ethiopia	356
21	Togo	351
22	Burundi	346
23	Afghanistan	333
24	Central African Rep	325

Note: Statistics are not available for all countries. The number of cases diagnosed and reported depends on the quality of medical practice and administration and can be under-reported in a number of countries.

Diabetes

Prevalence among pop. aged
20–79, 2001, %

1	Mexico	14.2
2	Trinidad and Tobago	14.1
3	Saudi Arabia	12.3
4	Hong Kong	12.1
	Mauritius	12.1
6	Jamaica	11.7
	Papua New Guinea	11.7
8	Cuba	11.5
9	Puerto Rico	11.3
	Singapore	11.3
11	Pakistan	9.2
12	United Arab Emirates	8.7
13	Slovakia	8.6
14	India	8.0
	Slovenia	8.0
	United States	8.0
17	Japan	7.4
	Russia	7.4
	Turkey	7.4

Measles immunisation

Lowest % of children aged
12–23 months, 2003

1	Central African Rep	35
	Nigeria	35
3	Somalia	40
4	Laos	42
5	Papua New Guinea	49
6	Afghanistan	50
	Congo-Brazzaville	50
8	Ethiopia	52
	Guinea	52
10	Haiti	53
	Liberia	53
12	Congo	54
13	Gabon	55
	Madagascar	55
15	Côte d'Ivoire	56
16	Sudan	57
17	Togo	58
18	Senegal	60

HIV/AIDS

Prevalence among population
aged 15–49, %, 2003

1	Swaziland	38.8
2	Botswana	37.3
3	Lesotho	28.9
4	Zimbabwe	24.6
5	Namibia	21.3
6	South Africa[a]	15.6
	Zambia[b]	15.6
8	Malawi	14.2
9	Central African Rep	13.5
10	Mozambique	12.2
11	Tanzania	8.8
12	Gabon	8.1
13	Côte d'Ivoire	7.0
14	Kenya	6.7
15	Burundi	6.0
16	Liberia	5.9
17	Haiti	5.6
18	Cameroon[c]	5.5
19	Nigeria	5.4
20	Rwanda	5.1
21	Congo-Brazzaville	4.9
22	Chad	4.8
23	Ethiopia	4.4
24	Congo	4.2

AIDS

Estimated deaths per 100,000
pop., 2003

1	Botswana	1,849
2	Lesotho	1,609
3	Swaziland	1,578
4	Zimbabwe	1,319
5	Zambia	823
6	South Africa	822
7	Namibia	805
8	Malawi	694
9	Central African Rep	595
10	Mozambique	583
11	Kenya	469
12	Tanzania	433
13	Burundi	366
14	Cameroon	306
15	Uganda	302
16	Haiti	288
17	Côte d'Ivoire	283
18	Rwanda	262
19	Congo-Brazzaville	260
20	Nigeria	250
21	Gabon	226
22	Burkina Faso	223
23	Liberia	214
24	Chad	209

a 2002   b 2001–02   c 2004

Health

Highest health spending
As % of GDP

1	United States	14.6
2	Cambodia	12.0
3	Lebanon	11.5
4	Switzerland	11.2
5	Germany	10.9
6	Uruguay	10.0
7	Iceland	9.9
8	Malawi	9.8
9	France	9.7
	Malta	9.7
11	Canada	9.6
	Norway	9.6
13	Australia	9.5
	Greece	9.5
15	Costa Rica	9.3
	Jordan	9.3
	Portugal	9.3
18	Bosnia	9.2
	Sweden	9.2
20	Belgium	9.1
	Israel	9.1
22	Argentina	8.9
	Panama	8.9
24	Denmark	8.8
	Netherlands	8.8
26	South Africa	8.7
27	Italy	8.5
	New Zealand	8.5
	Suriname	8.5
	Zimbabwe	8.5

Lowest health spending
As % of GDP

1	Iraq	1.5
2	Equatorial Guinea	1.8
3	Liberia	2.1
	Madagascar	2.1
5	Congo	2.2
	Myanmar	2.2
7	Laos	2.9
	Mauritius	2.9
	Philippines	2.9
10	Sierra Leone	2.9
11	Burundi	3.0
12	Bangladesh	3.1
	Qatar	3.1
	United Arab Emirates	3.1
15	Indonesia	3.2
	Pakistan	3.2
17	Libya	3.3
	Tajikistan	3.3
19	Albania	3.4
	Oman	3.4
21	Brunei	3.5
	Kazakhstan	3.5
23	Azerbaijan	3.7
	Sri Lanka	3.7
	Trinidad & Tobago	3.7
	Yemen	3.7
27	Georgia	3.8
	Kuwait	3.8
	Malaysia	3.8
30	Central African Rep	3.9
	Mauritania	3.9

Highest pop. per doctor

1	Malawi	88,321
2	Congo	71,642
3	Liberia	61,818
4	Rwanda	54,194
5	Tanzania	45,012
6	Mozambique	43,448
7	Chad	41,951
8	Eritrea	41,837
9	Ethiopia	35,870
10	Central African Rep	33,333
	Gambia, The	33,333
12	Somalia	31,935
13	Niger	31,088
14	Burkina Faso	26,531
15	Mali	24,575
16	Bhutan	22,330
17	Uganda	21,957

Lowest pop. per doctor

1	Italy	165
2	Cuba	170
3	United States	188
4	Belarus	220
5	Greece	229
6	Russia	237
7	Belgium	240
8	Lithuania	242
9	Georgia	252
10	Israel	265
11	Uruguay	275
12	Denmark	276
13	Germany	277
14	Norway	282
15	Armenia	285
16	Switzerland	286
17	Azerbaijan	289

Most hospital beds
Beds per 1,000 pop.

1	Switzerland	17.9	16	Romania	8.0
2	Japan	17.3	17	Australia	7.9
3	Norway	14.6	18	Finland	7.5
4	Russia	14.4	19	Thailand	7.4
5	Belarus	12.6	20	Bulgaria	7.2
6	Netherlands	10.8	21	Turkmenistan	7.1
7	Ireland	9.7	22	Kazakhstan	7.0
8	Ukraine	9.4	23	Estonia	6.7
9	Germany	9.1	24	Tajikistan	6.4
10	Czech Republic	8.8	25	Austria	6.3
11	Azerbaijan	8.5	26	Croatia	6.0
12	France	8.2	27	Moldova	5.9
	Hungary	8.2	28	Israel	5.8
14	Latvia	8.1		New Zealand	5.8
	Lithuania	8.1	30	South Korea	5.7

Obesity[a]

Men, % of total population

1	Lebanon	36.3
2	Qatar	34.6
3	Panama	27.9
4	United States	27.7
5	Greece	27.5
	Kuwait	27.5
7	Cyprus	26.6
8	Saudi Arabia	26.4
9	United Arab Emirates	25.6
10	Czech Republic	24.7
11	Bahrain	23.3
12	Albania	22.8
13	Germany	22.5
14	England	22.2
15	Malta	22.0
16	Ireland	20.1
17	Finland	19.8
18	Mexico	19.4
19	Australia	19.3
	Slovakia	19.3
21	Scotland	19.0
22	Uruguay	17.0
	Wales	17.0
24	Turkey	16.5
25	Dominican Republic	16.4
26	Oman	16.2
27	Canada	16.0
28	Luxembourg	15.3
29	Israel	14.7

Women, % of total population

1	Qatar	45.3
2	Saudi Arabia	44.0
3	United Arab Emirates	39.9
4	Lebanon	38.3
5	Greece	38.1
6	Panama	36.1
7	Albania	35.6
8	Malta	35.0
9	Bahrain	34.1
10	United States	34.0
11	Uzbekistan	33.0
12	Egypt	32.4
13	Iran	30.0
14	Kuwait	29.9
15	Turkey	29.4
16	Mexico	29.0
17	South Africa	27.9
18	Czech Republic	26.2
19	Portugal	26.1
20	Mongolia	24.6
21	Cyprus	23.7
22	Germany	23.3
23	England	23.0
24	Tunisia	22.7
25	Romania	22.4
26	Australia	22.2
27	Scotland	22.0
28	Morocco	21.7
29	Russia	21.6

Note: Data for these health rankings refer to the latest year available, 1998–2002.
a Defined as body mass index of 30 or more – see Glossary, page 246.

Marriage and divorce

Highest marriage rates
Number of marriages per 1,000 population

1	Bermuda	14.9			Singapore	6.3
2	Barbados	13.1	33	Denmark		6.2
3	Cyprus	12.9	34	Bosnia		6.1
4	Vietnam	12.1		Brunei		6.1
5	Egypt	10.8		Costa Rica		6.1
6	Jamaica	10.4	37	Croatia		6.0
7	Fiji	10.1		Moldova		6.0
8	Iran	9.9	39	Bahamas		5.8
9	Bangladesh	9.7		Japan		5.8
10	Cayman Islands	9.6		Ukraine		5.8
11	Sri Lanka	9.3	42	Algeria		5.7
12	Mauritius	8.7		Bahrain		5.7
13	Turkey	8.4		Channel Islands[a]		5.7
14	United States	8.3	45	Iceland		5.6
15	Guam	8.0		Malta		5.6
16	Albania	7.4	47	Guatemala		5.5
17	Iraq	7.3		Mongolia		5.5
	Taiwan	7.3		Romania		5.5
19	Belarus	7.2		Suriname		5.5
20	Macedonia	7.1	51	Norway		5.4
21	Aruba	6.9		Serbia & Montenegro		5.4
22	Uzbekistan	6.8		Turkmenistan		5.4
23	Australia	6.7	54	Kazakhstan		5.3
24	Mexico	6.6		Trinidad & Tobago		5.3
	Philippines	6.6	56	Ireland		5.2
	Puerto Rico	6.6		United Kingdom		5.2
	Thailand	6.6	58	Cuba		5.1
28	Portugal	6.5		Ecuador		5.1
29	South Korea	6.4		France		5.1
30	China	6.3		Spain		5.1
	Kirgizstan	6.3		Tunisia		5.1

Lowest marriage rates
Number of marriages per 1,000 population

1	Georgia	2.7	12	Tajikistan	3.5
2	Andorra	2.8	13	Argentina	3.6
	Macau	2.8		Slovenia	3.6
4	Dominican Republic	2.9	15	Bulgaria	3.7
	Saudi Arabia	2.9	16	Hong Kong	3.9
6	Latvia	3.1		Martinique	3.9
	Panama	3.1	18	Belgium	4.0
8	Armenia	3.2		Czech Republic	4.0
	United Arab Emirates	3.2		El Salvador	4.0
10	Estonia	3.3		Peru	4.0
	Poland	3.3			

Note: The data are based on latest available figures and hence will be affected by the population age structure at the time. Marriage rates refer to registered marriages only and, therefore, reflect the customs surrounding registry and efficiency of administration.

Highest divorce rates
Number of divorces per 1,000 population

1	Aruba	5.3		Kazakhstan	2.3
2	United States	4.8	32	Austria	2.2
3	Belarus	4.4		Costa Rica	2.2
4	Guam	4.3	34	Guadeloupe	2.1
5	Puerto Rico	3.8		Israel	2.1
6	Moldova	3.5		Sweden	2.1
7	Lithuania	3.3	37	Netherlands	2.0
	New Zealand	3.3		Romania	2.0
	Ukraine	3.3		Uruguay	2.0
10	Cuba	3.2	40	Taiwan	1.9
	Czech Republic	3.2	41	France	1.8
	Estonia	3.2		Hong Kong	1.8
13	South Korea	3.1		Iceland	1.8
14	United Kingdom	3.0		Singapore	1.8
15	Channel Islands[a]	2.9	45	Bahamas	1.7
	Russia	2.9		Cyprus	1.7
17	Australia	2.8		Portugal	1.7
	Switzerland	2.8		Slovakia	1.7
19	Denmark	2.7	49	Cayman Islands	1.6
	Finland	2.7	50	Egypt	1.5
21	Netherlands Antilles	2.6		Kuwait	1.5
22	Hungary	2.5	52	Barbados	1.4
	Latvia	2.5	53	Bulgaria	1.3
	Luxembourg	2.5		Jordan	1.3
25	Belgium	2.4	55	Bahrain	1.2
	Bermuda	2.4		Kirgizstan	1.2
	Germany	2.4		Martinique	1.2
	Norway	2.4		Réunion	1.2
29	Canada	2.3		Turkmenistan	1.2
	Japan	2.3			

Lowest divorce rates
Number of divorces per 1,000 population

1	Colombia	0.2	16	Azerbaijan	0.7
2	Libya	0.3		Ecuador	0.7
	Mongolia	0.3		El Salvador	0.7
4	Georgia	0.4		Panama	0.7
	Jamaica	0.4		Qatar	0.7
6	Armenia	0.5		Syria	0.7
	Bosnia	0.5	22	Brunei	0.8
	Chile	0.5		China	0.8
	Mexico	0.5		Italy	0.8
	Vietnam	0.5		Serbia & Montenegro	0.8
11	Brazil	0.6		Spain	0.8
	Macedonia	0.6	27	Greece	0.9
	Nicaragua	0.6		Macau	0.9
	Turkey	0.6		South Africa	0.9
	Uzbekistan	0.6		Suriname	0.9

[a] Guernsey only

Living standards

Biggest households[a]
Population per dwelling

1	Congo-Brazzaville	8.1		Uzbekistan	5.8
2	Pakistan	7.2	16	Jordan	5.7
3	Papua New Guinea	6.8		Kirgizstan	5.7
4	Gabon	6.4	18	Guinea-Bissau	5.6
	Kuwait	6.4	19	Burundi	5.5
	United Arab Emirates	6.4		Chad	5.5
7	Guinea	6.3		Iran	5.5
8	Cambodia	6.2		Mauritius	5.5
	Réunion	6.2		Swaziland	5.5
10	Algeria	6.1	24	Central African Rep	5.4
	Sudan	6.1		Fiji	5.4
12	Bangladesh	5.9		Laos	5.4
	Saudi Arabia	5.9		New Caledonia	5.4
14	French Polynesia	5.8		Sri Lanka	5.4

Highest cost of living[b]
December 2004, USA=100

1	Japan	138	10	Hong Kong	109
2	Norway	126	11	Netherlands	103
3	France	125		Sweden	103
4	Denmark	122	13	Germany	101
5	United Kingdom	119	14	Singapore	100
6	Iceland	114	15	Ireland	99
	Switzerland	114	16	Belgium	98
8	Finland	111	17	Australia	97
9	Austria	110		South Korea	97

Highest quality of life[c]
Ten is best, one is worst

1	Ireland	8.33	16	Netherlands	7.43
2	Switzerland	8.07	17	Japan	7.39
3	Norway	8.05	18	Hong Kong	7.35
4	Luxembourg	8.02	19	Portugal	7.31
5	Sweden	7.94	20	Austria	7.27
6	Australia	7.93	21	Taiwan	7.26
7	Iceland	7.91	22	Greece	7.16
8	Italy	7.81	23	Belgium	7.10
9	Denmark	7.80		Cyprus	7.10
10	Spain	7.73	25	France	7.08
11	Singapore	7.72	26	Germany	7.05
12	Finland	7.62	27	Slovenia	6.99
13	United States	7.62	28	Malta	6.93
14	Canada	7.60	29	United Kingdom	6.92
15	New Zealand	7.44	30	South Korea	6.88

a Latest available year.
b The cost of living index shown is compiled by the Economist Intelligence Unit for use
   by companies in determining expatriate compensation: it is a comparison of the cost
   of maintaining a typical international lifestyle in the country rather than a
   comparison of the purchasing power of a citizen of the country. The index is based on
   typical urban prices an international executive and family will face abroad. The prices

Smallest households[a]
Population per dwelling

1	Germany	2.1		Belarus		2.5
	Sweden	2.1		Lithuania		2.5
3	Denmark	2.2	18	Canada		2.6
	Finland	2.2		Italy		2.6
	Switzerland	2.2		Slovakia		2.6
6	Iceland	2.3		United States		2.6
	Netherlands	2.3		Uruguay		2.6
	Norway	2.3	23	Australia		2.7
9	Austria	2.4		Bulgaria		2.7
	Belgium	2.4		Czech Republic		2.7
	Estonia	2.4		Japan		2.7
	France	2.4		New Zealand		2.7
	Ukraine	2.4		Russia		2.7
	United Kingdom	2.4		Spain		2.7
15	Azerbaijan	2.5				

Lowest cost of living[b]
December 2004, USA=100

1	Iran	31		Sri Lanka	51
2	Philippines	37	11	Bangladesh	53
3	India	44		Serbia & Montenegro	53
	Pakistan	44		Venezuela	53
5	Paraguay	45	14	Brazil	54
6	Libya	47		Romania	54
7	Kazakhstan	50		Zambia	54
8	Argentina	51	17	Algeria	55
	Egypt	51		Uruguay	55

Lowest quality of life[c]
ten is best, one is worst

1	Zimbabwe	3.89	14	Ukraine	5.03
2	Haiti	4.09	15	Syria	5.05
3	Tanzania	4.50	16	Kazakhstan	5.08
4	Nigeria	4.51	17	Ghana	5.17
5	Tajikistan	4.75	18	Bosnia	5.22
6	Uzbekistan	4.77	19	Pakistan	5.23
7	Russia	4.80	20	Honduras	5.25
8	Botswana	4.81		South Africa	5.25
9	Kirgizstan	4.85	22	Guatemala	5.32
10	Turkmenistan	4.87	23	Iran	5.34
11	Uganda	4.88		Macedonia	5.34
12	Belarus	4.98	25	Georgia	5.37
13	Moldova	5.01	26	Azerbaijan	5.38

are for products of international comparable quality found in a supermarket or department store. Prices found in local markets and bazaars are not used unless the available merchandise is of the specified quality and the shopping area itself is safe for executive and family members. New York City prices are used as the base, so United States = 100.

The index is based on nine factors: GDP per head, life expectancy, political stability, family life, job security, community life, climate and geography, gender equality, political freedom

Consumer goods ownership

TV
Colour TVs per 100 households

1	United States	99.5	26	South Korea	93.3
2	Belgium	99.4	27	Hungary	92.8
3	Finland	99.3	28	Jordan	92.6
	Ireland	99.3	29	Denmark	92.4
	Taiwan	99.3		Slovenia	92.4
6	Hong Kong	99.1	31	Australia	91.8
	Saudi Arabia	99.1	32	Greece	91.5
8	Japan	99.0	33	Croatia	90.9
9	Canada	98.8	34	Argentina	90.6
	United Kingdom	98.8	35	Czech Republic	90.5
11	Singapore	98.6	36	Kuwait	90.3
12	Netherlands	98.5	37	Malaysia	90.2
	Spain	98.5	38	Tunisia	90.1
14	Austria	97.9	39	Mexico	90.0
	Portugal	97.9	40	Brazil	87.
16	New Zealand	97.8	41	Colombia	86.
17	Sweden	97.3	42	Slovakia	86.
18	Germany	97.2	43	Estonia	85.
19	Switzerland	97.1	44	Poland	84.
20	United Arab Emirates	96.6	45	Thailand	83.
21	Israel	96.1	46	Belarus	78.
22	France	95.9	47	Russia	75.
23	Italy	94.8	48	Ukraine	75.
24	Venezuela	93.9	49	Lithuania	75.
25	Norway	93.4	50	Latvia	72.

Telephone
Telephone lines per 100 people

1	Luxembourg	79.8	23	Italy	48.
2	Sweden	73.6	24	Austria	48.
3	Switzerland	72.8	25	Japan	47.
4	Norway	71.4	26	Israel	45.
5	Denmark	66.9	27	Greece	45.
6	Iceland	66.0	28	Singapore	45.
7	Germany	65.7	29	New Zealand	44.
8	Canada	65.1	30	Spain	42.
9	United States	62.4	31	Croatia	41.
10	Netherlands	61.4	32	Bahamas	41.
11	Taiwan	59.1	33	Portugal	41.
	United Kingdom	59.1	34	Slovenia	40.
13	Cyprus	57.2	35	Macau	38.
14	France	56.6	36	Bulgaria	38.
15	Hong Kong	55.9	37	Czech Republic	36.
16	Australia	54.2	38	Hungary	34.
17	South Korea	53.8	39	Estonia	34.
18	Malta	52.1	40	Poland	31.
19	Barbados	49.7	41	Belarus	31.
20	Finland	49.2	42	Latvia	28.
21	Ireland	49.1	43	United Arab Emirates	28.
22	Belgium	48.9	44	Uruguay	28.

CD player
CD players per 100 households

1	Norway	90.0	13	Belgium	66.5
2	Denmark	88.8	14	Finland	63.1
3	Netherlands	88.1	15	Switzerland	60.7
4	New Zealand	87.1	16	United Arab Emirates	58.7
5	Germany	86.4	17	Hong Kong	56.8
6	United Kingdom	85.3		Singapore	56.8
7	Sweden	85.0	19	Portugal	41.9
8	Australia	84.1	20	Ireland	41.5
9	Canada	79.5	21	Spain	39.1
10	Taiwan	70.8	22	Peru	34.1
11	Austria	70.1	23	Saudi Arabia	32.7
12	Japan	67.3	24	Hungary	30.5

Computer
Computers per 100 people

1	Switzerland	70.9	18	Ireland	42.1
2	United States	66.0	19	New Zealand	41.4
3	Singapore	62.2	20	United Kingdom	40.6
4	Sweden	62.1	21	Japan	38.2
5	Luxembourg	62.0	22	Austria	37.4
6	Australia	60.2	23	France	34.7
7	Denmark	57.7	24	Slovenia	32.6
8	South Korea	55.8	25	Belgium	31.8
9	Norway	52.8	26	French Polynesia	28.5
10	Canada	48.7	27	Cyprus	27.0
11	Germany	48.5	28	Macau	26.1
12	Taiwan	47.1	29	Malta	25.5
13	Netherlands	46.7	30	Israel	24.3
14	Iceland	45.1	31	Slovakia	23.6
15	Finland	44.2	32	Italy	23.1
16	Estonia	44.0	33	Costa Rica	21.8
17	Hong Kong	42.2	34	Spain	19.6

Mobile telephone
Subscribers per 100 people

1	Luxembourg	119.4	16	Ireland	88.0
2	Taiwan	114.1	17	Austria	87.9
3	Hong Kong	107.9	18	Slovenia	87.1
4	Italy	101.8	19	Singapore	85.3
5	Sweden	98.1	20	Switzerland	84.3
6	Iceland	96.6	21	Macau	81.2
7	Czech Republic	96.5	22	Belgium	79.3
8	Israel	96.1	23	Germany	78.5
9	Spain	91.6	24	Estonia	77.7
0	United Kingdom	91.2	25	Hungary	76.8
1	Finland	91.0		Netherlands	76.8
2	Norway	90.9	27	Cyprus	74.4
3	Greece	90.2	28	United Arab Emirates	73.6
4	Portugal	89.9	29	Malta	72.5
5	Denmark	88.3	30	Australia	72.0

Books and newspapers

Book sales

$m

1	United States	32,264
2	Japan	20,818
3	Germany	12,214
4	United Kingdom	5,348
5	Mexico	3,567
6	China	3,495
7	France	3,390
8	Italy	3,266
9	Spain	3,051
10	Canada	1,991
11	Australia	1,516
12	Belgium	1,205
13	Sweden	883
14	India	852
15	South Korea	821
16	Switzerland	809
17	Norway	751
18	Venezuela	710
19	Finland	647
20	Taiwan	646
21	Colombia	550
22	Netherlands	533
23	Portugal	494
24	Poland	475
25	Denmark	471
26	Singapore	459
27	Austria	425
28	Chile	394
29	New Zealand	360
30	Russia	358

Per head, $

1	Japan	551
2	Norway	544
3	Sweden	481
4	Finland	431
5	Bulgaria	385
6	Switzerland	353
7	Denmark	347
8	United Kingdom	314
9	Austria	311
10	Germany	274
11	Netherlands	261
12	Singapore	234
13	Luxembourg	230
14	Hong Kong	207
15	Estonia	193
16	New Zealand	189
17	United States	188
18	Slovenia	174
19	Czech Republic	163
20	Canada	157
21	Latvia	156
22	Hungary	156
23	Belgium	143
24	Italy	138
25	Ireland	136
26	France	134
27	Croatia	115
28	Australia	110
29	Spain	105
30	Poland	102

Daily newspapers

Copies per '000 population, latest year

1	Japan	551	16	New Zealand	18
2	Norway	544	17	United States	188
3	Sweden	481	18	Slovenia	174
4	Finland	431	19	Czech Republic	16
5	Bulgaria	385	20	Canada	15
6	Switzerland	353	21	Latvia	156
7	Denmark	347	22	Hungary	15
8	United Kingdom	314	23	Belgium	14
9	Austria	311	24	Italy	13
10	Germany	274	25	Ireland	13
11	Netherlands	261	26	France	13
12	Singapore	234	27	Croatia	11
13	Luxembourg	230	28	Australia	11
14	Hong Kong	207	29	Spain	10
15	Estonia	193	30	Poland	10

Music and the internet

Music sales[a]

$m, 2004		
1	United States	12,153
2	Japan	5,168
3	United Kingdom	3,509
4	Germany	2,149
5	France	1,979
6	Australia	717
7	Canada	694
8	Italy	653
9	Spain	573
10	Netherlands	508
11	Russia	491
12	Brazil	374
13	Mexico	360
14	Austria	289
15	Belgium	275
16	Norway	274
17	Sweden	268
18	Switzerland	259
19	South Africa	237
20	China	212
21	Denmark	187
22	Turkey	166

$ per head, 2004		
1	Norway	61
2	United Kingdom	59
3	United States	41
4	Japan	40
5	Australia	36
	Austria	36
	Ireland	36
	Switzerland	36
9	Denmark	35
10	France	33
11	Netherlands	32
12	New Zealand	30
	Sweden	30
14	Belgium	27
15	Germany	26
	Finland	26
17	Canada	22
18	Spain	14
19	Portugal	13
20	Hong Kong	12
21	Italy	11
	Singapore	11

Internet hosts

By country, January 2005		
1	United States[b]	200,042,089
2	Japan	19,543,034
3	Italy	9,343,663
4	Netherlands	6,443,558
5	Germany	6,127,262
6	France	4,999,770
7	Australia	4,820,646
8	United Kingdom	4,449,190
9	Brazil	3,934,577
10	Canada	3,839,173
11	Taiwan	3,516,215
12	Sweden	2,668,816
13	Poland	2,482,546
14	Belgium	2,012,283
15	Finland	1,915,506
16	Denmark	1,908,737
17	Mexico	1,868,583
18	Switzerland	1,785,427
19	Austria	1,594,059
20	Spain	1,304,558
21	Norway	1,237,270
22	Russia	1,135,833
23	Argentina	1,050,639

Per 1,000 pop., January 2005		
1	United States[b]	680.4
2	Iceland	482.1
3	Netherlands	400.2
4	Finland	368.4
5	Denmark	353.5
6	Sweden	299.9
7	Norway	274.9
8	Switzerland	248.0
9	Australia	244.7
10	Austria	196.8
11	Belgium	195.4
12	Estonia	182.7
13	New Zealand	166.9
14	Italy	162.8
15	Israel	156.9
16	Taiwan	155.6
17	Japan	153.0
18	Singapore	142.0
19	Hong Kong	122.3
20	Bermuda	122.1
21	Canada	121.9
22	France	83.2
23	Faroe Islands	78.2

a CDs and DVDs.
b Includes all hosts ending ".com", ".net" and ".org", which exaggerates the numbers.

Media habits[a]

Watching television
Average number of hours per week spent

1	Thailand	22.4		
2	Philippines	21.0		
3	Egypt	20.9		
4	Turkey	20.2		
5	Indonesia	19.7		
6	United States	19.0		
7	Taiwan	18.9		
8	Brazil	18.4		
9	United Kingdom	18.0		
10	Japan	17.9		
11	Saudi Arabia	17.7		
12	France	17.3		
13	Hong Kong	16.7		
14	Czech Republic	16.2		
15	Poland	15.9		
	Spain	15.9		
17	China	15.7		
18	South Korea	15.4		

Reading
Average number of hours per week spent

1	India	10.7
2	Thailand	9.4
3	China	8.0
4	Philippines	7.6
5	Egypt	7.5
6	Czech Republic	7.4
7	Russia	7.1
8	France	6.9
	Sweden	6.9
10	Hungary	6.8
	Saudi Arabia	6.8
12	Hong Kong	6.7
13	Poland	6.5
14	Venezuela	6.4
15	Australia	6.3
	South Africa	6.3
17	Indonesia	6.0

Listening to radio
Average number of hours per week spent

1	Argentina	20.8
2	Brazil	17.2
3	South Africa	15.0
4	Czech Republic	13.3
	Thailand	13.3
	Turkey	13.3
7	Poland	12.5
8	Hungary	12.1
9	Germany	11.5
10	Australia	11.3
11	Mexico	11.1
12	Sweden	10.9
13	United Kingdom	10.5
14	United States	10.2
15	Spain	9.9
16	Philippines	9.5
17	Canada	9.1

On a computer/the internet[b]
Average number of hours per week spent

1	Taiwan	12.6
2	Thailand	11.7
3	Spain	11.5
4	Hungary	10.9
5	China	10.8
6	Hong Kong	10.7
7	Poland	10.6
	Turkey	10.6
9	Brazil	10.5
10	Egypt	10.3
11	Philippines	9.8
12	South Korea	9.6
13	Saudi Arabia	9.3
14	South Africa	9.0
15	Argentina	8.9
	Russia	8.9
17	France	8.8
	United Kingdom	8.8
	United States	8.8
20	Canada	8.3

a Aged 13 years and over. Thirty countries surveyed between December 2004 and February 2005.
b Non-work related.

Teenagers

15-year-olds who watch TV 4+ hours a day on weekdays

Males, %

1	Ukraine	45.4
2	Estonia	40.8
3	Latvia	40.7
4	Lithuania	39.1
5	Russia	34.7
6	Israel	33.7
7	Poland	33.3
8	Macedonia	32.4

Females, %

1	Ukraine	39.2
2	Israel	33.4
3	Portugal	32.0
4	Latvia	31.6
5	United Kingdom	29.5
6	Estonia	29.2
7	Italy	27.3
	Russia	27.3

15-year-olds who communicate electronically every day[a]

Males, %

1	Greece	50.0
2	Greenland	46.9
	Norway	46.9
4	Denmark	45.4
5	Israel	44.2
6	Croatia	41.9
7	United Kingdom	39.8
8	Russia	39.3
9	Malta	38.3

Females, %

1	Greece	62.7
2	Croatia	60.1
3	Italy	58.8
4	Norway	57.1
5	Denmark	56.5
	Israel	56.5
7	Russia	55.4
8	United States	52.8
9	Macedonia	52.6

15-year-olds who are obese[b]

Males, %

1	United States	10.5
2	Malta	9.3
3	Canada	4.3
	United Kingdom	4.3
5	Hungary	3.7
6	Austria	3.3
7	Spain	2.9
8	Finland	2.8
9	Greece	2.7
	Greenland	2.7
	Israel	2.7
12	Italy	2.5

Females, %

1	United States	5.3
2	Malta	4.8
3	Canada	4.6
4	United Kingdom	2.7
5	France	2.4
6	Belgium	1.8
	Hungary	1.8
	Ireland	1.8
9	Finland	1.4
10	Greenland	1.2
	Macedonia	1.2
	Switzerland	1.2

15-year-olds who have used cannabis within the past year

Males, %

1	Canada	43.3
2	Switzerland	40.3
3	United States	36.5
4	United Kingdom	36.3
5	Greenland	36.1
6	Spain	31.6
7	France	31.2
8	Czech Republic	30.9
9	Slovenia	27.3

Females, %

1	Canada	37.5
2	Switzerland	35.3
3	United Kingdom	31.7
4	Greenland	31.1
5	Spain	30.0
6	United States	26.2
7	France	23.8
8	Czech Republic	23.2
9	Slovenia	21.4

Note: Tables cover Europe and North America only, 2001–02.
a Telephone, e-mail or text
b According to body-mass-index measures – see Glossary, page 246.

Nobel prize winners: 1901–2002

Peace

1	United States	17
2	United Kingdom	11
3	France	9
4	Sweden	5
5	Belgium	4
	Germany	4
7	Norway	3
	South Africa	3
9	Argentina	2
	Austria	2
	Israel	2
	Russia	2
	Switzerland	2

Economics[a]

1	United States	28
2	United Kingdom	8
3	Norway	2
	Sweden	2
5	France	1
	Germany	1
	Netherlands	1
	Russia	1

Literature

1	France	14
2	United States	12
3	United Kingdom	9
4	Germany	7
5	Sweden	6
6	Italy	5
	Spain	5
8	Norway	3
	Poland	3
	Russia	3

Physiology or medicine

1	United States	49
2	United Kingdom	21
3	Germany	14
4	Sweden	7
5	France	6
	Switzerland	6
7	Austria	5
	Denmark	5
9	Belgium	3
	Italy	3

Physics

1	United States	46
2	United Kingdom	19
3	Germany	17
4	France	8
5	Netherlands	6
	Russia	6
7	Japan	4
	Sweden	4
	Switzerland	4
10	Austria	3
	Italy	3
12	Canada	2
	Denmark	2
14	Colombia	1
	India	1
	Ireland	1
	Pakistan	1
	Poland	1

Chemistry

1	United States	40
2	United Kingdom	22
3	Germany	14
4	France	6
	Switzerland	6
6	Sweden	5
7	Canada	4
	Japan	4
9	Argentina	1
	Austria	1
	Belgium	1
	Czech Republic	1
	Denmark	1
	Finland	1
	Israel	1
	Italy	1
	Netherlands	1
	Norway	1
	Russia	1

a Since 1969.
Notes: Prizes by country of residence at time awarded. When prizes have been shared in the same field, one credit given to each country. Only top rankings in each field are included.

Olympic medal winners

Summer games, 1896–2004

		Gold	Silver	Bronze
1	United States	895	690	604
2	Soviet Union[a]	440	357	325
3	United Kingdom	180	233	225
4	France	173	187	203
5	Italy	172	136	153
6	Germany[b]	162	191	205
7	Germany (East)	153	129	127
8	Hungary	148	130	154
9	Sweden	138	154	171
10	China	112	96	78
11	Australia	100	106	131
12	Finland	100	80	113
13	Japan	98	97	103
14	Romania	74	86	106
15	Netherlands	60	65	84
16	Russia[c]	59	53	47
17	Poland	56	72	113
18	Germany (West)	56	67	81
19	Cuba	56	46	41
20	Canada	52	79	99

Winter games, 1924–2002

		Gold	Silver	Bronze
1	Germany	108	105	87
2	Norway	94	94	75
3	Soviet Union[a]	87	63	67
4	United States	69	72	52
5	Finland	42	51	49
6	Austria	41	57	63
7	Sweden	39	30	29
8	Switzerland	32	33	38
9	Italy	31	31	27
10	Canada	31	28	37
11	Russia	27	20	13
12	Netherlands	22	28	19
13	France	22	22	28
14	South Korea	11	5	4
15	Japan	8	10	13
16	United Kingdom	8	4	15
17	Croatia	3	1	0
18	China	2	12	8
19	Czech Republic	2	1	2
20	Australia	2	0	1

a 1952–1992.
b Germany 1896–1936, unified teams in 1956–64, then since 1992.
c Russia 1896–1912, then since 1996.
Note: Figures exclude mixed teams in 1896, 1900 and 1904 and Australasia teams in 1908 and 1912.

Drinking and smoking

Beer drinkers
Litres consumed per head

1	Czech Republic[a]	157.0
2	Ireland	141.2
3	Germany	117.5
4	Austria	110.6
5	Luxembourg[a]	101.6
6	United Kingdom	101.5
7	Belgium	96.2
	Denmark	96.2
9	Australia[a]	91.5
10	Slovakia[a]	88.4
11	Venezuela[a]	82.1
12	United States	81.6
13	Finland	80.2
14	Poland[a]	79.0
15	Netherlands	78.7
16	Spain	78.3
17	Estonia[a]	75.0
18	New Zealand	72.8
19	Hungary[a]	72.2
20	Canada	67.8
21	Romania[a]	67.0
22	Cyprus[a]	60.0
23	Portugal	58.7

Wine drinkers
Litres consumed per head

1	Luxembourg[a]	66.1
2	France	48.5
3	Italy	47.5
4	Portugal[a]	42.0
5	Switzerland	40.9
6	Hungary[a]	37.4
7	Argentina	34.6
8	Greece[a]	33.8
9	Uruguay[a]	33.3
10	Denmark[a]	32.6
11	Spain[a]	30.6
12	Austria[a]	29.8
13	Finland[a]	26.3
14	Germany	23.6
15	Belgium	23.0
	Romania[a]	23.0
17	Malta[a]	22.3
18	Bulgaria[a]	21.3
19	Australia[a]	20.4
20	United Kingdom	20.1
21	Netherlands	19.6
22	New Zealand	19.1
23	Chile[a]	18.0

Alcoholic drinks
Litres of pure alcohol consumed per head

1	Luxembourg	12.6
2	Hungary	11.4
3	Czech Republic	11.0
4	Ireland	10.8
5	Germany	10.2
6	Spain	10.0
7	Portugal	9.6
	United Kingdom	9.6
9	Denmark	9.5
10	Austria	9.3
	France	9.3
12	Cyprus	9.0
	Switzerland	9.0
14	Belgium	8.8
15	Russia	8.7
16	Slovakia	8.5
17	Latvia	8.1
	Romania	8.1
19	Finland	7.9
	Netherlands	7.9
21	Greece	7.7
22	Australia	7.2

Smokers
Av. ann. consumption of cigarettes per head per day

1	Greece	8.6
2	Bulgaria	7.4
3	Macedonia	7.1
4	Bosnia	6.6
5	Japan	6.4
6	Spain	6.2
7	South Korea	6.1
8	Slovenia	6.0
9	Albania	5.8
10	Czech Republic	5.7
	Estonia	5.7
12	Russia	5.6
13	Armenia	5.5
14	Ukraine	5.4
15	Belgium	5.3
	Cyprus	5.3
17	Croatia	5.2
	Switzerland	5.2
19	Hungary	5.0
	Serbia & Montenegro	5.0

a Estimate.

Crime and punishment

Police
Total police personnel per 100,000 pop.

1	Kuwait	1,116
2	Cyprus	618
3	Italy	559
4	Uruguay	541
5	Panama	519
6	Mexico	492
7	Czech Republic	458
8	Malta	452
9	Portugal	450
10	Croatia	446
11	Latvia	442
12	Azerbaijan	402
13	Albania	381
14	Slovakia	376
15	Slovenia	364
16	Belgium	358
17	Lithuania	337
18	United States	326
19	Moldova	324
20	Austria	305

Crime[a]
Tot. recorded crimes per 100,000 pop.

1	Iceland	21,211
2	Sweden	13,837
3	United Kingdom	11,014
4	Finland	10,005
5	Belgium	9,422
6	Denmark	9,137
7	Netherlands	8,813
8	Canada	8,025
9	Germany	7,888
10	Austria	6,464
11	South Africa	5,915
12	Luxembourg	5,866
13	Malta	4,288
14	Switzerland	4,220
15	Slovenia	4,160
16	Hungary	4,142
17	United States	4,119
18	Uruguay	3,987
19	Italy	3,868
20	Chile	3,810

Prisoners
Total prison pop., latest available year

1	United States	2,085,620
2	China	1,548,498
3	Russia	763,054
4	Brazil	330,642
5	India	313,635
6	Ukraine	198,386
7	Mexico	191,890
8	South Africa	186,739
9	Thailand	168,264
10	Iran	133,658
11	Rwanda[b]	112,000
12	Pakistan[b]	86,000
13	Indonesia	84,357
14	United Kingdom	83,337
15	Egypt[b]	80,000
16	Poland	79,807
17	Germany	79,329
18	Bangladesh	74,170
19	Japan	73,734
20	Philippines	70,383
21	Colombia	68,545
22	Turkey	67,772
23	Ethiopia[b]	65,000

Per 100,000 pop., latest available year

1	United States	714
2	Belarus	532
	Bermuda	532
	Russia	532
5	Virgin Islands	490
6	Turkmenistan[b]	489
7	Cuba[b]	487
8	Suriname	437
9	Cayman Islands	429
10	Ukraine	416
11	South Africa	413
12	Bahamas	410
13	Singapore	392
14	Kirgizstan	390
15	Kazakhstan	386
	Puerto Rico	386
17	Barbados	367
18	Netherlands Antilles	364
19	Panama	354
20	Guam	353
21	Botswana	339
	Estonia	339
23	Latvia	337

a Including attempted crimes.
b Estimate.

Stars...

Space missions
Firsts and selected events

1957 Man-made satellite   Dog in space, Laika
1961 Human in space, Yuri Gagarin
    Entire day in space, Gherman Titov
1963 Woman in space, Valentina Tereshkova
1964 Space crew, one pilot and two passengers
1965 Space walk, Alexei Leonov
    Computer guidance system
    Eight days in space achieved (needed to travel to moon and back)
1966 Docking between space craft and target vehicle
    Autopilot re-entry and landing
1968 Live television broadcast from space
    Moon orbit
1969 Astronaut transfer from one craft to another in space
    Moon landing
1971 Space station, Salyut
    Drive on the moon
1973 Space laboratory, Skylab
1978 Non-American, non-Soviet, Vladimir Remek (Czechoslovakia)
1982 Space shuttle, Columbia (first craft to carry four crew members)
1983 Five crew mission
1984 Space walk, untethered
    Capture, repair and redeployment of satellite in space
    Seven crew mission
1986 Space shuttle explosion, Challenger
    Mir space station activated
1990 Hubble telescope deployed
2001 Dennis Tito, first paying space tourist
2003 Space shuttle explosion, Columbia. Shuttle programme suspended.
    China's first manned space flight, Yang Liwei
2004 SpaceShipOne, first successful private manned space flight

Space vehicle launches
By host country

2001

1	United States	23
2	Russia	21
3	France	8
4	India	2
5	China	1
	Japan	1

2002

1	Russia	23
2	United States	18
3	France	11
4	China	3
5	Japan	2
6	India	1
	Israel	1

2003

1	United States	24
2	Russia	19
3	China	6
4	France	4
5	India	2
	Japan	2

2004

1	United States	21
2	Russia	17
3	China	2
	France	2
5	India	1
	Sweden	1

...and Wars

Defence spending
As % of GDP

1	North Korea	25.0	16	Angola		5.7
2	Oman	11.6	17	Bahrain		5.6
3	Liberia	11.4	18	Singapore		5.2
4	Qatar	10.0	19	Brunei		5.1
5	Myanmar	9.6	20	Uzbekistan		5.0
6	Israel	9.5	21	Ethiopia		4.9
7	Kuwait	9.4		Russia		4.9
8	Eritrea	9.2		Turkey		4.9
9	Saudi Arabia	8.9	24	Pakistan		4.5
10	Jordan	8.7	25	Colombia		4.2
11	Vietnam	7.4	26	Libya		4.2
12	Burundi	7.2		Morocco		4.2
13	Syria	7.0	28	Greece		4.1
	Yemen	7.0		Rwanda		4.1
15	Armenia	6.4				

Armed forces
'000

		Regulars	Reserves			Regulars	Reserves
1	China	2,250	550	16 Ukraine		296	1,000
2	USA	1,427	1,238	17 Taiwan		290	1,657
3	India	1,325	535	18 Brazil		288	1,115
4	North Korea	1,082	4,700	19 Germany		285	359
5	Russia	961	2,400	20 France		259	100
6	South Korea	686	4,500	21 UK		213	273
7	Pakistan	620	513	22 Eritrea		202	120
8	Iran	540	350	23 Colombia		200	61
9	Turkey	515	379	24 Italy		200	63
10	Myanmar	488		25 Saudi Arabia		200	
11	Vietnam	484	3,000	26 Morocco		196	150
12	Egypt	450	410	27 Mexico		193	300
13	Syria	319	354	28 Greece		178	291
14	Thailand	314	200	29 Israel		167	358
15	Indonesia	302	400	30 Poland		163	234

Current UN peacekeeping missions[a]

		Military	Civilian police	Staff	Fatalities
1	Middle East (May 1948)	165	0	217	40
2	India/Pakistan (January 1949)	44	0	70	9
3	Cyprus (March 1964)	894	43	152	173
4	Syria (May 1974)	1,030	0	143	40
5	Lebanon (March 1978)	2,044	0	399	250
6	Western Sahara (April 1991)	231	6	238	10
7	Georgia (August 1993)	119	11	282	7
8	Kosovo (June 1999)	37	3,391	3,434	32
9	Sierra Leone (October 1999)	3,543	79	760	159
10	Congo-Kinshasa (November 1999)	16,095	175	1,888	54
11	Ethiopia and Eritrea (July 2000)	3,335	0	463	8

March 2005. Dates in brackets refer to missions' start dates.

Environment

Environmental sustainability index[a]

Highest			*Lowest*		
1	Finland	75.1	1	North Korea	29.2
2	Norway	73.4	2	Taiwan	32.7
3	Uruguay	71.8	3	Turkmenistan	33.1
4	Sweden	71.7	4	Iraq	33.6
5	Iceland	70.8	5	Uzbekistan	34.4
6	Canada	64.4	6	Haiti	34.8
7	Switzerland	63.7	7	Sudan	35.9
8	Argentina	62.7	8	Trinidad & Tobago	36.3
	Austria	62.7	9	Kuwait	36.6
10	Brazil	62.2	10	Yemen	37.3
11	Gabon	61.7	11	Saudi Arabia	37.8
12	Australia	61.0	12	Ethiopia	37.9
13	New Zealand	60.9	13	China	38.6
14	Latvia	60.4		Tajikistan	38.6
	Peru	60.4	15	Iran	39.8
16	Paraguay	59.7	16	Burundi	40.0
17	Costa Rica	59.6	17	Lebanon	40.5
18	Bolivia	59.5	18	Zimbabwe	41.2
	Croatia	59.5	19	Libya	42.3
20	Ireland	59.2		Philippines	42.3
21	Colombia	58.9		Vietnam	42.3
	Lithuania	58.9	22	Mauritania	42.6
23	Albania	58.8	23	Angola	42.9
24	Central African Rep	58.7	24	South Korea	43.0
25	Denmark	58.2	25	Liberia	43.4
	Estonia	58.2		Sierra Leone	43.4
27	Slovenia	57.5	27	Dominican Republic	43.7
28	Japan	57.3	28	El Salvador	43.8
29	Germany	56.9		Syria	43.8
30	Namibia	56.7	30	Belgium	44.0
31	Russia	56.1		Egypt	44.0
32	Botswana	55.9		Guatemala	44.0

Environmental social and institutional capacity index[b]

Highest

1	Finland	91.7	11	Austria	81.
2	Sweden	91.6	12	New Zealand	79.
3	Norway	91.3		Spain	79.
4	Switzerland	91.0	14	United States	78.
5	Japan	88.7	15	France	77.
6	Denmark	87.5	16	Canada	77.
7	Iceland	86.7	17	Australia	76.
8	Netherlands	85.7	18	South Korea	74.
9	Germany	85.4	19	Slovenia	73.
10	United Kingdom	84.8	20	Belgium	73.

a Based on 20 key indicators, including: environmental systems and stresses; human
  vulnerability to environmental risks; institutional capacities on environmental issues
  shared resources.
b Includes government policies, policies of the science and technology sector and the
  responsiveness of the private sector towards the environment.

Personal safety and security city index
New York=100, November 2004

Highest

1	Luxembourg	122.5
2	Bern, Switzerland	120.0
	Geneva, Switzerland	120.0
	Helsinki, Finland	120.0
	Zurich, Switzerland	120.0
6	Stockholm, Sweden	116.0
	Vienna, Austria	116.0
8	Copenhagen, Denmark	113.0
	Dusseldorf, Germany	113.0
	Frankfurt, Germany	113.0
	Munich, Germany	113.0
	Nurnberg, Germany	113.0
	Oslo, Norway	113.0

Lowest

1	Baghdad, Iraq	5.0
2	Abidjan, Côte d'Ivoire	24.0
3	Bangui, Cen. Afr. Rep.	26.5
4	Lagos, Nigeria	32.5
	Port Harcourt, Nigeria	32.5
6	Bogota, Colombia	33.0
7	Brazzaville, Congo-Braz.	35.0
	Pointe Noire, Congo-Braz.	35.0
9	Kinshasa, Congo	35.5
10	Khartoum, Sudan	36.0
11	Medellin, Colombia	37.5
12	Jerusalem, Israel	38.0

Rural population
Av. annual rate of change, 2000–05, %

Highest

1	Andorra	5.3
2	Somalia	3.4
3	Afghanistan	3.3
	Iraq	3.3
5	Uganda	3.2
6	Eritrea	3.1
	Yemen	3.1
8	Liberia	2.9
	Niger	2.9
10	Aruba	2.8
11	Bhutan	2.7
	Burundi	2.7
	Gambia, The	2.7
	Sierra Leone	2.7
15	Madagascar	2.6
16	Burkina Faso	2.5
17	Chad	2.4
18	Syria	2.3
	West Bank and Gaza	2.3
20	Congo	2.2
	Ethiopia	2.2
	Papua New Guinea	2.2
23	Angola	2.0
	Jordan	2.0
	Mali	2.0
26	Egypt	1.9
	Pakistan	1.9
28	French Polynesia	1.8
	Guatemala	1.8
	Uzbekistan	1.8

Lowest

1	Puerto Rico	-14.5
2	Guadeloupe	-9.8
3	Martinique	-4.9
4	Réunion	-4.1
5	Australia	-3.8
	Norway	-3.8
7	Virgin Islands	-3.6
8	Gabon	-2.7
9	Brazil	-2.4
	Malta	-2.4
11	Uruguay	-2.1
12	Bulgaria	-2.0
13	Luxembourg	-1.9
14	Suriname	-1.8
15	Belarus	-1.7
16	Bahamas	-1.6
	Hungary	-1.6
18	Germany	-1.5
19	Chile	-1.4
	Trinidad and Tobago	-1.4
21	Croatia	-1.2
	Estonia	-1.2
	Greenland	-1.2
24	Guam	-1.1
25	Canada	-1.0
	Iceland	-1.0
	Portugal	-1.0
28	Argentina	-0.9
	Indonesia	-0.9
	Iran	-0.9
	Netherlands	-0.9
	Ukraine	-0.9

Sulphur dioxide emissions

Tonnes per populated square km[a]

1	Benin	21.39	16	United States	4.68
2	Trinidad & Tobago	20.99	17	Bulgaria	4.61
3	Australia	11.86	18	Egypt	4.09
4	South Korea	11.58	19	United Kingdom	4.04
5	Jamaica	8.95	20	Iceland	3.85
6	Lebanon	8.07	21	Portugal	3.84
7	North Korea	7.64	22	Greece	3.79
8	Canada	7.52	23	Cuba	3.74
9	Kuwait	7.12	24	Georgia	3.62
10	Chile	6.70	25	Slovenia	3.59
11	Taiwan	6.29	26	Spain	3.57
12	Hungary	5.31	27	Estonia	3.35
13	Belgium	5.14	28	Czech Republic	3.33
	Romania	5.14	29	Israel	3.31
15	Poland	4.85	30	Libya	3.22

Nitrogen oxide emissions

Tonnes per populated square km[a]

1	Paraguay	50.70	16	Denmark	4.71
2	Taiwan	14.77	17	Italy	4.63
3	Australia	14.28	18	Germany	4.49
4	Netherlands	10.15	19	Portugal	4.47
5	Belgium	9.88	20	Jordan	3.49
6	Iceland	8.76	21	Spain	3.36
7	South Korea	8.60	22	New Zealand	3.30
8	Trinidad & Tobago	7.33	23	France	3.26
9	United States	7.13	24	Slovenia	3.23
10	United Kingdom	6.39	25	Jamaica	2.80
11	Libya	6.34	26	Poland	2.69
12	Japan	5.59	27	Botswana	2.65
13	Lebanon	5.25	28	Switzerland	2.50
14	Czech Republic	5.00	29	Armenia	2.55
15	United Arab Emirates	4.99	30	Greece	2.52

Vehicles per populated land[a]

Number of cars, trucks and buses per square km

1	Japan	197.1	13	France	73.
2	Belgium	172.8	14	United States	65.
3	Netherlands	166.9	15	Austria	65.
4	Taiwan	161.8	16	Iceland	63.
5	Italy	145.0	17	Australia	59.
6	Lebanon	139.1	18	Trinidad & Tobago	56.
7	Germany	132.4	19	Spain	53.
8	United Kingdom	112.9	20	Denmark	52.
9	South Korea	112.4	21	Czech Republic	49.
10	Switzerland	104.1	22	Canada	49.
11	Israel	83.3	23	Slovenia	47
12	Portugal	79.2	24	Kuwait	43.

a Five or more people per square km.

Severe water stress

% of country where water consumption exceeds 40% of available water

1	Kuwait	100.0	16	Iran	87.3
2	Trinidad & Tobago	99.9	17	Armenia	87.1
3	Syria	99.6	18	Uzbekistan	86.7
4	Israel	97.6	19	Iraq	86.2
5	Nepal	97.5	20	Lebanon	84.9
6	Azerbaijan	96.3	21	Libya	83.7
7	Tajikistan	94.8	22	Morocco	82.3
8	Turkmenistan	93.9	23	Jordan	81.2
9	Kirgizstan	93.6	24	India	80.4
10	Belgium	93.5	25	Pakistan	76.4
11	United Arab Emirates	92.7	26	South Africa	68.4
12	Tunisia	92.0	27	Algeria	67.9
13	Saudi Arabia	90.7	28	Turkey	64.4
14	Egypt	88.7	29	Yemen	64.3
15	Spain	87.8	30	Portugal	63.2

Population with access to improved drinking water source

Lowest, %

1	Cambodia	34.0		Uganda	56.0
2	Papua New Guinea	39.0	17	Romania	57.0
3	Mozambique	42.0		Sierra Leone	57.0
4	Latvia	43.0	19	Tajikistan	58.0
5	Madagascar	45.0	20	Guinea-Bissau	59.0
6	Niger	46.0	21	Nigeria	60.0
7	Congo	46.0	22	Bhutan	62.0
	Congo-Brazzaville	46.0		Kenya	62.0
9	Mali	48.0		Liberia	62.0
10	Angola	50.0		Mongolia	62.0
11	Burkina Faso	51.0	26	Cameroon	63.0
	Guinea	51.0	27	Malawi	67.0
	Togo	51.0	28	Benin	68.0
14	Zambia	55.0	29	Sudan	69.0
15	Mauritania	56.0		Yemen	69.0

Freshwater availability

'000 cubic meters per person, long-term average, highest

1	Congo-Brazzaville	543.3	15	Norway	60.8
2	Iceland	301.4	16	Venezuela	60.5
3	Uruguay	265.0	17	Central African Rep	57.7
4	Gabon	192.8	18	Namibia	54.8
5	Papua New Guinea	151.7	19	Brazil	53.1
6	Angola	140.5	20	Cambodia	45.7
7	Paraguay	110.3	21	Croatia	33.6
8	Colombia	90.6	22	Australia	33.2
9	Canada	86.6	23	Nicaragua	32.1
10	Bolivia	80.9	24	Congo	30.4
11	New Zealand	79.9		Yemen	30.4
12	Laos	75.0	26	Ecuador	29.5
	Liberia	75.0	27	Panama	28.9
13	Peru	65.4	28	Mongolia	28.3

Total land area under protected status

Highest, %

1	Colombia	72.3		15	Ecuador	26.0
2	Venezuela	70.3		16	Costa Rica	25.6
3	Saudi Arabia	41.8			Denmark	25.6
4	Zambia	41.4		18	Guatemala	25.3
5	Tanzania	39.6		19	Dominican Republic	24.5
6	Austria	36.4		20	New Zealand	24.4
7	Germany	31.7		21	Cambodia	23.7
8	Malaysia	30.6		22	Poland	23.5
9	Bhutan	30.2		23	Benin	22.7
	Botswana	30.2		24	Slovakia	22.5
11	Switzerland	28.8		25	Nicaragua	21.8
12	Sri Lanka	26.5		26	Honduras	20.8
13	Uganda	26.4		27	Estonia	19.6
14	Netherlands	26.2		28	Papua New Guinea	19.5

Mammal species under threat

As % of mammal species in each country

1	New Zealand	80.0		15	Ireland	24.0
2	Iceland	63.6			United Kingdom	24.0
3	Cuba	35.5		17	Chile	23.1
	Madagascar	35.5		18	Bhutan	22.2
5	Indonesia	32.2		19	Jamaica	20.8
6	Philippines	31.7		20	China	20.3
7	Spain	29.3		21	Bangladesh	20.
8	India	27.2			Romania	20.
9	Portugal	27.0		23	Japan	19.
10	South Korea	26.5			Vietnam	19.
11	Papua New Guinea	26.1		25	Oman	19.
12	Dominican Republic	25.0		26	Cambodia	19.
	Sri Lanka	25.0		27	France	19.
14	Australia	24.2		28	Belgium	19.

Threatened bird species

As % of bird species in each country

1	New Zealand	42.0		17	Bangladesh	7.
2	Kuwait	35.0			India	7.
3	Philippines	34.2		19	Brazil	7.
4	South Korea	22.3			Indonesia	7.
5	Haiti	18.7		21	Chile	7.
6	North Korea	16.5		22	Malaysia	7.
7	Japan	14.0		23	Vietnam	6.
8	Madagascar	13.4		24	China	6.
9	Cuba	13.1		25	Israel	6.
10	United Arab Emirates	11.9		26	Iraq	6.
11	Dominican Republic	11.0		27	Cambodia	6.
12	Jamaica	10.6		28	Russia	6.
13	Saudi Arabia	9.7		29	Thailand	6.
14	Oman	9.4		30	Jordan	5.
15	United States	8.6		31	Sri Lanka	5.
16	Yemen	8.4		32	Australia	5.

Country profiles

ALGERIA

Area	2,381,741 sq km	Capital	Algiers
Arable as % of total land	3	Currency	Algerian dinar (AD)

People

Population	31.8m	Life expectancy: men	70.9 yrs
Pop. per sq km	13.3	women	73.7 yrs
Av. ann. growth		Adult literacy	68.9%
in pop. 2000–05	1.51%	Fertility rate (per woman)	2.5
Pop. under 15	29.6%	Urban population	58.8%
Pop. over 60	6.5%		per 1,000 pop.
No. of men per 100 women	102	Crude birth rate	22.8
Human Development Index	70.4	Crude death rate	4.9

The economy

GDP	AD5,149bn	GDP per head	$2,090
GDP	$66.5bn	GDP per head in purchasing	
Av. ann. growth in real		power parity (USA=100)	15.7
GDP 1993–2003	3.2%	Economic freedom index	3.49

Origins of GDP		Components of GDP	
	% of total		% of total
Agriculture	10	Private consumption	41.2
Industry, of which:	55	Public consumption	14.8
manufacturing	7	Investment	29.8
Services	35	Exports	38.8
		Imports	-24.6

Structure of employment

	% of total		% of labour force
Agriculture	10	Unemployed 2002	27.
Industry	58	Av. ann. rate 1995–2002	27.
Services	32		

Energy

	m TOE		
Total output	150.3	Net energy imports as %	
Total consumption	30.8	of energy use	-38
Consumption per head,			
kg oil equivalent	985		

Inflation and finance

		av. ann. increase 1997–200	
Consumer price			
inflation 2004	3.6%	Narrow money (M1)	14.9
Av. ann. inflation 1999–2004	2.4%	Broad money	20.6
Money market rate, 2004	1.09%		

Exchange rates

	end 2004		December 20
		Effective rates	1995 = 1
AD per $	72.61	– nominal	77.
AD per SDR	112.77	– real	79.
AD per €	98.91		

Trade

Principal exports

	$bn fob
Crude oil	11.6
Natural gas	6.1
Condensate	4.2
Total incl. others	**26.0**

Principal imports

	$bn cif
Capital goods	5.0
Food	2.7
Semi-finished goods	2.4
Total incl. others	**14.4**

Main export destinations

	% of total
Italy	18.9
United States	17.9
France	13.2
Spain	10.9

Main origins of imports

	% of total
France	32.9
Italy	10.2
Spain	6.5
Germany	6.1

Balance of payments[a], reserves and debt, $bn

Visible exports fob	20.0	Change in reserves	10.3
Visible imports fob	-12.0	Level of reserves	
Trade balance	8.0	end Dec.	35.5
Invisibles inflows	2.0	No. months of import cover	22.8
Invisibles outflows	-5.4	Official gold holdings, m oz	5.6
Net transfers	1.1	Foreign debt	23.4
Current account balance	5.7	– as % of GDP	41
– as % of GDP	8.5	– as % of total exports	103
Capital balance[b]	-2.0	Debt service ratio	19
Overall balance[b]	5.0		

Health and education

Health spending, % of GDP	4.3	Education spending, % of GDP	...
Doctors per 1,000 pop.	0.9	Enrolment, %: primary	108
Hospital beds per 1,000 pop.	2.1	secondary	80
Improved-water source access,		tertiary	15
% of pop.	87		

Society

No. of households	5.1m	Colour TVs per 100 households	72.7
Av. no. per household	6.1	Telephone lines per 100 pop.	6.4
Marriages per 1,000 pop.	5.7	Mobile telephone subscribers	
Divorces per 1,000 pop.	...	per 100 pop.	4.5
Cost of living, Dec. 2004		Computers per 100 pop.	0.8
New York = 100	55	Internet hosts per 1,000 pop.	...

ARGENTINA

Area	2,766,889 sq km	Capital	Buenos Aires
Arable as % of total land	12	Currency	Peso (P)

People

Population	38.4m	Life expectancy: men	71.6 yrs
Pop. per sq km	13.9	women	79.1 yrs
Av. ann. growth		Adult literacy	97.0%
in pop. 2000–05	0.98%	Fertility rate (per woman)	2.4
Pop. under 15	26.4%	Urban population	90.1%
Pop. over 60	13.9%		per 1,000 pop.
No. of men per 100 women	96	Crude birth rate	19.0
Human Development Index	85.3	Crude death rate	7.7

The economy

GDP	P375bn	GDP per head	$3,380
GDP	$130bn	GDP per head in purchasing	
Av. ann. growth in real		power parity (USA=100)	30.2
GDP 1993–2003	0.8%	Economic freedom index	3.49

Origins of GDP

	% of total
Agriculture	11.0
Industry, of which:	34.8
manufacturing	24.0
Services	54.2

Components of GDP

	% of total
Private consumption	63.2
Public consumption	11.4
Investment	14.6
Exports	25.0
Imports	-14.2

Structure of employment

	% of total		% of labour force
Agricultural	1	Unemployed 2003	15.6
Industry	23	Av. ann. rate 1995–2003	16.2
Services	76		

Energy

	m TOE		
Total output	81.7	Net energy imports as %	
Total consumption	56.3	of energy use	-45
Consumption per head			
kg oil equivalent	1,543		

Inflation and finance

		av. ann. increase 1998–2003	
Consumer price			
inflation 2004	4.4%	Narrow money (M1)	14.8%
Av. ann. inflation 1999–2004	7.9%	Broad money	5.7%
Money market rate, 2004	1.96%		

Exchange rates

	end 2004		December 200
			1995 = 100
P per $	2.96	Effective rates	
P per SDR	4.60	– nominal	..
P per €	4.03	– real	..

Trade

Principal exports

	$bn fob
Agricultural products	10.0
Manufactures	7.7
Primary products	6.5
Fuels	5.4
Total incl. others	**29.6**

Principal imports

	$bn cif
Intermediate goods	6.3
Capital goods	2.5
Consumer goods	1.7
Total incl. others	**13.8**

Main export destinations

	% of total
Brazil	20.8
Chile	11.7
United States	10.6
China	8.4

Main origins of imports

	% of total
Brazil	22.1
United States	19.4
Germany	5.8
Italy	3.9

Balance of payments, reserves and debt, $bn

Visible exports fob	29.6	Change in reserves	3.7
Visible imports fob	-13.1	Level of reserves	
Trade balance	16.4	end Dec.	14.2
Invisibles inflows	7.1	No. months of import cover	5.8
Invisibles outflows	-16.8	Official gold holdings, m oz	0.0
Net transfers	0.6	Foreign debt	166.2
Current account balance	7.4	– as % of GDP	104
– as % of GDP	6.0	– as % of total exports	473
Capital balance	-15.7	Debt service ratio	40
Overall balance	-10.7		

Health and education

Health spending, % of GDP	8.9	Education spending, % of GDP	4.6
Doctors per 1,000 pop.	3.0	Enrolment, %: primary	120
Hospital beds per 1,000 pop.	3.7	secondary	100
Improved-water source access,		tertiary	56
% of pop.	79		

Society

No. of households	10.3m	Colour TVs per 100 households	90.6
Av. no. per household	3.6	Telephone lines per 100 pop.	21.9
Marriages per 1,000 pop.	3.6	Mobile telephone subscribers	
Divorces per 1,000 pop.	...	per 100 pop.	17.8
Cost of living, Dec. 2004		Computers per 100 pop.	8.2
New York = 100	51	Internet hosts per 1,000 pop.	27.3

AUSTRALIA

Area	7,682,300 sq km	Capital	Canberra
Arable as % of total land	6	Currency	Australian dollar (A$)

People

Population	19.7m	Life expectancy: men		78.5 yrs
Pop. per sq km	2.6	women		83.4 yrs
Av. ann. growth		Adult literacy		99.0%
in pop. 2000–05	1.11%	Fertility rate (per woman)		1.8
Pop. under 15	19.6%	Urban population		92.0%
Pop. over 60	17.3%			per 1,000 pop.
No. of men per 100 women	98	Crude birth rate		12.3
Human Development Index	94.6	Crude death rate		7.0

The economy

GDP	A$805bn	GDP per head	$26,520
GDP	$522bn	GDP per head in purchasing	
Av. ann. growth in real		power parity (USA=100)	76.2
GDP 1993–2003	3.7%	Economic freedom index	1.79

Origins of GDP		Components of GDP	
	% of total		% of total
		Private consumption	60.8
Agriculture & mining	8.2	Public consumption	17.9
Manufacturing	11.5	Investment	25.9
Other	80.3	Exports	20.2
		Imports	-24.8

Structure of employment

	% of total		% of labour force
Agriculture	4	Unemployed 2003	6.0
Industry	26	Av. ann. rate 1995–2003	7.3
Services	70		

Energy

	m TOE		
Total output	255.2	Net energy imports as %	
Total consumption	112.7	of energy use	-12
Consumption per head,			
kg oil equivalent	5,732		

Inflation and finance

		av. ann. increase 1998–200	
Consumer price			
inflation 2004	2.3%	Narrow money (M1)	15.0%
Av. ann. inflation 1999–2004	2.0%	Broad money	9.4%
Money market, 2004	5.25%	Household saving rate, 2003	-3.4

Exchange rates

	end 2004		December 200
			1995 = 10
A$ per $	1.28	Effective rates	114.
A$ per SDR	1.99	– nominal	112
A$ per €	1.74	– real	

Trade

Principal exports		**Principal imports**	
	$bn fob		*$bn cif*
Minerals & metals	31.8	Intermediate & other goods	32.4
Manufacturing goods	16.9	Consumption goods	27.0
Rural goods	14.6	Capital goods	20.2
Other goods	7.6	Fuels and lubricants	6.4
Total incl. others	71.6	Total incl. others	89.0

Main export destinations		**Main origins of imports**	
	% of total		*% of total*
Developing countries	46.5	Developing countries	31.6
Japan	18.9	EU15	23.6
EU15	13.6	United States	16.9
Asean[a]	12.0	Asean[a]	15.6
United States	9.0	Japan	12.3

Balance of payments, reserves and aid, $bn

Visible exports fob	70.5	Overall balance	6.9
Visible imports fob	-85.9	Change in reserves	11.7
Trade balance	-15.3	Level of reserves	
Invisibles inflows	31.1	end Dec.	33.3
Invisibles outflows	-46.2	No. months of import cover	3.0
Net transfers	-0.1	Official gold holdings, m oz	2.6
Current account balance	-30.4	Aid given	1.22
– as % of GDP	-5.8	– as % of GDP	0.25
Capital balance	36.6		

Health and education

Health spending, % of GDP	9.5	Education spending, % of GDP	4.8
Doctors per 1,000 pop.	2.5	Enrolment, %: primary	104
Hospital beds per 1,000 pop.	7.9	secondary	154
Improved-water source access,		tertiary	74
% of pop.	100		

Society

No. of households	7.3m	Colour TVs per 100 households	91.8
Av. no. per household	2.7	Telephone lines per 100 pop.	54.2
Marriages per 1,000 pop.	6.7	Mobile telephone subscribers	
Divorces per 1,000 pop.	2.8	per 100 pop.	72.0
Cost of living, Dec. 2004		Computers per 100 pop.	60.2
New York = 100	97	Internet hosts per 1,000 pop.	244.7

a Brunei, Indonesia, Laos, Malaysia, Myanmar, Philippines, Singapore, Thailand, Vietnam.

AUSTRIA

Area	83,855 sq km	Capital	Vienna
Arable as % of total land	17	Currency	Euro (€)

People

Population	8.1m	Life expectancy: men	76.9 yrs
Pop. per sq km	96.6	women	82.4 yrs
Av. ann. growth		Adult literacy	99.0%
in pop. 2000–05	0.23%	Fertility rate (per woman)	1.4
Pop. under 15	15.5%	Urban population	65.8%
Pop. over 60	22.7%		per 1,000 pop.
No. of men per 100 women	96	Crude birth rate	8.6
Human Development Index	93.4	Crude death rate	9.8

The economy

GDP	€224bn	GDP per head	$31,410
GDP	$253bn	GDP per head in purchasing	
Av. ann. growth in real		power parity (USA=100)	78.8
GDP 1993–2003	2.0%	Economic freedom index	2.09

Origins of GDP		Components of GDP	
	% of total		% of total
Agriculture	2.4	Private consumption	56.6
Industry, of which:	31.5	Public consumption	18.3
manufacturing	...	Investment	22.9
Services	66.1	Exports	56.4
		Imports	-54.2

Structure of employment

	% of total		% of labour force
Agriculture	4	Unemployed 2003	4.3
Industry	29	Av. ann. rate 1995–2003	3.9
Services	67		

Energy

	m TOE		
Total output	9.9	Net energy imports as %	
Total consumption	30.4	of energy use	67
Consumption per head,			
kg oil equivalent	3,774		

Inflation and finance

		av. ann. increase 1998–2003	
Consumer price			
inflation 2004	2.1%	Euro area:	
Av. ann. inflation 1999–2004	2.0%	Narrow money (M1)	8.9%
Deposit rate, h'holds, 2004	1.72%	Broad money	6.7%
		Household saving rate, 2003	8.9%

Exchange rates

	end 2004		December 2004
			1995 = 100
€ per $	0.73	Effective rates	
€ per SDR	1.14	– nominal	106.
		– real	105.

Trade

Principal exports

	$bn fob
Consumer goods	42.5
Investment goods	24.3
Intermediate goods	11.9
Food & beverages	5.1
Total incl. others	**87.4**

Principal imports

	$bn cif
Consumer goods	41.4
Investment goods	22.7
Intermediate goods	11.7
Raw materials (incl. fuels)	10.6
Total incl. others	**88.1**

Main export destinations

	% of total
EU25	71.4
Germany	31.9
Italy	8.8
United States	5.1

Main origins of imports

	% of total
EU25	77.3
Germany	40.8
Italy	7.0
France	4.8
United States	4.8

Balance of payments, reserves and aid, $bn

Visible exports fob	89.6	Overall balance	-2.0
Visible imports fob	-88.5	Change in reserves	-0.5
Trade balance	1.1	Level of reserves	
Invisibles inflows	59.2	end Dec.	12.7
Invisibles outflows	-59.4	No. months of import cover	1.0
Net transfers	-6.7	Official gold holdings, m oz	10.2
Current account balance	-1.4	Aid given	0.51
– as % of GDP	-0.5	– as % of GDP	0.20
Capital balance	-0.5		

Health and education

Health spending, % of GDP	7.7	Education spending, % of GDP	5.8
Doctors per 1,000 pop.	3.2	Enrolment, %: primary	103
Hospital beds per 1,000 pop.	6.3	secondary	100
Improved-water source access, % of pop.	100	tertiary	48

Society

No. of households	3.4m	Colour TVs per 100 households	97.9
Av. no. per household	2.4	Telephone lines per 100 pop.	48.1
Marriages per 1,000 pop.	4.1	Mobile telephone subscribers	
Divorces per 1,000 pop.	2.2	per 100 pop.	87.9
Cost of living, Dec. 2004		Computers per 100 pop.	37.4
New York = 100	110	Internet hosts per 1,000 pop.	196.7

BANGLADESH

Area	143,998 sq km	Capital	Dhaka
Arable as % of total land	62	Currency	Taka (Tk)

People

Population	146.7m	Life expectancy: men	63.8 yrs
Pop. per sq km	1,018.8	women	65.8 yrs
Av. ann. growth		Adult literacy	41.1%
in pop. 2000–05	1.91%	Fertility rate (per woman)	3.3
Pop. under 15	35.5%	Urban population	24.2%
Pop. over 60	5.7%		per 1,000 pop.
No. of men per 100 women	104	Crude birth rate	28.9
Human Development Index	50.9	Crude death rate	7.2

The economy

GDP	Tk3,006bn	GDP per head	$350
GDP	$51.9bn	GDP per head in purchasing	
Av. ann. growth in real		power parity (USA=100)	5.0
GDP 1993–2003	5.0%	Economic freedom index	3.95

Origins of GDP[a]		Components of GDP[a]	
	% of total		% of total
Agriculture	23.4	Private consumption	76.8
Industry, of which:	27.2	Public consumption	5.0
manufacturing	15.9	Investment	23.2
Services	49.4	Exports	13.3
		Imports	-18.8

Structure of employment

	% of total		% of labour force
Agriculture	63	Unemployed 2001	2.3
Industry	11	Av. ann. rate 1995–2001	2.4
Services	26		

Energy

			m TOE
Total output	16.7	Net energy imports as %	
Total consumption	21.0	of energy use	20
Consumption per head,			
kg oil equivalent	155		

Inflation and finance

		av. ann. increase 1998–2003	
Consumer price			
inflation 2004	5.7%	Narrow money (M1)	10.8%
Av. ann. inflation 1999–2003	3.3%	Broad money	15.1%
Deposit rate, mid-2004	6.56%		

Exchange rates

	end 2004		December 2004
			1995 = 100
Tk per $	60.74	Effective rates	
Tk per SDR	94.33	– nominal	..
Tk per €	82.73	– real	..

Trade

Principal exports[a]

	$bn fob
Clothing	3.6
Fish & fish products	0.3
Jute goods	0.2
Leather	0.2
Total incl. others	5.3

Principal imports[a]

	$bn cif
Capital goods	2.7
Textiles & yarn	1.9
Fuels	0.9
Cereal & dairy products	0.5
Total incl. others	9.5

Main export destinations[b]

	% of total
United States	27.6
Germany	10.4
United Kingdom	9.8
France	5.7
Italy	3.8

Main origins of imports[b]

	% of total
India	14.6
China	11.6
Singapore	11.5
Japan	7.6
Hong Kong	5.4

Balance of payments, reserves and debt, $bn

Visible exports fob	7.1	Change in reserves	0.9
Visible imports fob	-9.5	Level of reserves	
Trade balance	-2.4	end Dec.	2.6
Invisibles inflows	1.1	No. months of import cover	2.8
Invisibles outflows	-2.1	Official gold holdings, m oz	0.1
Net transfers	3.6	Foreign debt	18.8
Current account balance	0.1	– as % of GDP	37
– as % of GDP	0.4	– as % of total exports	188
Capital balance	0.7	Debt service ratio	7
Overall balance	0.9		

Health and education

Health spending, % of GDP	3.1	Education spending, % of GDP	2.3
Doctors per 1,000 pop.	0.2	Enrolment, %: primary	98
Hospital beds per 1,000 pop.	...	secondary	47
Improved-water source access, % of pop.	75	tertiary	6

Society

No. of households	24.6m	Colour TVs per 100 households	2.7
Av. no. per household	5.9	Telephone lines per 100 pop.	0.6
Marriages per 1,000 pop.	9.7	Mobile telephone subscribers	
Divorces per 1,000 pop.	...	per 100 pop.	1.0
Cost of living, Dec. 2004		Computers per 100 pop.	0.8
New York = 100	53	Internet hosts per 1,000 pop.	...

a Fiscal year ending June 30 2003.
b 2002

BELGIUM

Area	30,520 sq km	Capital	Brussels
Arable as % of total land	26	Currency	Euro (€)

People

Population	10.3m	Life expectancy: men	76.5 yrs
Pop. per sq km	337.5	women	82.7 yrs
Av. ann. growth		Adult literacy	99.0%
in pop. 2000–05	0.22%	Fertility rate (per woman)	1.7
Pop. under 15	16.8%	Urban population	97.2%
Pop. over 60	22.4%		per 1,000 pop.
No. of men per 100 women	96	Crude birth rate	10.8
Human Development Index	94.2	Crude death rate	10.2

The economy

GDP	€267bn	GDP per head	$29,170
GDP	$302bn	GDP per head in purchasing	
Av. ann. growth in real		power parity (USA=100)	76.6
GDP 1993–2003	2.2%	Economic freedom index	2.13

Origins of GDP		Components of GDP	
	% of total		% of total
Agriculture	1.6	Private consumption	54.5
Industry, of which:	26.8	Public consumption	22.8
manufacturing	...	Investment	18.8
Services	71.6	Exports	81.6
		Imports	-77.6

Structure of employment

	% of total		% of labour force
Agriculture	2	Unemployed 2003	8.2
Industry	25	Av. ann. rate 1995–2003	8.3
Services	73		

Energy

	m TOE		
Total output	13.2	Net energy imports as %	
Total consumption	56.9	of energy use	77
Consumption per head,			
kg oil equivalent	5,505		

Inflation and finance

		av. ann. increase 1998–2003	
Consumer price			
inflation 2004	2.1%	Euro area:	
Av. ann. inflation 1999–2004	2.1%	Narrow money (M1)	8.9%
Treasury bill rate, 2004	1.97%	Broad money	6.7%
		Household saving rate, 2003	14.0%

Exchange rates

	end 2004		December 2004
			1995 = 100
€ per $	0.73	Effective rates	
€ per SDR	1.14	– nominal	108.
		– real	105.

Trade

Principal exports

	$bn fob
Chemicals	69.8
Transport equipment	32.7
Machinery	30.4
Food & animals	21.2
Total incl. others	254.9

Principal imports

	$bn cif
Chemicals	55.4
Machinery	34.1
Transport equipment	28.1
Food & animals	17.4
Total incl. others	234.3

Main export destinations

	% of total
Germany	19.5
France	17.3
Netherlands	11.7
United Kingdom	9.2
Euro area	63.3

Main origins of imports

	% of total
Germany	17.6
Netherlands	16.6
France	13.3
United Kingdom	7.5
Euro area	61.2

Balance of payments, reserves and aid, $bn

Visible exports fob	203.3	Overall balance	-1.7
Visible imports fob	-193.8	Change in reserves	-0.2
Trade balance	9.5	Level of reserves	
Invisibles inflows	83.3	end Dec.	14.4
Invisibles outflows	-73.5	No. months of import cover	0.6
Net transfers	-6.6	Official gold holdings, m oz	8.3
Current account balance	12.8	Aid given	1.85
– as % of GDP	4.2	– as % of GDP	0.60
Capital balance	-0.3		

Health and education

Health spending, % of GDP	9.1	Education spending, % of GDP	5.9
Doctors per 1,000 pop.	4.2	Enrolment, %: primary	105
Hospital beds per 1,000 pop.	4.1	secondary	161
Improved-water source access, % of pop.	...	tertiary	60

Society

No. of households	4.4m	Colour TVs per 100 households	99.4
Av. no. per household	2.4	Telephone lines per 100 pop.	48.4
Marriages per 1,000 pop.	4.0	Mobile telephone subscribers	
Divorces per 1,000 pop.	2.4	per 100 pop.	79.3
Cost of living, Dec. 2004		Computers per 100 pop.	31.8
New York = 100	98	Internet hosts per 1,000 pop.	195.3

BRAZIL

Area	8,511,965 sq km	Capital	Brasilia
Arable as % of total land	7	Currency	Real (R)

People

Population	178.5m	Life expectancy: men	68.2 yrs
Pop. per sq km	21.0	women	75.7 yrs
Av. ann. growth		Adult literacy	88.2%
in pop. 2000–05	1.39%	Fertility rate (per woman)	2.4
Pop. under 15	27.9%	Urban population	83.1%
Pop. over 60	8.8%		per 1,000 pop.
No. of men per 100 women	97	Crude birth rate	19.7
Human Development Index	77.5	Crude death rate	6.5

The economy

GDP	R1,515n	GDP per head	$2,760
GDP	$492bn	GDP per head in purchasing	
Av. ann. growth in real		power parity (USA=100)	19.9
GDP 1993–2003	2.4%	Economic freedom index	3.25

Origins of GDP

Components of GDP

	% of total		% of total
		Private consumption	56.7
Agriculture	9.9	Public consumption	19.9
Industry, of which:	38.8	Investment	19.8
manufacturing	...	Exports	16.4
Services	51.3	Imports	-12.8

Structure of employment

	% of total		% of labour force
Agriculture	20	Unemployed 2002	9.7
Industry	14	Av. ann. rate 1995–2002	8.3
Services	66		

Energy

			m TOE
Total output	161.7	Net energy imports as %	
Total consumption	190.7	of energy use	15
Consumption per head,			
kg oil equivalent	1,093		

Inflation and finance

		av. ann. increase 1998–2003	
Consumer price			
inflation 2004	6.6%	Narrow money (M1)	15.3%
Av. ann. inflation 1999–2004	8.7%	Broad money	9.4%
Money market rate, 2004	16.24%		

Exchange rates

	end 2004		December 2004
			1995 = 100
R per $	2.65	Effective rates	
R per sdr	4.12	– nominal	..
R per 7	3.62	– real	..

Trade

Principal exports

	$bn fob
Transport equipment & parts	11.2
Soyabeans etc.	7.9
Metal goods	7.2
Chemical products	1.7
Total incl. others	**73.1**

Principal imports

	$bn cif
Machines & electrical equipment	11.9
Chemical products	8.8
Oil & derivatives	6.6
Transport equipment & parts	4.9
Total incl. others	**50.7**

Main export destinations

	% of total
United States	23.1
Argentina	6.2
China	6.2
Netherlands	5.8

Main origins of imports

	% of total
United States	20.1
Argentina	9.7
Germany	8.7
Japan	5.2

Balance of payments, reserves and debt, $bn

Visible exports fob	73.1	Change in reserves	11.8
Visible imports fob	-48.3	Level of reserves	
Trade balance	24.8	end Dec.	49.6
Invisibles inflows	13.8	No. months of import cover	6.9
Invisibles outflows	-37.4	Official gold holdings, m oz	0.5
Net transfers	2.9	Foreign debt	235.4
Current account balance	4.0	– as % of GDP	50
– as % of GDP	0.8	– as % of total exports	299
Capital balance	0.3	Debt service ratio	72
Overall balance	3.6		

Health and education

Health spending, % of GDP	7.9	Education spending, % of GDP	4.3
Doctors per 1,000 pop.	2.1	Enrolment, %: primary	148
Hospital beds per 1,000 pop.	2.8	secondary	110
Improved-water source access, % of pop.	89	tertiary	18

Society

No. of households	50.6m	Colour TVs per 100 households	87.1
Av. no. per household	3.5	Telephone lines per 100 pop.	22.3
Marriages per 1,000 pop.	4.3	Mobile telephone subscribers	
Divorces per 1,000 pop.	0.6	per 100 pop.	26.4
Cost of living, Dec. 2004		Computers per 100 pop.	7.5
New York = 100	54	Internet hosts per 1,000 pop.	22.0

BULGARIA

Area	110,994 sq km	Capital	Sofia
Arable as % of total land	30	Currency	Lev (BGL)

People

Population	7.9m	Life expectancy: men	69.8 yrs
Pop. per sq km	71.2	women	76.3 yrs
Av. ann. growth		Adult literacy	98.6%
in pop. 2000–05	-0.69%	Fertility rate (per woman)	1.2
Pop. under 15	13.8%	Urban population	69.8%
Pop. over 60	22.4%		per 1,000 pop.
No. of men per 100 women	94	Crude birth rate	7.9
Human Development Index	79.6	Crude death rate	14.5

The economy

GDP	BGL34.4bn	GDP per head	$2,510
GDP	$19.9bn	GDP per head in purchasing	
Av. ann. growth in real		power parity (USA=100)	20.0
GDP 1993–2003	1.3%	Economic freedom index	2.74

Origins of GDP		Components of GDP	
	% of total		% of total
Agriculture	11.4	Private consumption	77.8
Industry, of which:	30.0	Public consumption	10.3
manufacturing	...	Investment	21.7
Services	58.6	Exports	53.2
		Imports	-63.0

Structure of employment

	% of total		% of labour force
Agriculture	11	Unemployed 2003	17.6
Industry	33	Av. ann. rate 1995–2003	15.6
Services	56		

Energy

		m TOE	
		Net energy imports as %	
Total output	10.5	of energy use	45
Total consumption	19.0		
Consumption per head,			
kg oil equivalent	2,417		

Inflation and finance

		av. ann change 1998–200	
Consumer price			
inflation 2004	6.4%	Narrow money (M1)	16.7%
Av. ann. inflation 1999–2004	6.4%	Broad money	20.3%
Money market rate 2004	1.95%		

Exchange rates

	end 2004		December 200
			1995 = 10
BGL per $	1.44	Effective rates	
BGL per SDR	2.23	– nominal	126.5
BGL per €	1.96	– real	124.9

Trade

Principal exports		Principal imports	
	$bn fob		*$bn cif*
Clothing	1.6	Mineral fuels	1.5
Metals (excl. iron & steel)	0.6	Textiles	1.1
Iron & steel	0.6	Machinery & equipment	1.0
Chemicals	0.4	Chemicals	0.7
Total incl. others	**7.5**	Total incl. others	**10.8**

Main export destinations		Main origins of imports	
	% of total		*% of total*
Italy	14.0	Germany	14.3
Germany	10.8	Russia	12.5
Greece	10.4	Italy	10.2
Turkey	9.1	Greece	6.6

Balance of payments, reserves and debt, $bn

Visible exports fob	7.4	Change in reserves	2.0
Visible imports fob	-9.9	Level of reserves	
Trade balance	-2.5	end Dec.	6.8
Invisibles inflows	3.5	No. months of import cover	6.2
Invisibles outflows	-3.4	Official gold holdings, m oz	1.3
Net transfers	0.7	Foreign debt	13.3
Current account balance	-1.7	– as % of GDP	83
– as % of GDP	-8.4	– as % of total exports	148
Capital balance	2.1	Debt service ratio	13
Overall balance	0.7		

Health and education

Health spending, % of GDP	7.3	Education spending, % of GDP	3.5
Doctors per 1,000 pop.	3.4	Enrolment, %: primary	99
Hospital beds per 1,000 pop.	7.2	secondary	98
Improved-water source access,		tertiary	38
% of pop.	100		

Society

No. of households	2.9m	Colour TVs per 100 households	65.8
Av. no. per household	2.7	Telephone lines per 100 pop.	38.1
Marriages per 1,000 pop.	3.7	Mobile telephone subscribers	
Divorces per 1,000 pop.	1.3	per 100 pop.	46.6
Cost of living, Dec. 2004		Computers per 100 pop.	5.2
New York = 100	58	Internet hosts per 1,000 pop.	10.1

CAMEROON

Area	475,442 sq km	Capital	Yaoundé
Arable as % of total land	13	Currency	CFA franc (CFAfr)

People

Population	16.0m	Life expectancy: men	45.8 yrs
Pop. per sq km	33.7	women	46.7 yrs
Av. ann. growth		Adult literacy	67.9%
in pop. 2000–05	1.88%	Fertility rate (per woman)	4.7
Pop. under 15	41.2%	Urban population	51.4%
Pop. over 60	5.6%		per 1,000 pop.
No. of men per 100 women	99	Crude birth rate	35.4
Human Development Index	50.1	Crude death rate	16.8

The economy

GDP	CFAfr7,260bn	GDP per head	$780
GDP	$12.5bn	GDP per head in purchasing	
Av. ann. growth in real		power parity (USA=100)	5.3
GDP 1993–2003	3.8%	Economic freedom index	3.60

Origins of GDP		Components of GDP[a]	
	% of total		% of total
Agriculture	27.9	Private consumption	67.8
Industry, of which:	30.0	Public consumption	8.0
manufacturing	...	Investment	27.1
Services	42.1	Exports	20.7
		Imports	-23.7

Structure of employment

	% of total		% of labour force
Agriculture	70	Unemployed 2003	...
Industry	13	Av. ann. rate 1995–2003	...
Services	17		

Energy

	m TOE		
Total output	12.0	Net energy imports as %	
Total consumption	6.6	of energy use	-83
Consumption per head,			
kg oil equivalent	417		

Inflation and finance

		av. ann. change 1998–200	
Consumer price			
inflation 2002	2.8%	Narrow money (M1)	9.7%
Av. ann. inflation 1999–2002	1.7%	Broad money	12.8%
Deposit rate, 2004	5.00%		

Exchange rates

	end 2004		December 200
			1995 = 10
CFAfr per $	481.58	Effective rates	
CFAfr per SDR	747.90	– nominal	116.
CFAfr per €	655.96	– real	114.

Trade

Principal exports	$bn fob	Principal imports	$bn cif
Crude oil	0.9	Intermediate goods	0.8
Timber	0.3	Capital goods	0.5
Cocoa	0.2	Food & consumer goods	0.4
Total incl. others	2.2	Total incl. others	1.8

Main export destinations	% of total	Main origins of imports	% of total
Spain	20.3	France	30.4
Italy	15.0	Nigeria	13.4
Netherlands	11.9	Belgium	5.3
France	10.6		

Balance of payments[b], reserves and debt, $bn

Visible exports fob	2.3	Change in reserves	0.0
Visible imports fob	-1.4	Level of reserves	
Trade balance	0.9	end Dec.	0.7
Invisibles inflows	0.6	No. months of import cover	2.5
Invisibles outflows	-1.2	Official gold holdings, m oz	0.0
Net transfers	0.1	Foreign debt	9.2
Current account balance	0.5	– as % of GDP	96
– as % of GDP[c]	-4.8	– as % of total exports	335
Capital balance[d]	-0.1	Debt service ratio	16
Overall balance[d]	-0.3		

Health and education

Health spending, % of GDP	4.6	Education spending, % of GDP	3.2
Doctors per 1,000 pop.	0.1	Enrolment, %: primary	107
Hospital beds per 1,000 pop.	...	secondary	31
Improved-water source access, % of pop.	63	tertiary	5

Society

No. of households	4.2m	Colour TVs per 100 households	2.3
Av. no. per household	3.8	Telephone lines per 100 pop.	0.7
Marriages per 1,000 pop.	...	Mobile telephone subscribers	
Divorces per 1,000 pop.	...	per 100 pop.	6.6
Cost of living, Dec. 2004		Computers per 100 pop.	0.6
New York = 100	...	Internet hosts per 1,000 pop.	...

Fiscal year ending June 30 2002.
2000
2002
Fiscal year ending June 30 2000.

CANADA

Area[a]	9,970,610 sq km	Capital	Ottawa
Arable as % of total land	5	Currency	Canadian dollar (C$)

People

Population	31.5m	Life expectancy: men		78.2 yrs
Pop. per sq km	3.2	women		83.1 yrs
Av. ann. growth		Adult literacy		99.0%
in pop. 2000–05	1.00%	Fertility rate (per woman)		1.5
Pop. under 15	17.6%	Urban population		80.4%
Pop. over 60	17.9%			per 1,000 pop.
No. of men per 100 women	98	Crude birth rate		10.3
Human Development Index	94.3	Crude death rate		7.4

The economy

GDP	C$1,200bn	GDP per head	$27,190
GDP	$857bn	GDP per head in purchasing	
Av. ann. growth in real		power parity (USA=100)	79.6
GDP 1993–2003	3.4%	Economic freedom index	1.91

Origins of GDP		Components of GDP	
	% of total		% of total
Agriculture	2.3	Private consumption	56.8
Industry, of which:	29.0	Public consumption	19.0
manufacturing & mining	21.0	Investment	21.1
Services	68.7	Exports	37.8
		Imports	-33.8

Structure of employment

	% of total		% of labour force
Agriculture	3	Unemployed 2003	7.6
Industry	23	Av. ann. rate 1995–2003	8.2
Services	74		

Energy

	m TOE		
Total output	385.4	Net energy imports as %	
Total consumption	250.0	of energy use	-54
Consumption per head,			
kg oil equivalent	7,973		

Inflation and finance

		av. ann. increase 1998–2003	
Consumer price			
inflation 2004	1.8%	Narrow money (M1)	9.6%
Av. ann. inflation 1999–2004	2.4%	Broad money	7.7%
Money market rate, 2004	2.25%	Household saving rate, 2003	1.4%

Exchange rates

	end 2004		December 2004
			1995 = 100
C$ per $	1.20	Effective rates	114.4
C$ per SDR	1.87	– nominal	
C$ per €	1.63	– real	120

Trade

Principal exports		Principal imports	
	$bn fob		*$bn fob*
Machinery & industrial		Machinery & industrial	
equipment	63.7	equipment	70.1
Motor vehicles and parts	62.8	Motor vehicles & parts	54.6
Industrial goods	47.6	Industrial goods	46.5
Energy products	43.8	Consumer goods	33.0
Forest products	24.6	Agric. products	15.4
Agricultural products	20.9	Energy products	14.0
Total incl. others	**272.4**	Total incl. others	**238.6**

Main export destinations		Main origins of imports	
	% of total		*% of total*
United States	82.5	United States	70.1
EU15 (excl. UK)	4.3	EU15	10.2
Japan	2.5	China	5.4
United Kingdom	1.7	Japan	3.1

Balance of payments, reserves and aid, $bn

Visible exports fob	285.8	Overall balance	-3.3
Visible imports fob	-244.3	Change in reserves	-0.9
Trade balance	41.5	Level of reserves	
Invisibles inflows	66.4	end Dec.	36.3
Invisibles outflows	-90.9	No. months of import cover	1.3
Net transfers	0.2	Official gold holdings, m oz	0.1
Current account balance	17.3	Aid given	2.03
– as % of GDP	2.0	– as % of GDP	0.24
Capital balance	-18.0		

Health and education

Health spending, % of GDP	9.6	Education spending, % of GDP	5.3
Doctors per 1,000 pop.	1.9	Enrolment, %: primary	101
Hospital beds per 1,000 pop.	3.2	secondary	105
Improved-water source access,		tertiary	58
% of pop.	100		

Society

No. of households	11.8m	Colour TVs per 100 households	98.8
Av. no. per household	2.6	Telephone lines per 100 pop.	65.1
Marriages per 1,000 pop.	4.7	Mobile telephone subscribers	
Divorces per 1,000 pop.	2.3	per 100 pop.	41.9
Cost of living, Dec. 2004		Computers per 100 pop.	48.7
New York = 100	84	Internet hosts per 1,000 pop.	121.9

Including freshwater.

CHILE

Area	756,945 sq km	Capital	Santiago
Arable as % of total land	3	Currency	Chilean peso (Ps)

People

Population	15.8m	Life expectancy: men	75.5 yrs
Pop. per sq km	20.9	women	81.5 yrs
Av. ann. growth		Adult literacy	95.7%
in pop. 2000–05	1.12%	Fertility rate (per woman)	2.0
Pop. under 15	24.9%	Urban population	87.0%
Pop. over 60	11.6%		per 1,000 pop.
No. of men per 100 women	98	Crude birth rate	18.2
Human Development Index	83.9	Crude death rate	5.4

The economy

GDP	50,068bn pesos	GDP per head	$4,590
GDP	$72.4bn	GDP per head in purchasing	
Av. ann. growth in real		power parity (USA=100)	26.0
GDP 1993–2003	4.6%	Economic freedom index	1.81

Origins of GDP		Components of GDP	
	% of total		% of total
Agriculture	6.4	Private consumption	62.5
Industry, of which:	38.6	Public consumption	12.6
manufacturing	17.7	Investment	21.8
Services	55.0	Exports	36.4
		Imports	-33.3

Structure of employment

	% of total		% of labour force
Agriculture	14	Unemployed 2003	7.4
Industry	23	Av. ann. rate 1995–2003	7.0
Services	63		

Energy

	m TOE		
Total output	8.8	Net energy imports as %	
Total consumption	24.7	of energy use	6
Consumption per head,			
kg oil equivalent	1,585		

Inflation and finance

			av. ann. increase 1998–2003
Consumer price			
inflation 2004	1.1%	Narrow money (M1)	10.9%
Av. ann. inflation 1999–2004	2.7%	Broad money	4.7%
Money market rate, 2004	1.88%		

Exchange rates

	end 2004		December 2004
Ps per $	559.83	Effective rates	1995 = 100
Ps per SDR	869.42	– nominal	83
Ps per Ecu	767.54	– real	83

Trade

Principal exports		Principal imports	
	$bn fob		*$bn cif*
Copper	7.5	Intermediate goods	11.0
Fruit	1.7	Capital goods	3.7
Paper products	1.2	Consumer goods	3.2
Total incl. others	**21.5**	**Total incl. others**	**19.4**

Main export destinations		Main origins of imports	
	% of total		*% of total*
United States	16.5	Argentina	19.4
Japan	10.7	United States	13.0
China	8.8	Brazil	10.4
Mexico	4.8	China	6.6

Balance of payments, reserves and debt, $bn

Visible exports fob	21.5	Change in reserves	0.5
Visible imports fob	-18.0	Level of reserves	
Trade balance	3.5	end Dec.	15.8
Invisibles inflows	6.4	No. months of import cover	6.8
Invisibles outflows	-11.6	Official gold holdings, m oz	0.0
Net transfers	0.6	Foreign debt	43.2
Current account balance	-1.1	– as % of GDP	66
– as % of GDP	-0.8	– as % of total exports	174
Capital balance	1.7	Debt service ratio	34
Overall balance	-0.4		

Health and education

Health spending, % of GDP	5.8	Education spending, % of GDP	4.4
Doctors per 1,000 pop.	1.2	Enrolment, %: primary	100
Hospital beds per 1,000 pop.	2.8	secondary	91
Improved-water source access,		tertiary	42
% of pop.	95		

Society

No. of households	4.2m	Colour TVs per 100 households	61.7
Av. no. per household	3.7	Telephone lines per 100 pop.	22.1
Marriages per 1,000 pop.	4.8	Mobile telephone subscribers	
Divorces per 1,000 pop.	0.5	per 100 pop.	51.1
Cost of living, Dec. 2004		Computers per 100 pop.	11.9
New York = 100	61	Internet hosts per 1,000 pop.	18.6

CHINA

Area	9,560,900 sq km	Capital	Beijing
Arable as % of total land	15	Currency	Yuan

People

Population	1,304.2m	Life expectancy: men		70.8 yrs
Pop. per sq km	136.4	women		74.6 yrs
Av. ann. growth		Adult literacy[a]		90.9%
in pop. 2000–05	0.65%	Fertility rate (per woman)		1.7
Pop. under 15	21.4%	Urban population		38.6%
Pop. over 60	10.9%			per 1,000 pop.
No. of men per 100 women	106	Crude birth rate		14.5
Human Development Index	74.5	Crude death rate		7.1

The economy

GDP	Yuan11,729bn	GDP per head	$1,090
GDP	$1,417bn	GDP per head in purchasing	
Av. ann. growth in real		power parity (USA=100)	13.2
GDP 1993–2003	8.9%	Economic freedom index	3.46

Origins of GDP		Components of GDP	
	% of total		% of total
Agriculture	15	Private consumption	4
Industry, of which:	52	Public consumption	1
manufacturing	39	Investment	4
Services	33	Exports	3
		Imports	-3

Structure of employment

	% of total		% of labour force
Agriculture	49	Unemployed 2002	4
Industry	22	Av. ann. rate 1995–2002	3
Services	29		

Energy

	m TOE		
Total output	1,220.8	Net energy imports as %	
Total consumption	1,228.6	of energy use	
Consumption per head,			
kg oil equivalent	960		

Inflation and finance

		av. ann. increase 1998–200	
Consumer price			
inflation 2003	1.2%	Narrow money (M1)	17.5
Av. ann. inflation 1999–2003	0.3%	Broad money	16.2
Deposit rate, 2004	2.25%		

Exchange rates

	end 2004		December 20
			1995 = 1
Yuan per $	8.28	Effective rates	
Yuan per SDR	12.85	– nominal	88.
Yuan per €	11.28	– real	91

Trade

Principal exports

	$bn fob
Office equipment	62.6
Apparel & clothing	52.1
Telecoms equipment	45.0
Electrical machinery	42.4
Footwear	13.0
Total incl. others	**437.9**

Principal imports

	$bn cif
Electrical machinery	79.8
Petroleum products	26.7
Office equipment	24.2
Other machinery	21.0
Telecoms equipment	19.5
Total incl. others	**413.1**

Main export destinations

	% of total
United States	21.1
Hong Kong	17.4
Japan	13.6
South Korea	4.6
Germany	4.0

Main origins of imports

	% of total
Japan	18.0
Taiwan	12.0
South Korea	10.4
United States	8.2
Germany	5.9

Balance of payments, reserves and debt, $bn

Visible exports fob	438.3	Change in reserves	118.5
Visible imports fob	-393.6	Level of reserves	
Trade balance	44.7	end Dec.	416.2
Invisibles inflows	62.8	No. months of import cover	10.6
Invisibles outflows	-79.2	Official gold holdings, m oz	19.3
Net transfers	17.6	Foreign debt	193.6
Current account balance	45.9	– as % of GDP	15
– as % of GDP	3.2	– as % of total exports	49
Capital balance	52.7	Debt service ratio	9
Overall balance	116.6		

Health and education

Health spending, % of GDP	5.8	Education spending, % of GDP	2.1
Doctors per 1,000 pop.	1.6	Enrolment, %: primary	116
Hospital beds per 1,000 pop.	2.5	secondary	70
Improved-water source access,		tertiary	13
% of pop.	77		

Society

No. of households	371.6m	Colour TVs per 100 households	45.9
Av. no. per household	3.5	Telephone lines per 100 pop.	20.9
Marriages per 1,000 pop.	6.3	Mobile telephone subscribers	
Divorces per 1,000 pop.	0.8	per 100 pop.	21.5
Cost of living, Dec. 2004		Computers per 100 pop.	2.8
New York = 100	85	Internet hosts per 1,000 pop.	0.1

Note: Data excludes Special Administrative Regions ie, Hong Kong and Macau.
2000

COLOMBIA

| Area | 1,141,748 sq km | Capital | Bogota |
| Arable as % of total land | 2 | Currency | Colombian peso (peso) |

People

Population	44.2m	Life expectancy: men	70.3 yrs
Pop. per sq km	38.7	women	76.3 yrs
Av. ann. growth		Adult literacy	92.1%
in pop. 2000–05	1.59%	Fertility rate (per woman)	2.6
Pop. under 15	31.0%	Urban population	76.5%
Pop. over 60	7.5%		per 1,000 pop.
No. of men per 100 women	98	Crude birth rate	22.2
Human Development Index	77.3	Crude death rate	5.4

The economy

GDP	226,330bn pesos	GDP per head	$1,780
GDP	$78.7bn	GDP per head in purchasing	
Av. ann. growth in real		power parity (USA=100)	17.0
GDP 1993–2003	2.2%	Economic freedom index	3.21

Origins of GDP

	% of total
Agriculture	12.9
Industry, of which:	30.3
manufacturing	14.5
Services	56.7

Components of GDP

	% of total
Private consumption	64.0
Public consumption	20.
Investment	17.
Exports	20.
Imports	-23.

Structure of employment

	% of total		% of labour force
Agriculture	22	Unemployed 2003	14.
Industry	18	Av. ann. rate 1995–2003	14.
Services	60		

Energy

	m TOE		
Total output	72.3	Net energy imports as %	
Total consumption	27.4	of energy use	-16
Consumption per head,			
kg oil equivalent	625		

Inflation and finance

		av. ann. increase 1998–20	
Consumer price			
inflation 2004	5.9%	Narrow money (M1)	18.2
Av. ann. inflation 1999–2004	7.3%	Broad money	13.
Money market rate, 2004	7.01%		

Exchange rates

	end 2004		December 20
			1995 = 1
Peso per $	2,412	Effective rates	
Peso per SDR	3,746	– nominal	7
Peso per €	3,285	– real	9

Trade

Principal exports

	$bn fob
Oil	3.4
Coal	1.4
Coffee	0.8
Total incl. others	12.7

Principal imports

	$bn cif
Intermediate goods & raw materials	6.4
Capital goods	4.8
Consumer goods	2.7
Total	13.9

Main export destinations

	% of total
United States	47.5
Venezuela	9.6
Ecuador	7.9
Peru	3.3

Main origins of imports

	% of total
United States	29.7
Venezuela	7.4
Japan	6.5
Mexico	5.3

Balance of payments, reserves and debt, $bn

Visible exports fob	13.7	Change in reserves	0.1
Visible imports fob	-13.3	Level of reserves	
Trade balance	0.4	end Dec.	10.9
Invisibles inflows	2.4	No. months of import cover	6.3
Invisibles outflows	-7.4	Official gold holdings, m oz	0.3
Net transfers	3.3	Foreign debt	34.0
Current account balance	-1.2	– as % of GDP	43
– as % of GDP	-1.5	– as % of total exports	182
Capital balance	0.8	Debt service ratio	46
Overall balance	-0.2		

Health and education

Health spending, % of GDP	8.1	Education spending, % of GDP	4.4
Doctors per 1,000 pop.	0.9	Enrolment, %: primary	110
Hospital beds per 1,000 pop.	1.0	secondary	71
Improved-water source access, % of pop.	92	tertiary	24

Society

No. of households	11.2m	Colour TVs per 100 households	86.2
Av. no. per household	3.9	Telephone lines per 100 pop.	17.9
Marriages per 1,000 pop.	...	Mobile telephone subscribers	
Divorces per 1,000 pop.	0.2	per 100 pop.	14.1
Cost of living, Dec. 2004		Computers per 100 pop.	4.9
New York = 100	62	Internet hosts per 1,000 pop.	7.4

CÔTE D'IVOIRE

Area	322,463 sq km	Capital	Abidjan/Yamoussoukro
Arable as % of total land	10	Currency	CFA franc (CFAfr)

People

Population	16.6m	Life expectancy: men	45.6 yrs
Pop. per sq km	51.5	women	47.0 yrs
Av. ann. growth		Adult literacy	48.1%
in pop. 2000–05	1.63%	Fertility rate (per woman)	5.1
Pop. under 15	41.9%	Urban population	44.9%
Pop. over 60	5.3%		per 1,000 pop.
No. of men per 100 women	103	Crude birth rate	35.5
Human Development Index	39.9	Crude death rate	16.7

The economy

GDP	CFAfr7,982bn	GDP per head	$830
GDP	$13.7bn	GDP per head in purchasing	
Av. ann. growth in real		power parity (USA=100)	3.9
GDP 1993–2003	1.9%	Economic freedom index	3.26

Origins of GDP		Components of GDP	
	% of total		% of total
Agriculture	29.0	Private consumption	63.7
Industry, of which:	26.0	Public consumption	14.3
manufacturing	...	Investment	11.5
Services	45.0	Exports	46.0
		Imports	-35.5

Structure of employment

	% of total		% of labour force
Agriculture	...	Unemployed 2002	..
Industry	...	Av. ann. rate 1995–2002	..
Services	...		

Energy

	m TOE		
		Net energy imports as %	
Total output	6.5	of energy use	
Total consumption	6.6		
Consumption per head,			
kg oil equivalent	397		

Inflation and finance

			av. ann. change 1998–200
Consumer price			
inflation 2003	3.4%	Narrow money (M1)	5.9
Av. ann. inflation 1999–2003	3.3%	Broad money	5.7
Money market rate, 2004	4.95%		

Exchange rates

	end 2004		December 200
			1995 = 10
CFAfr per $	481.6	Effective rates	
CFAfr per SDR	747.9	– nominal	116.
CFAfr per €	655.9	– real	120

Trade

Principal exports

	$bn fob
Cocoa beans & products	2.4
Petroleum products	0.7
Timber	0.2
Coffee & products	0.1
Total incl. others	**5.8**

Principal imports

	$bn cif
Capital goods	0.8
Capital equip. & raw materials	0.7
Consumer goods	0.6
Fuel & lubricants	0.6
Total incl. others	**3.3**

Main export destinations

	% of total
Netherlands	11.9
France	10.4
United States	7.6
Germany	5.2
Spain	5.0

Main origins of imports

	% of total
France	20.2
Nigeria	18.5
China	7.2
Italy	3.6
United States	3.2

Balance of payments, reserves and debt, $bn

Visible exports fob	5.8	Change in reserves	0.4
Visible imports fob	-3.3	Level of reserves	
Trade balance	2.5	end Dec.	2.2
Invisibles inflows	0.9	No. months of import cover	4.5
Invisibles outflows	-2.6	Official gold holdings, m oz	0.0
Net transfers	-0.5	Foreign debt	12.2
Current account balance	0.4	– as % of GDP	107
– as % of GDP	2.6	– as % of total exports	210
Capital balance	-1.1	Debt service ratio	10
Overall balance	-0.8		

Health and education

Health spending, % of GDP	6.2	Education spending, % of GDP	4.6
Doctors per 1,000 pop.	0.1	Enrolment, %: primary	80
Hospital beds per 1,000 pop.	...	secondary	26
Improved-water source access,		tertiary	7
% of pop.	84		

Society

No. of households	3.4m	Colour TVs per 100 households	28.0
Av. no. per household	4.8	Telephone lines per 100 pop.	1.4
Marriages per 1,000 pop.	...	Mobile telephone subscribers	
Divorces per 1,000 pop.	...	per 100 pop.	7.7
Cost of living, Dec. 2004		Computers per 100 pop.	0.9
New York = 100	92	Internet hosts per 1,000 pop.	0.1

CZECH REPUBLIC

Area	78,864 sq km	Capital	Prague
Arable as % of total land	40	Currency	Koruna (Kc)

People

Population	10.2m	Life expectancy: men	73.1 yrs
Pop. per sq km	129.3	women	79.4 yrs
Av. ann. growth		Adult literacy	99.0%
in pop. 2000–05	-0.09	Fertility rate (per woman)	1.2
Pop. under 15	14.6%	Urban population	74.3%
Pop. over 60	20.0%		per 1,000 pop.
No. of men per 100 women	95	Crude birth rate	8.8
Human Development Index	86.8	Crude death rate	11.1

The economy

GDP	Kc2,532bn	GDP per head	$8,790
GDP	$89.7bn	GDP per head in purchasing	
Av. ann. growth in real		power parity (USA=100)	41.3
GDP 1993–2003	2.3%	Economic freedom index	2.30

Origins of GDP		Components of GDP	
	% of total		% of total
Agriculture	3.5	Private consumption	50.
Industry, of which:	35.4	Public consumption	23.
manufacturing	...	Investment	27.
Services	61.0	Exports	62.
		Imports	-65.

Structure of employment

	% of total		% of labour force
Agriculture	4	Unemployed 2002	7.
Industry	38	Av. ann. rate 1995–2002	6.
Services	58		

Energy

	m TOE		
Total output	30.7	Net energy imports as %	
Total consumption	41.7	of energy use	2
Consumption per head,			
kg oil equivalent	4,090		

Inflation and finance

		av. ann. increase 1998–2004	
Consumer price			
inflation 2004	2.8%	Narrow money (M1)	19.0
Av. ann. inflation 1999–2004	2.7%	Broad money	8.7
Money market rate, 2004	2.56%		

Exchange rates

	end 2004		December 2004
			1995 = 100
Kc per $	22.37	Effective rates	
Kc per SDR	34.73	– nominal	125
Kc per €	30.47	– real	121

Trade

Principal exports		Principal imports	
	$bn fob		*$bn cif*
Machinery & transport		Machinery & transport	
equipment	24.3	equipment	21.9
Semi-manufactures	11.2	Semi-manufactures	10.3
Chemicals	2.9	Chemicals	5.8
Raw materials & fuels	2.8	Raw materials & fuels	5.3
Total incl. others	**48.6**	Total incl. others	**51.1**

Main export destinations		Main origins of imports	
	% of total		*% of total*
Germany	36.9	Germany	32.4
Slovakia	7.9	Italy	5.3
Austria	6.2	China	5.2
United Kingdom	5.4	Slovakia	5.2
Poland	4.8	France	4.9
EU15	69.8	EU15	59.3

Balance of payments, reserves and debt, $bn

Visible exports fob	48.7	Change in reserves	3.2
Visible imports fob	-51.2	Level of reserves	
Trade balance	-2.5	end Dec.	27.0
Invisibles inflows	10.4	No. months of import cover	4.9
Invisibles outflows	-14.1	Official gold holdings, m oz	0.4
Net transfers	0.5	Foreign debt	34.6
Current account balance	-5.7	– as % of GDP	48
– as % of GDP	-6.3	– as % of total exports	69
Capital balance	5.9	Debt service ratio	11
Overall balance	0.4		

Health and education

Health spending, % of GDP	7.0	Education spending, % of GDP	4.4
Doctors per 1,000 pop.	3.4	Enrolment, %: primary	104
Hospital beds per 1,000 pop.	8.8	secondary	97
Improved-water source access,		tertiary	34
% of pop.	...		

Society

No. of households	3.8m	Colour TVs per 100 households	90.5
Av. no. per household	2.7	Telephone lines per 100 pop.	36.0
Marriages per 1,000 pop.	4.0	Mobile telephone subscribers	
Divorces per 1,000 pop.	3.2	per 100 pop.	96.5
Cost of living, Dec. 2004		Computers per 100 pop.	17.7
New York = 100	74	Internet hosts per 1,000 pop.	71.0

DENMARK

Area	43,075 sq km	Capital	Copenhagen
Arable as % of total land	54	Currency	Danish krone (DKr)

People

Population	5.4m	Life expectancy: men	75.5 yrs
Pop. per sq km	125.4	women	80.1 yrs
Av. ann. growth		Adult literacy	99.0%
in pop. 2000–05	0.34	Fertility rate (per woman)	1.8
Pop. under 15	18.8%	Urban population	85.3%
Pop. over 60	21.1%		per 1,000 pop.
No. of men per 100 women	98	Crude birth rate	11.8
Human Development Index	93.2	Crude death rate	10.6

The economy

GDP	DKr1,396bn	GDP per head	$39,330
GDP	$211.9bn	GDP per head in purchasing	
Av. ann. growth in real		power parity (USA=100)	82.3
GDP 1993–2003	2.6%	Economic freedom index	1.76

Origins of GDP		**Components of GDP**	
	% of total		% of total
Agriculture	2.3	Private consumption	47.
Industry, of which:	26.2	Public consumption	26.
manufacturing	...	Investment	19.
Services	71.5	Exports	43.
		Imports	-36.

Structure of employment

	% of total		% of labour force
Agriculture	3	Unemployed 2003	5.
Industry	26	Av. ann. rate 1995–2003	5.
Services	71		

Energy

	m TOE		
Total output	28.8	Net energy imports as %	
Total consumption	19.7	of energy use	-4
Consumption per head,			
kg oil equivalent	3,675		

Inflation and finance

		av. ann. increase 1998–200	
Consumer price			
inflation 2004	1.2%	Narrow money (M1)	5.4
Av. ann. inflation 1999–2004	2.2%	Broad money	1.5
Money market rate, 2004	2.16%	Household saving rate, 2003	0.3

Exchange rates

	end 2004		December 20
			1995 = 1
DKr per $	5.47	Effective rates	
DKr per SDR	8.49	– nominal	10
DKr per €	7.45	– real	11

Trade

Principal exports

	$bn fob
Manufactured goods	49.6
Agric. products	6.4
Energy & products	4.7
Ships	0.3
Total incl. others	**65.2**

Principal imports

	$bn cif
Intermediate goods	24.3
Consumer goods	16.6
Capital goods	7.3
Transport equipment	3.2
Total incl. others	**56.1**

Main export destinations

	% of total
Germany	18.6
Sweden	12.7
United Kingdom	8.5
United States	6.1
Norway	5.7
Netherlands	5.1
France	4.6
EU25	69.0

Main origins of imports

	% of total
Germany	23.1
Sweden	12.9
United Kingdom	7.0
Netherlands	6.9
France	4.8
Norway	4.5
Italy	4.1
EU25	74.5

Balance of payments, reserves and aid, $bn

Visible exports fob	64.5	Overall balance	4.7
Visible imports fob	-54.8	Change in reserves	10.3
Trade balance	9.7	Level of reserves	
Invisibles inflows	42.9	end Dec.	37.9
Invisibles outflows	-32.1	No. months of import cover	4.7
Net transfers	-3.5	Official gold holdings, m oz	2.0
Current account balance	7.0	Aid given	1.75
– as % of GDP	3.3	– as % of GDP	0.84
Capital balance	-5.1		

Health and education

Health spending, % of GDP	8.8	Education spending, % of GDP	8.4
Doctors per 1,000 pop.	3.7	Enrolment, %: primary	105
Hospital beds per 1,000 pop.	3.3	secondary	129
Improved-water source access,		tertiary	63
% of pop.	100		

Society

No. of households	2.5m	Colour TVs per 100 households	92.4
Av. no. per household	2.2	Telephone lines per 100 pop.	66.9
Marriages per 1,000 pop.	6.2	Mobile telephone subscribers	
Divorces per 1,000 pop.	2.7	per 100 pop.	88.3
Cost of living, Dec. 2004		Computers per 100 pop.	57.7
New York = 100	122	Internet hosts per 1,000 pop.	353.5

EGYPT

Area	1,000,250 sq km	Capital	Cairo
Arable as % of total land	3	Currency	Egyptian pound (£E)

People

Population	71.9m	Life expectancy: men	68.9 yrs
Pop. per sq km	71.9	women	73.5 yrs
Av. ann. growth		Adult literacy	55.6%
in pop. 2000–05	1.91%	Fertility rate (per woman)	3.3
Pop. under 15	33.6%	Urban population	42.1%
Pop. over 60	7.1%		per 1,000 pop.
No. of men per 100 women	101	Crude birth rate	26.6
Human Development Index	65.3	Crude death rate	5.7

The economy

GDP	£E415bn	GDP per head	$1,150
GDP	$82.4bn	GDP per head in purchasing	
Av. ann. growth in real		power parity (USA=100)	10.4
GDP 1993–2003	4.5%	Economic freedom index	3.38

Origins of GDP		**Components of GDP**[a]	
	% of total		% of total
Agriculture	16	Private consumption	72.9
Industry, of which:	34	Public consumption	12.8
manufacturing	19	Investment	17.0
Services	50	Exports	21.0
		Imports	-24.

Structure of employment

	% of total		% of labour force
Agriculture	32	Unemployed 2003	11.
Industry	17	Av. ann. rate 1995–2003	9.
Services	51		

Energy

	m TOE		
Total output	59.8	Net energy imports as %	
Total consumption	52.4	of energy use	-1
Consumption per head,			
kg oil equivalent	789		

Inflation and finance

		av. ann. increase 1998–200	
Consumer price			
inflation 2004	11.3%	Narrow money (M1)	9.8
Av. ann. inflation 1999–2004	4.6%	Broad money	12.8
Treasury bill rate, 2004	9.9%		

Exchange rates

	end 2004		December 20
			1995 = 1
£E per $	9.52	Effective rates	
£E per SDR	6.13	– nominal	
£E per €	12.97	– real	

Trade

Principal exports[b]

	$bn fob
Petroleum & products	3.9
Cotton yarn & textiles	0.7
Metals	0.5
Agricultural products	0.1
Total incl. others	**6.3**

Principal imports[b]

	$bn fob
Intermediate goods	5.2
Investment goods	3.5
Consumer goods	2.9
Fuels	2.6
Total incl. others	**11.1**

Main export destinations

	% of total
United States	13.7
Italy	12.6
United Kingdom	8.1
France	4.8

Main origins of imports

	% of total
United States	13.5
Germany	7.6
Italy	6.9
France	6.5

Balance of payments, reserves and debt, $bn

Visible exports fob	9.0	Change in reserves	0.5
Visible imports fob	-13.2	Level of reserves	
Trade balance	-4.2	end Dec.	14.6
Invisibles inflows	11.7	No. months of import cover	8.6
Invisibles outflows	-7.3	Official gold holdings, m oz	2.4
Net transfers	3.6	Foreign debt	31.4
Current account balance	3.7	– as % of GDP	35
– as % of GDP	4.5	– as % of total exports	147
Capital balance	-5.7	Debt service ratio	13
Overall balance	-0.4		

Health and education

Health spending, % of GDP	4.9	Education spending, % of GDP	...
Doctors per 1,000 pop.	2.2	Enrolment, %: primary	97
Hospital beds per 1,000 pop.	2.0	secondary	85
Improved-water source access,		tertiary	38
% of pop.	98		

Society

No. of households	15.1m	Colour TVs per 100 households	49.7
Av. no. per household	4.4	Telephone lines per 100 pop.	12.7
Marriages per 1,000 pop.	10.8	Mobile telephone subscribers	
Divorces per 1,000 pop.	1.5	per 100 pop.	8.5
Cost of living, Dec. 2004		Computers per 100 pop.	2.9
New York = 100	51	Internet hosts per 1,000 pop.	0.3

b Year ending June 30, 2003.
Year ending June 30, 2004.

ESTONIA

Area	45,200 sq km	Capital	Tallinn
Arable as % of total land	14	Currency	Kroon (EEK)

People

Population	1.3m	Life expectancy: men	67.0 yrs
Pop. per sq km	28.8	women	78.0 yrs
Av. ann. growth		Adult literacy[a]	99.8%
in pop. 2000–05	-0.55%	Fertility rate (per woman)	1.4
Pop. under 15	15.2%	Urban population	69.4%
Pop. over 60	21.6%		per 1,000 pop.
No. of men per 100 women	85	Crude birth rate	8.7
Human Development Index	85.3	Crude death rate	13.6

The economy

GDP	EEK126bn	GDP per head	$6,990
GDP	$9.1bn	GDP per head in purchasing	
Av. ann. growth in real		power parity (USA=100)	33.6
GDP 1993–2003	4.4%	Economic freedom index	1.65

Origins of GDP

Components of GDP

	% of total		% of total
Agriculture	4	Private consumption	56.6
Industry, of which:	28	Public consumption	19.0
manufacturing	18	Investment	31.1
Services	67	Exports	75.0
		Imports	-83.0

Structure of employment

	% of total		% of labour force
Agriculture	7	Unemployed 2003	10.0
Industry	33	Av. ann. rate 1995–2003	10.9
Services	60		

Energy

	m TOE		
Total output	3.2	Net energy imports as %	
Total consumption	4.5	of energy use	30
Consumption per head,			
kg oil equivalent	3,324		

Inflation and finance

		av. ann. increase 1998–2003	
Consumer price			
inflation 2004	3.1%	Narrow money (M1)	18.6%
Av. ann. inflation 1999–2004	3.5%	Broad money	18.7%
Money market rate, 2004	2.50%		

Exchange rates

	end 2004		December 2004
			1995 = 100
EEK per $	11.47	Effective rates	
EEK per SDR	17.92	– nominal	
EEK per €	15.62	– real	

Trade

Principal exports	$bn fob	Principal imports	$bn cif
Machinery & equipment	1.1	Machinery & equipment	1.8
Wood & paper	0.8	Transport equipment	1.0
Clothing & footwear	0.6	Chemicals	0.8
Furniture	0.4	Clothing & footwear	0.6
Food	0.3	Food	0.6
Total incl. others	4.5	Total incl. others	6.5

Main export destinations	% of total	Main origins of imports	% of total
Finland	25.9	Finland	15.9
Sweden	15.2	Germany	11.3
Germany	9.9	Sweden	8.8
Latvia	7.0	Russia	8.6
United Kingdom	4.2	China	4.5

Balance of payments, reserves and debt, $bn

Visible exports fob	4.6	Change in reserves	0.4
Visible imports fob	-6.2	Level of reserves	
Trade balance	-1.6	end Dec.	1.4
Invisibles inflows	2.5	No. months of import cover	2.0
Invisibles outflows	-2.2	Official gold holdings, m oz	0.0
Net transfers	0.1	Foreign debt	7.0
Current account balance	-1.2	– as % of GDP	100
– as % of GDP	-13.2	– as % of total exports	118
Capital balance	1.4	Debt service ratio	21
Overall balance	0.2		

Health and education

Health spending, % of GDP	5.1	Education spending, % of GDP	7.4
Doctors per 1,000 pop.	3.1	Enrolment, %: primary	101
Hospital beds per 1,000 pop.	6.7	secondary	96
Improved-water source access, % of pop.	...	tertiary	64

Society

No. of households	0.6m	Colour TVs per 100 households	85.6
Av. no. per household	2.4	Telephone lines per 100 pop.	34.1
Marriages per 1,000 pop.	3.3	Mobile telephone subscribers	
Divorces per 1,000 pop.	3.2	per 100 pop.	77.7
Cost of living, Dec. 2004		Computers per 100 pop.	44.0
New York = 100	...	Internet hosts per 1,000 pop.	182.6

FINLAND

Area	338,145 sq km	Capital	Helsinki
Arable as % of total land	7	Currency	Euro (€)

People

Population	5.2m	Life expectancy: men	76.0 yrs
Pop. per sq km	15.4	women	82.4 yrs
Av. ann. growth		Adult literacy	99.0%
in pop. 2000–05	0.28%	Fertility rate (per woman)	1.7
Pop. under 15	17.3%	Urban population	60.9%
Pop. over 60	21.3%		per 1,000 pop.
No. of men per 100 women	96	Crude birth rate	10.8
Human Development Index	93.5	Crude death rate	9.8

The economy

GDP	€143bn	GDP per head	$31,070
GDP	$161.9bn	GDP per head in purchasing	
Av. ann. growth in real		power parity (USA=100)	72.7
GDP 1993–2003	3.6%	Economic freedom index	1.90

Origins of GDP		**Components of GDP**	
	% of total		% of total
Agriculture	3.2	Private consumption	52.4
Industry, of which:	29.1	Public consumption	22.3
manufacturing & mining	22.7	Investment	18.5
Services	67.7	Exports	37.3
		Imports	-30.7

Structure of employment

	% of total		% of labour force
Agriculture	8	Unemployed 2003	9.0
Industry	28	Av. ann. rate 1995–2003	11.2
Services	64		

Energy

	m TOE		
Total output	16.1	Net energy imports as %	
Total consumption	35.6	of energy use	55
Consumption per head,			
kg oil equivalent	6,852		

Inflation and finance

		av. ann. increase 1998–200.	
Consumer price			
inflation 2004	0.2%	Euro area:	
Av. ann. inflation 1999–2004	1.7%	Narrow money (M1)	8.9%
Money market rate, 2004	2.11%	Broad money	6.7%
		Household saving rate, 2003	0.6%

Exchange rates

	end 2004		December 200
			1995 = 10
€ per $	0.73	Effective rates	
€ per SDR	1.44	– nominal	109.
		– real	103.

Trade

Principal exports		Principal imports	
	$bn fob		*$bn cif*
Electrical & optical equipment	22.1	Raw materials	15.7
Metals, machinery &		Consumer goods	5.1
transport equipment	16.5	Capital goods	5.0
Paper & products	3.8	Energy	4.9
Chemicals	3.5		
Total incl. others	**52.4**	Total incl. others	**41.5**

Main export destinations		Main origins of imports	
	% of total		*% of total*
Germany	11.8	Germany	15.0
United Kingdom	9.6	Sweden	11.9
Russia	8.1	Russia	11.1
Sweden	8.1	United States	5.3
United States	7.5	United Kingdom	4.8
France	4.7	Japan	4.7

Balance of payments, reserves and aid, $bn

Visible exports fob	52.5	Overall balance	-0.5
Visible imports fob	-39.9	Change in reserves	1.3
Trade balance	12.6	Level of reserves	
Invisibles inflows	17.9	end Dec.	11.2
Invisibles outflows	-22.7	No. months of import cover	2.1
Net transfers	-1.0	Official gold holdings, m oz	1.6
Current account balance	6.8	Aid given	0.56
– as % of GDP	4.2	– as % of GDP	0.35
Capital balance	-11.3		

Health and education

Health spending, % of GDP	7.3	Education spending, % of GDP	6.3
Doctors per 1,000 pop.	3.1	Enrolment, %: primary	102
Hospital beds per 1,000 pop.	7.5	secondary	128
Improved-water source access,		tertiary	86
% of pop.	100		

Society

No. of households	2.4m	Colour TVs per 100 households	99.3
Av. no. per household	2.2	Telephone lines per 100 pop.	49.2
Marriages per 1,000 pop.	4.3	Mobile telephone subscribers	
Divorces per 1,000 pop.	2.7	per 100 pop.	91.0
Cost of living, Dec. 2004		Computers per 100 pop.	44.2
New York = 100	111	Internet hosts per 1,000 pop.	368.4

FRANCE

Area	543,965 sq km	Capital	Paris
Arable as % of total land	34	Currency	Euro (€)

People

Population	60.1m	Life expectancy: men	76.6 yrs
Pop. per sq km	110.5	women	83.5 yrs
Av. ann. growth		Adult literacy	99.0%
in pop. 2000–05	0.41%	Fertility rate (per woman)	1.9
Pop. under 15	18.2%	Urban population	76.3%
Pop. over 60	21.1%		per 1,000 pop.
No. of men per 100 women	95	Crude birth rate	12.8
Human Development Index	93.2	Crude death rate	9.6

The economy

GDP	€1,557bn	GDP per head	$29,240
GDP	$1,758bn	GDP per head in purchasing	
Av. ann. growth in real		power parity (USA=100)	73.2
GDP 1993–2003	2.0%	Economic freedom index	2.63

Origins of GDP		Components of GDP	
	% of total		% of total
Agriculture	2.8	Private consumption	55.5
Industry, of which:	25.8	Public consumption	24.3
manufacturing	...	Investment	19.2
Services	71.4	Exports	25.9
		Imports	-24.7

Structure of employment

	% of total		% of labour force
Agriculture	2	Unemployed 2003	9.7
Industry	24	Av. ann. rate 1995–2003	11.2
Services	74		

Energy

	m TOE		
Total output	134.4	Net energy imports as %	
Total consumption	265.9	of energy use	49
Consumption per head,			
kg oil equivalent	4,470		

Inflation and finance

		av. ann. increase 1998–2003	
Consumer price			
inflation 2004	2.1%	Euro area:	
Av. ann. inflation 1999–2004	1.9%	Narrow money (M1)	8.9%
Deposit rate, 2004	2.25%	Broad money	6.7%
		Household saving rate, 2003	11.1%

Exchange rates

	end 2004		December 2004
			1995 = 100
€ per $	0.73	Effective rates	
€ per SDR	1.14	– nominal	109.4
		– real	105.1

Trade

Principal exports		Principal imports	
	$bn fob		*$bn cif*
Intermediate goods	109.9	Intermediate goods	112.8
Capital goods	83.9	Capital goods	76.5
Motor vehicles & other		Consumer goods	62.8
transport equipment	55.5	Motor vehicles & other	
Consumer goods	55.3	transport equipment	42.3
Food & drink	45.0	Energy	35.6
Total incl. others	**365.0**	Total incl. others	**369.8**

Main export destinations		Main origins of imports	
	% of total		*% of total*
Germany	15.0	Germany	17.4
Spain	10.2	Italy	9.4
United Kingdom	9.7	Spain	7.6
Italy	9.3	Belgium-Luxembourg	7.5
Belgium-Luxembourg	8.3	United Kingdom	6.8
EU15	63.1	EU15	60.4

Balance of payments, reserves and aid, $bn

Visible exports fob	361.9	Overall balance	1.3
Visible imports fob	-360.8	Change in reserves	9.1
Trade balance	1.0	Level of reserves	
Invisibles inflows	188.3	end Dec.	70.8
Invisibles outflows	-165.8	No. months of import cover	1.6
Net transfers	-19.1	Official gold holdings, m oz	97.3
Current account balance	4.4	Aid given[a]	7.25
– as % of GDP	0.2	– as % of GDP	0.41
Capital balance	-8.9		

Health and education

Health spending, % of GDP	9.7	Education spending, % of GDP	5.7
Doctors per 1,000 pop.	3.3	Enrolment, %: primary	105
Hospital beds per 1,000 pop.	8.2	secondary	109
Improved-water source access, % of pop.	...	tertiary	54

Society

No. of households	24.7m	Colour TVs per 100 households	95.9
Av. no. per household	2.4	Telephone lines per 100 pop.	56.6
Marriages per 1,000 pop.	5.1	Mobile telephone subscribers	
Divorces per 1,000 pop.	1.8	per 100 pop.	69.6
Cost of living, Dec. 2004		Computers per 100 pop.	34.7
New York = 100	125	Internet hosts per 1,000 pop.	83.2

Including aid to French overseas territories.

GERMANY

Area	357,868 sq km	Capital	Berlin
Arable as % of total land	34	Currency	Euro (€)

People

Population	82.5m	Life expectancy: men	76.4 yrs
Pop. per sq km	230.5	women	82.1 yrs
Av. ann. growth		Adult literacy	99.0%
in pop. 2000–05	0.08%	Fertility rate (per woman)	1.3
Pop. under 15	14.3%	Urban population	88.1%
Pop. over 60	25.1%		per 1,000 pop.
No. of men per 100 women	95	Crude birth rate	8.7
Human Development Index	92.5	Crude death rate	10.7

The economy

GDP	€2,129bn	GDP per head	$29,130
GDP	$2,403bn	GDP per head in purchasing	
Av. ann. growth in real		power parity (USA=100)	73.1
GDP 1993–2003	1.4%	Economic freedom index	2.00

Origins of GDP		**Components of GDP**	
	% of total		% of total
Agriculture	1.1	Private consumption	59.0
Industry, of which:	28.6	Public consumption	19.2
manufacturing	...	Investment	17.4
Services	70.3	Exports	36.1
		Imports	-31.8

Structure of employment

	% of total		% of labour force
Agriculture	3	Unemployed 2003	10.0
Industry	34	Av. ann. rate 1995–2003	9.1
Services	63		

Energy

	m TOE		
Total output	134.8	Net energy imports as %	
Total consumption	346.4	of energy use	61
Consumption per head,			
kg oil equivalent	4,198		

Inflation and finance

		av. ann. increase 1998–2003	
Consumer price			
inflation 2004	1.7%	Euro area:	
Av. ann. inflation 1999–2004	1.5%	Narrow money (M1)	8.9%
Money market rate, 2004	2.05%	Broad money	6.7%
		Household saving rate, 2003	10.7%

Exchange rates

	end 2004		December 2004
			1995 = 100
€ per $	0.73	Effective rates	
€ per SDR	1.14	– nominal	110.9
		– real	105.1

Trade

Principal exports	
	$bn fob
Road vehicles	145.5
Machinery	102.9
Chemicals	92.9
Electricity devices	36.2
Telecoms technology	35.1
Total incl. others	**749.6**

Principal imports	
	$bn cif
Road vehicles	64.4
Chemicals	63.2
Machinery	41.8
Fuels	39.9
Computer technology	30.5
Total incl. others	**600.4**

Main export destinations	
	% of total
France	10.6
United States	9.3
United Kingdom	8.4
Italy	7.4
Netherlands	6.2
Austria	5.3
Belgium	5.0

Main origins of imports	
	% of total
France	9.0
Netherlands	7.8
United States	7.3
Italy	6.1
United Kingdom	6.1
Belgium	4.9
Austria	3.8

Balance of payments, reserves and aid, $bn

Visible exports fob	753.1	Overall balance	-0.7
Visible imports fob	-601.4	Change in reserves	7.7
Trade balance	151.7	Level of reserves	
Invisibles inflows	233.6	end Dec.	96.8
Invisibles outflows	-247.4	No. months of import cover	1.3
Net transfers	-32.5	Official gold holdings, m oz	110.6
Current account balance	54.9	Aid given	6.78
– as % of GDP	2.3	– as % of GDP	0.28
Capital balance	-79.3		

Health and education

Health spending, % of GDP	10.9	Education spending, % of GDP	4.6
Doctors per 1,000 pop.	3.6	Enrolment, %: primary	100
Hospital beds per 1,000 pop.	9.1	secondary	100
Improved-water source access, % of pop.	...	tertiary	48

Society

No. of households	38.9m	Colour TVs per 100 households	97.2
Av. no. per household	2.1	Telephone lines per 100 pop.	65.7
Marriages per 1,000 pop.	4.5	Mobile telephone subscribers	
Divorces per 1,000 pop.	2.4	per 100 pop.	78.5
Cost of living, Dec. 2004		Computers per 100 pop.	48.5
New York = 100	101	Internet hosts per 1,000 pop.	74.3

GREECE

Area	131,957 sq km	Capital	Athens
Arable as % of total land	21	Currency	Euro (€)

People

Population	11.0m	Life expectancy: men	76.1 yrs
Pop. per sq km	83.4	women	81.3 yrs
Av. ann. growth		Adult literacy	99.0%
in pop. 2000–05	0.26%	Fertility rate (per woman)	1.3
Pop. under 15	14.3%	Urban population	60.8%
Pop. over 60	23.0%		per 1,000 pop.
No. of men per 100 women	98	Crude birth rate	9.1
Human Development Index	90.2	Crude death rate	10.5

The economy

GDP	€153bn	GDP per head	$15,650
GDP	$172.2bn	GDP per head in purchasing	
Av. ann. growth in real		power parity (USA=100)	52.7
GDP 1993–2003	3.4%	Economic freedom index	2.80

Origins of GDP

	% of total
Agriculture	7.3
Industry, of which:	24.0
manufacturing	...
Services	68.7

Components of GDP

	% of total
Private consumption	66.8
Public consumption	16.4
Investment	25.8
Exports	20.5
Imports	-29.4

Structure of employment

	% of total		% of labour force
Agriculture	12	Unemployed 2002	9.6
Industry	20	Av. ann. rate 1995–2002	10.5
Services	68		

Energy

	m TOE		
Total output	10.2	Net energy imports as %	
Total consumption	29.0	of energy use	65
Consumption per head,			
kg oil equivalent	2,637		

Inflation and finance

Consumer price		av. ann. increase 1998–2003	
inflation 2004	2.9%	Euro area:	
Av. ann. inflation 1999–2004	3.3%	Narrow money (M1)	8.9%
Treasury bill rate, 2004	2.27%	Broad money	6.7%

Exchange rates

	end 2004		December 2004
€ per $	0.73	Effective rates	1995 = 100
€ per SDR	1.14	– nominal	105.3
		– real	113.5

Trade

Principal exports

	$bn fob
Manufactures	7.7
Food & beverages	2.9
Fuel	0.9
Ores & metals	1.8
Total incl. others	13.2

Principal imports

	$bn cif
Manufactures	31.0
Fuels	6.1
Food	5.2
Total incl. others	43.7

Main export destinations[a]

	% of total
Germany	10.4
Italy	8.5
United Kingdom	6.3
Bulgaria	5.4
EU15	38.7

Main origins of imports[a]

	% of total
Germany	12.2
Italy	11.5
France	5.7
Netherlands	5.6
EU15	52.5

Balance of payments, reserves and debt, $bn

Visible exports fob	12.6	Overall balance	-4.7
Visible imports fob	-38.2	Change in reserves	-3.6
Trade balance	-25.6	Level of reserves	
Invisibles inflows	26.1	end Dec.	5.8
Invisibles outflows	-16.0	No. months of import cover	1.3
Net transfers	4.3	Official gold holdings, m oz	3.5
Current account balance	-11.2	Aid given	0.36
– as % of GDP	-6.5	– as % of GDP	0.21
Capital balance	7.6		

Health and education

Health spending, % of GDP	9.5	Education spending, % of GDP	3.9
Doctors per 1,000 pop.	4.4	Enrolment, %: primary	99
Hospital beds per 1,000 pop.	4.9	secondary	97
Improved-water source access, % of pop.	...	tertiary	68

Society

No. of households	3.7m	Colour TVs per 100 households	91.5
Av. no. per household	2.8	Telephone lines per 100 pop.	45.4
Marriages per 1,000 pop.	4.3	Mobile telephone subscribers	
Divorces per 1,000 pop.	0.9	per 100 pop.	84.5
Cost of living, Dec. 2004		Computers per 100 pop.	8.2
New York = 100	82	Internet hosts per 1,000 pop.	34.3

HONG KONG

Area	1,075 sq km	Capital	Victoria
Arable as % of total land	5	Currency	Hong Kong dollar (HK$)

People

Population	7.0m	Life expectancy: men	79.3 yrs
Pop. per sq km	6,511.6	women	85.1 yrs
Av. ann. growth		Adult literacy	93.5%
in pop. 2000–05	1.18%	Fertility rate (per woman)	0.9
Pop. under 15	14.4%	Urban population	100.0%
Pop. over 60	15.4%		per 1,000 pop.
No. of men per 100 women	89	Crude birth rate	8.5
Human Development Index	90.3	Crude death rate	5.9

The economy

GDP	HK$1,220bn	GDP per head	$22,380
GDP	$156.7bn	GDP per head in purchasing	
Av. ann. growth in real		power parity (USA=100)	76.0
GDP 1993–2003	3.3%	Economic freedom index	1.35

Origins of GDP

	% of total
Agriculture	0
Industry, of which:	12
manufacturing	5
Services	88

Components of GDP

	% of total
Private consumption	55.8
Public consumption	9.8
Investment	25.8
Exports	166.8
Imports	-158.2

Structure of employment

	% of total		% of labour force
Agriculture	0	Unemployed 2003	7.9
Industry	20	Av. ann. rate 1995–2003	4.9
Services	80		

Energy

	m TOE		
Total output	0.05	Net energy imports as %	
Total consumption	16.4	of energy use	100
Consumption per head,			
kg oil equivalent	2,413		

Inflation and finance

			av. ann. increase 1998–2003
Consumer price			
inflation 2004	-0.4%	Narrow money (M1)	15.2%
Av. ann. inflation 1999–2004	-2.3%	Broad money	4.8%
Money market rate, 2004	0.13%		

Exchange rates

	end 2004		December 2004
HK$ per $	7.78	Effective rates	1995 = 100
HK$ per SDR	12.16	– nominal	...
HK$ per €	10.66	– real	...

Trade

Principal exports[a]

	$bn fob
Clothing	8.2
Electrical machinery & apparatus	1.3
Textiles	0.8
Jewellery	0.7
Printed matter	0.3
Total incl. others	**19.6**

Principal imports

	$bn cif
Raw materials & semi-manufactures	84.0
Consumer goods	73.9
Capital goods	61.9
Food	7.5
Fuel	4.5
Total incl. others	**231.8**

Main export destinations

	% of total
China	42.6
United States	18.6
Japan	5.4
United Kingdom	3.3

Main origins of imports

	% of total
China	43.5
Japan	11.8
Taiwan	6.9
United States	5.5

Balance of payments, reserves and debt, $bn

Visible exports fob	224.7	Change in reserves	6.5
Visible imports fob	-230.4	Level of reserves	
Trade balance	-5.8	end Dec.	118.4
Invisibles inflows	89.7	No. months of import cover	4.8
Invisibles outflows	-65.1	Official gold holdings, m oz	0.1
Net transfers	-1.8	Foreign debt	59.2
Current account balance	17.0	– as % of GDP	38
– as % of GDP	10.8	– as % of total exports	19
Capital balance	-22.0	Debt service ratio	2
Overall balance	1.0		

Health and education

Health spending, % of GDP	...	Education spending, % of GDP	4.1
Doctors per 1,000 pop.	1.6	Enrolment, %: primary	108
Hospital beds per 1,000 pop.	5.5	secondary	80
Improved-water source access, % of pop.	98	tertiary	26

Society

No. of households	2.1m	Colour TVs per 100 households	99.1
Av. no. per household	3.3	Telephone lines per 100 pop.	55.9
Marriages per 1,000 pop.	3.9	Mobile telephone subscribers	
Divorces per 1,000 pop.	1.8	per 100 pop.	107.9
Cost of living, Dec. 2004		Computers per 100 pop.	42.2
New York = 100	109	Internet hosts per 1,000 pop.	122.3

a Domestic, excluding re-exports.
Note: Hong Kong became a Special Administrative Region of China on July 1 1997.

HUNGARY

Area	93,030 sq km	Capital	Budapest
Arable as % of total land	50	Currency	Forint (Ft)

People

Population	9.9m	Life expectancy: men	69.8 yrs
Pop. per sq km	106.4	women	77.7 yrs
Av. ann. growth		Adult literacy	99.1%
in pop. 2000–05	-0.25%	Fertility rate (per woman)	1.3
Pop. under 15	15.7%	Urban population	65.1%
Pop. over 60	20.8%		per 1,000 pop.
No. of men per 100 women	91	Crude birth rate	8.8
Human Development Index	84.8	Crude death rate	12.9

The economy

GDP	Ft18,568bn	GDP per head	$8,360
GDP	$82.7bn	GDP per head in purchasing	
Av. ann. growth in real		power parity (USA=100)	36.7
GDP 1993–2003	3.5%	Economic freedom index	2.40

Origins of GDP

Components of GDP

	% of total		% of total
Agriculture	3.3	Private consumption	68.0
Industry, of which:	27.5	Public consumption	10.8
manufacturing	...	Investment	24.8
Services	69.2	Exports	62.0
		Imports	-66.2

Structure of employment

	% of total		% of labour force
Agriculture	6	Unemployed 2003	5.3
Industry	27	Av. ann. rate 1995–2003	7.4
Services	67		

Energy

	m TOE		
Total output	10.8	Net energy imports as %	
Total consumption	25.4	of energy use	57
Consumption per head,			
kg oil equivalent	2,505		

Inflation and finance

			av. ann. increase 1998–2003
Consumer price			
inflation 2004	6.8%	Narrow money (M1)	15.2%
Av. ann. inflation 1999–2004	7.1%	Broad money	14.2%
Treasury bill rate, 2004	11.32%		

Exchange rates

	end 2004		December 2004
			1995 = 100
Ft per $	180.3	Effective rates	
Ft per SDR	279.9	– nominal	115.0
Ft per €	247.0	– real	136.3

Trade

Principal exports	$bn fob	Principal imports	$bn cif
Machinery & transport equipment	25.6	Machinery & transport equipment	24.4
Other manufactures	12.1	Other manufactures	16.9
Food & beverages	2.8	Fuels	3.7
Raw materials	0.9	Food & food products	1.5
Total incl. others	**42.5**	Total incl. others	**47.5**

Main export destinations	% of total	Main origins of imports	% of total
Germany	30.4	Germany	28.6
Austria	11.2	Austria	8.7
United States	5.8	Italy	7.5
Italy	4.5	Russia	6.7

Balance of payments, reserves and debt, $bn

Visible exports fob	43.5	Change in reserves	2.4
Visible imports fob	-46.8	Level of reserves	
Trade balance	-3.3	end Dec.	12.8
Invisibles inflows	9.4	No. months of import cover	2.5
Invisibles outflows	-14.2	Official gold holdings, m oz	0.1
Net transfers	0.7	Foreign debt	45.8
Current account balance	-7.5	– as % of GDP	73
– as % of GDP	-9.0	– as % of total exports	102
Capital balance	7.5	Debt service ratio	34
Overall balance	0.3		

Health and education

Health spending, % of GDP	7.8	Education spending, % of GDP	5.1
Doctors per 1,000 pop.	3.6	Enrolment, %: primary	101
Hospital beds per 1,000 pop.	8.2	secondary	106
Improved-water source access, % of pop.	99	tertiary	44

Society

No. of households	3.7m	Colour TVs per 100 households	92.8
Av. no. per household	2.7	Telephone lines per 100 pop.	34.9
Marriages per 1,000 pop.	4.3	Mobile telephone subscribers	
Divorces per 1,000 pop.	2.5	per 100 pop.	76.9
Cost of living, Dec. 2004		Computers per 100 pop.	10.8
New York = 100	69	Internet hosts per 1,000 pop.	61.8

INDIA

Area	3,287,263 sq km	Capital	New Delhi
Arable as % of total land	54	Currency	Indian rupee (Rs)

People

Population	1,065.5m	Life expectancy: men	63.2 yrs
Pop. per sq km	324.0	women	66.7 yrs
Av. ann. growth		Adult literacy	61.3%
in pop. 2000–05	1.55%	Fertility rate (per woman)	3.1
Pop. under 15	32.1%	Urban population	28.3%
Pop. over 60	7.9%		per 1,000 pop.
No. of men per 100 women	105	Crude birth rate	23.8
Human Development Index	59.5	Crude death rate	8.3

The economy

GDP	Rs27,600bn	GDP per head	$560
GDP	$600.6bn	GDP per head in purchasing	
Av. ann. growth in real		power parity (USA=100)	7.6
GDP 1993–2003	6.2%	Economic freedom index	3.53

Origins of GDP[a]		Components of GDP[a]	
	% of total		% of total
Agriculture	22	Private consumption	61.6
Industry, of which:	27	Public consumption	10.6
manufacturing	16	Investment	24.8
Services	51	Exports	19.1
		Imports	-16.3

Structure of employment

	% of total		% of labour force
Agriculture	60	Unemployed 2002	11.6
Industry	17	Av. ann. rate 1995–2002	11.6
Services	23		

Energy

	m TOE		
Total output	438.8	Net energy imports as %	
Total consumption	538.3	of energy use	18
Consumption per head,			
kg oil equivalent	513		

Inflation and finance

Consumer price			av. ann. increase 1998–200
inflation 2004	3.8%	Narrow money (M1)	13.2%
Av. ann. inflation 1999–2004	3.9%	Broad money	15.3%
Lending rate, 2004	10.92%		

Exchange rates

	end 2004		December 200
			1995 = 10
Rs per $	43.59	Effective rates	
Rs per SDR	67.69	– nominal	..
Rs per €	59.71	– real	..

Trade

Principal exports[a]

	$bn fob
Engineering goods	12.2
Gems & jewellery	10.5
Textiles	6.5
Chemicals	6.3
Ready-made garments	6.1
Total incl. others	57.0

Principal imports[a]

	$bn cif
Petroleum & products	20.6
Capital goods	9.8
Electronic goods	7.5
Gems	7.1
Total incl. others	71.1

Main export destinations

	% of total
United States	21.9
China	6.9
United Kingdom	5.6
Hong Kong	5.1

Main origins of imports

	% of total
United States	7.7
Belgium	6.4
United Kingdom	5.8
China	5.2

Balance of payments[b], reserves and debt, $bn

Visible exports fob	52.7	Change in reserves	32.1
Visible imports fob	-65.2	Level of reserves	
Trade balance	-12.4	end Dec.	103.7
Invisibles inflows	27.2	No. months of import cover	12.5
Invisibles outflows	-24.9	Official gold holdings, m oz	11.5
Net transfers	14.8	Foreign debt	113.5
Current account balance	4.7	– as % of GDP	22
– as % of GDP	0.9	– as % of total exports	120
Capital balance	11.5	Debt service ratio	22
Overall balance	16.9		

Health and education

Health spending, % of GDP	6.1	Education spending, % of GDP	4.1
Doctors per 1,000 pop.	0.5	Enrolment, %: primary	99
Hospital beds per 1,000 pop.	1.5	secondary	53
Improved-water source access,		tertiary	11
% of pop.	86		

Society

No. of households	199.4m	Colour TVs per 100 households	33.7
Av. no. per household	5.3	Telephone lines per 100 pop.	4.6
Marriages per 1,000 pop.	...	Mobile telephone subscribers	
Divorces per 1,000 pop.	...	per 100 pop.	2.5
Cost of living, Dec. 2004		Computers per 100 pop.	0.7
New York = 100	44	Internet hosts per 1,000 pop.	0.3

a Year ending March 31, 2004.
b 2002

INDONESIA

Area	1,904,443 sq km	Capital	Jakarta
Arable as % of total land	11	Currency	Rupiah (Rp)

People

Population	219.9m	Life expectancy: men	67.0 yrs
Pop. per sq km	115.5	women	70.5 yrs
Av. ann. growth		Adult literacy	87.9%
in pop. 2000–05	1.26%	Fertility rate (per woman)	2.4
Pop. under 15	28.3%	Urban population	45.6%
Pop. over 60	8.4%		per 1,000 pop.
No. of men per 100 women	100	Crude birth rate	20.7
Human Development Index	69.2	Crude death rate	7.1

The economy

GDP	Rp1,787trn	GDP per head	$950
GDP	$208.3bn	GDP per head in purchasing	
Av. ann. growth in real		power parity (USA=100)	8.5
GDP 1993–2003	3.0%	Economic freedom index	3.54

Origins of GDP		Components of GDP	
	% of total		% of total
Agriculture	16.3	Private consumption	69.3
Industry, of which:	48.2	Public consumption	9.2
manufacturing	30.1	Investment	15.9
Services	35.5	Exports	31.2
		Imports	-25.7

Structure of employment

	% of total		% of total
Agriculture	45	Unemployed 2002	9.1
Industry	16	Av. ann. rate 1995–2002	5.9
Services	39		

Energy

	m TOE		
Total output	240.9	Net energy imports as %	
Total consumption	156.1	of energy use	-54
Consumption per head,			
kg oil equivalent	737		

Inflation and finance

		av. ann. increase 1998–2003	
Consumer price			
inflation 2004	6.2%	Narrow money (M1)	19.4%
Av. ann. inflation 1999–2004	7.9%	Broad money	10.8%
Money market rate, 2004	5.38%		

Exchange rates

	end 2004		December 2004
			1995 = 100
Rp per $	9,290	Effective rates	
Rp per SDR	14,428	– nominal	..
Rp per €	12,727	– real	..

Trade

Principal exports

	$bn fob
Petroleum & products	7.2
Garments & textiles	7.1
Natural gas	6.5
Total incl. others	**64.1**

Principal imports

	$bn cif
Raw materials	25.5
Capital goods	4.2
Consumer goods	2.9
Total incl. others	**42.2**

Main export destinations

	% of total
Japan	24.0
United States	14.9
Singapore	10.4
South Korea	8.4

Main origins of imports

	% of total
Japan	18.8
China	14.9
Singapore	13.8
United States	8.4

Balance of payments, reserves and debt, $bn

Visible exports fob	63.3	Change in reserves	4.2
Visible imports fob	-39.5	Level of reserves	
Trade balance	23.7	end Dec.	36.3
Invisibles inflows	6.4	No. months of import cover	6.8
Invisibles outflows	-24.7	Official gold holdings, m oz	3.1
Net transfers	1.9	Foreign debt	134.4
Current account balance	7.3	– as % of GDP	80
– as % of GDP	3.5	– as % of total exports	196
Capital balance	-0.9	Debt service ratio	27
Overall balance	3.4		

Health and education

Health spending, % of GDP	3.2	Education spending, % of GDP	1.3
Doctors per 1,000 pop.	0.2	Enrolment, %: primary	111
Hospital beds per 1,000 pop.	0.6	secondary	61
Improved-water source access,		tertiary	15
% of pop.	78		

Society

No. of households	56.2m	Colour TVs per 100 households	50.4
Av. no. per household	3.9	Telephone lines per 100 pop.	3.9
Marriages per 1,000 pop.	...	Mobile telephone subscribers	
Divorces per 1,000 pop.	...	per 100 pop.	8.7
Cost of living, Dec. 2004		Computers per 100 pop.	1.2
New York = 100	67	Internet hosts per 1,000 pop.	0.6

IRAN

Area	1,648,000 sq km	Capital	Tehran
Arable as % of total land	9	Currency	Rial (IR)

People

Population	68.9m	Life expectancy: men	70.1 yrs
Pop. per sq km	41.8	women	73.4 yrs
Av. ann. growth		Adult literacy	79.4%
in pop. 2000–05	0.93%	Fertility rate (per woman)	2.1
Pop. under 15	28.7%	Urban population	66.7%
Pop. over 60	6.4%		per 1,000 pop.
No. of men per 100 women	103	Crude birth rate	20.3
Human Development Index	73.2	Crude death rate	5.2

The economy

GDP	IR1,124trn	GDP per head	$1,990
GDP	$137.1bn	GDP per head in purchasing	
Av. ann. growth in real		power parity (USA=100)	18.5
GDP 1993–2003	4.1%	Economic freedom index	4.16

Origins of GDP		Components of GDP[a]	
	% of total		% of total
Agriculture	11	Private consumption	45.2
Industry, of which:	41	Public consumption	12.5
manufacturing	13	Investment	39.3
Services	48	Exports	28.0
		Imports	-25.5

Structure of employment

	% of total		% of labour force
Agriculture	30	Unemployed 2002	12.3
Industry	25	Av. ann. rate 2000–2002	12.4
Services	45		

Energy

	m TOE		
Total output	240.5	Net energy imports as %	
Total consumption	134.0	of energy use	-80
Consumption per head,			
kg oil equivalent	2,044		

Inflation and finance

		av. ann. increase 1998–2003	
Consumer price			
inflation 2003	16.5%	Narrow money (M1)	22.3%
Av. ann. inflation 1999–2003	14.1%	Broad money	24.2%

Exchange rates

	end 2004		December 2004
			1995 = 100
IR per $	8,793	Effective rates	
IR per SDR	13,656	– nominal	73.2
IR per €	12,046	– real	116.5

Trade

Principal exports[b]	$bn fob	Principal imports[c]	$bn cif
Oil & gas	23.0	Transport, machinery & tools	7.6
Chemicals & petrochemicals	1.1	Chemicals & pharmaceuticals	2.4
Fruits	0.6	Food & animals	2.1
Total incl. others	**28.2**	**Total incl. others**	**17.6**

Main export destinations	% of total	Main origins of imports	% of total
Japan	22.4	Germany	12.3
China	10.4	France	9.3
Italy	6.7	China	9.2
South Korea	5.1	Italy	8.8
Netherlands	4.1	Switzerland	7.4

Balance of payments[d], reserves and debt, $bn

Visible exports fob	28.2	Change in reserves	...
Visible imports fob	-23.8	Level of reserves	
Trade balance	4.4	end Dec.	...
Invisibles inflows[e]	1.9	No. months of import cover	...
Invisibles outflows[e]	-2.9	Official gold holdings, m oz	...
Net transfers[e]	0.6	Foreign debt	11.6
Current account balance	3.7	– as % of GDP	9
– as % of GDP	1.5	– as % of total exports	33
Capital balance[e]	-10.2	Debt service ratio	5
Overall balance[e]	1.1		

Health and education

Health spending, % of GDP	6.0	Education spending, % of GDP	5.0
Doctors per 1,000 pop.	1.1	Enrolment, %: primary	92
Hospital beds per 1,000 pop.	...	secondary	78
Improved-water source access,		tertiary	20
% of pop.	93		

Society

No. of households	12.4m	Colour TVs per 100 households	9.5
Av. no. per household	5.5	Telephone lines per 100 pop.	22.0
Marriages per 1,000 pop.	9.9	Mobile telephone subscribers	
Divorces per 1,000 pop.	1.0	per 100 pop.	5.1
Cost of living, Dec. 2004		Computers per 100 pop.	9.1
New York = 100	31	Internet hosts per 1,000 pop.	–

Iranian year ending March 20, 2004.
2002
2001
Iranian year ending March 20, 2003.
Iranian year ending March 20, 2002.

IRELAND

Area	70,282 sq km	Capital	Dublin
Arable as % of total land	16	Currency	Euro (€)

People

Population	4.0m	Life expectancy: men	75.9 yrs
Pop. per sq km	56.9	women	81.1 yrs
Av. ann. growth		Adult literacy	99.0%
in pop. 2000–05	1.75%	Fertility rate (per woman)	1.9
Pop. under 15	20.2%	Urban population	59.9%
Pop. over 60	15.1%		per 1,000 pop.
No. of men per 100 women	99	Crude birth rate	14.4
Human Development Index	93.6	Crude death rate	7.3

The economy

GDP	€136bn	GDP per head	$38,430
GDP	$153.7bn	GDP per head in purchasing	
Av. ann. growth in real		power parity (USA=100)	81.9
GDP 1993–2003	7.9%	Economic freedom index	1.70

Origins of GDP		Components of GDP	
	% of total		% of total
Agriculture	4.6	Private consumption	46.
Industry, of which:	46.0	Public consumption	14.
manufacturing	...	Investment	23.
Services	49.4	Exports	83.
		Imports	-68.

Structure of employment

	% of total		% of labour force
Agriculture	8	Unemployed 2003	4.
Industry	29	Av. ann. rate 1995–2003	7.
Services	63		

Energy

	m TOE		
Total output	1.5	Net energy imports as %	
Total consumption	15.3	of energy use	9
Consumption per head,			
kg oil equivalent	3,894		

Inflation and finance

		av. ann. increase 1998–200	
Consumer price		Euro area:	
inflation 2004	2.2%	Narrow money (M1)	8.9
Av. ann. inflation 1999–2004	4.1%	Broad money	6.7
Money market rate, 2004	2.21%	Household saving rate, 2003	8.3

Exchange rates

	end 2004		December 20
			1995 = 1
€ per $	0.73	Effective rates	
€ per SDR	1.14	– nominal	115
		– real	

Trade

Principal exports	$bn fob	Principal imports	$bn cif
Chemicals	49.2	Machinery & transport	
Machinery & transport		equipment	49.3
equipment	32.2	Chemicals	16.3
Manufactured materials	13.0	Food, drink & tobacco	9.0
Food, drink & tobacco	4.6	Fuels	4.3
Total incl. others	**92.7**	Total incl. others	**54.1**

Main export destinations	% of total	Main origins of imports	% of total
United States	20.5	United Kingdom	34.6
United Kingdom	18.1	United States	15.7
Belgium	12.6	Germany	7.9
Germany	8.3	Netherlands	4.0

Balance of payments, reserves and aid, $bn

Visible exports fob	89.6	Overall balance	-1.9
Visible imports fob	-51.8	Change in reserves	-1.3
Trade balance	37.8	Level of reserves	
Invisibles inflows	70.2	end Dec.	4.2
Invisibles outflows	-110.6	No. months of import cover	0.3
Net transfers	0.5	Official gold holdings, m oz	0.2
Current account balance	-2.1	Aid given	0.50
– as % of GDP	-1.4	– as % of GDP	0.39
Capital balance	1.4		

Health and education

Health spending, % of GDP	7.3	Education spending, % of GDP	4.3
Doctors per 1,000 pop.	0.5	Enrolment, %: primary	105
Hospital beds per 1,000 pop.	9.7	secondary	107
Improved-water source access,		tertiary	50
% of pop.	...		

Society

No. of households	1.3m	Colour TVs per 100 households	99.3
Av. no. per household	3.0	Telephone lines per 100 pop.	49.1
Marriages per 1,000 pop.	5.2	Mobile telephone subscribers	
Divorces per 1,000 pop.	...	per 100 pop.	88.0
Cost of living, Dec. 2004		Computers per 100 pop.	42.1
New York = 100	99	Internet hosts per 1,000 pop.	34.7

ISRAEL

| Area | 20,770 sq km | Capital | Jerusalem |
| Arable as % of total land | 16 | Currency | New Shekel (NIS) |

People

Population	6.4m	Life expectancy: men	78.4 yrs
Pop. per sq km	308.1	women	82.6 yrs
Av. ann. growth		Adult literacy	95.3%
in pop. 2000–05	2.00%	Fertility rate (per woman)	2.9
Pop. under 15	27.8%	Urban population	91.6%
Pop. over 60	13.3%		per 1,000 pop
No. of men per 100 women	98	Crude birth rate	19.8
Human Development Index	90.8	Crude death rate	5.6

The economy

GDP	NIS502bn	GDP per head	$17,22(
GDP	$110.2bn	GDP per head in purchasing	
Av. ann. growth in real		power parity (USA=100)	51.
GDP 1993–2003	3.5%	Economic freedom index	2.3(

Origins of GDP	% of total	Components of GDP	% of tota
Agriculture	2.6	Private consumption	58.
Industry, of which:	34.8	Public consumption	30.
manufacturing	23.9	Investment	17.
Services	59.8	Exports	38.
		Imports	-44.

Structure of employment

	% of total		% of labour fore
Agriculture	19	Unemployed 2003	10.
Industry	24	Av. ann. rate 1995–2003	8.
Services	57		

Energy

	m TOE		
Total output	0.7	Net energy imports as %	
Total consumption	21.0	of energy use	9
Consumption per head,			
kg oil equivalent	3,181		

Inflation and finance

		av. ann. increase 1998–20(
Consumer price		
inflation 2004	-0.4%	Narrow money (M1)	11.2
Av. ann. inflation 1999–2004	1.6%	Broad money	7.8
Treasury bill rate, 2004	4.78%		

Exchange rates

	end 2004		December 20(
NIS per $	4.31	Effective rates	1995 = 1(
NIS per SDR	6.69	– nominal	75.
NIS per €	5.90	– real	75.

Trade

Principal exports

	$bn fob
Diamonds	9.0
Communications, medical & scientific equipment	4.6
Chemicals	4.5
Electronics	2.2
Total incl. others	31.6

Principal imports

	$bn fob
Diamonds	7.7
Machinery & equipment	4.4
Fuel	3.6
Chemicals	2.3
Total incl. others	32.3

Main export destinations

	% of total
United States	42.4
Belgium	6.1
United Kingdom	4.7
Germany	4.4
Netherlands	3.7

Main origins of imports

	% of total
United States	22.4
Germany	8.9
Belgium	8.4
United Kingdom	7.3
Switzerland	7.2

Balance of payments, reserves and debt, $bn

Visible exports fob	30.1	Change in reserves	2.2
Visible imports fob	-32.3	Level of reserves	
Trade balance	-2.2	end Dec.	26.3
Invisibles inflows	14.5	No. months of import cover	6.2
Invisibles outflows	-18.5	Official gold holdings, m oz	0.0
Net transfers	6.4	Foreign debt	71.0
Current account balance	0.1	– as % of GDP	64.3
– as % of GDP	0.1	– as % of total exports	153
Capital balance	-2.0	Debt service ratio	13.1
Overall balance	-0.5		

Health and education

Health spending, % of GDP	9.1	Education spending, % of GDP	7.3
Doctors per 1,000 pop.	3.8	Enrolment, %: primary	113
Hospital beds per 1,000 pop.	5.8	secondary	93
Improved-water source access, % of pop.	100	tertiary	58

Society

No. of households	1.9m	Colour TVs per 100 households	96.1
Av. no. per household	3.5	Telephone lines per 100 pop.	45.8
Marriages per 1,000 pop.	4.5	Mobile telephone subscribers	
Divorces per 1,000 pop.	2.1	per 100 pop.	96.1
Cost of living, Dec. 2004		Computers per 100 pop.	24.3
New York = 100	84	Internet hosts per 1,000 pop.	156.8

ITALY

Area	301,245 sq km	Capital	Rome
Arable as % of total land	28	Currency	Euro (€)

People

Population	57.4m	Life expectancy: men	77.5 yrs
Pop. per sq km	190.5	women	83.6 yrs
Av. ann. growth		Adult literacy	98.6%
in pop. 2000–05	0.13%	Fertility rate (per woman)	1.3
Pop. under 15	14.0%	Urban population	67.4%
Pop. over 60	25.6%		per 1,000 pop
No. of men per 100 women	94	Crude birth rate	8.8
Human Development Index	92.0	Crude death rate	10.6

The economy

GDP	€1,301bn	GDP per head	$25,58*
GDP	$1,468bn	GDP per head in purchasing	
Av. ann. growth in real		power parity (USA=100)	71.*
GDP 1993–2003	1.7%	Economic freedom index	2.2*

Origins of GDP		Components of GDP	
	% of total		% of total
Agriculture	2.3	Private consumption	59.
Industry, of which:	28.9	Public consumption	19.
manufacturing	...	Investment	19.
Services	68.9	Exports	25
		Imports	-24.

Structure of employment

	% of total		% of labour force
Agriculture	5	Unemployed 2003	8
Industry	32	Av. ann. rate 1995–2003	10.
Services	63		

Energy

	m TOE		
Total output	26.6	Net energy imports as %	
Total consumption	172.7	of energy use	8
Consumption per head,			
kg oil equivalent	2,994		

Inflation and finance

		av. ann. increase 1998–20	
Consumer price			
inflation 2004	2.2%	Euro area:	
Av. ann. inflation 1999–2004	2.5%	Narrow money (M1)	8.9
Money market rate, 2004	2.10%	Broad money	6.7
		Household saving rate, 2003	10.7

Exchange rates

	end 2004		December 20
€ per $	0.73	Effective rates	1995 = 1
€ per SDR	1.14	– nominal	10*
		– real	10*

Trade

Principal exports		**Principal imports**	
	$bn fob		*$bn cif*
Engineering products	85.4	Engineering products	59.2
Textiles & clothing	43.0	Transport equipment	43.7
Transport equipment	32.5	Chemicals	39.8
Chemicals	29.1	Energy products	29.1
Food, drink & tobacco	16.5	Food, drink & tobacco	20.5
Total incl. others	**294.5**	**Total incl. others**	**291.4**

Main export destinations		**Main origins of imports**	
	% of total		*% of total*
Germany	13.8	Germany	17.9
France	12.3	France	11.4
United States	9.6	Netherlands	5.9
United Kingdom	7.0	United Kingdom	5.1
Spain	6.3	United States	4.9
EU15	60.6	EU15	61.4

Balance of payments, reserves and aid, $bn

Visible exports fob	293.1	Overall balance	1.1
Visible imports fob	-282.9	Change in reserves	7.6
Trade balance	10.2	Level of reserves	
Invisibles inflows	124.7	end Dec.	63.3
Invisibles outflows	-147.4	No. months of import cover	1.8
Net transfers	-8.1	Official gold holdings, m oz	78.8
Current account balance	-20.6	Aid given	2.43
– as % of GDP	-1.4	– as % of GDP	0.17
Capital balance	22.8		

Health and education

Health spending, % of GDP	8.5	Education spending, % of GDP	5.0
Doctors per 1,000 pop.	6.1	Enrolment, %: primary	101
Hospital beds per 1,000 pop.	4.7	secondary	99
Improved-water source access, % of pop.	...	tertiary	53

Society

No. of households	22.8m	Colour TVs per 100 households	94.8
Av. no. per household	2.6	Telephone lines per 100 pop.	48.4
Marriages per 1,000 pop.	4.5	Mobile telephone subscribers	
Divorces per 1,000 pop.	0.8	per 100 pop.	101.8
Cost of living, Dec. 2004		Computers per 100 pop.	23.1
New York = 100	92	Internet hosts per 1,000 pop.	162.8

JAPAN

Area	377,727 sq km	Capital	Tokyo
Arable as % of total land	12	Currency	Yen (¥)

People

Population	127.7m	Life expectancy: men		79.1 yrs
Pop. per sq km	338.0		women	86.4 yrs
Av. ann. growth		Adult literacy		99.0%
in pop. 2000–05	0.17%	Fertility rate (per woman)		1.3
Pop. under 15	14.0%	Urban population[a]		78.9%
Pop. over 60	26.3%			per 1,000 pop.
No. of men per 100 women	96	Crude birth rate		9.2
Human Development Index	93.8	Crude death rate		8.8

The economy

GDP	¥499trn	GDP per head	$33,680
GDP	$4,301bn	GDP per head in purchasing	
Av. ann. growth in real		power parity (USA=100)	75.4
GDP 1993–2003	1.3%	Economic freedom index	2.46

Origins of GDP		Components of GDP	
	% of total		% of total
Agriculture	1.3	Private consumption	56.8
Industry, of which:	30.4	Public consumption	17.5
manufacturing	20.8	Investment	24.0
Services	68.3	Exports	11.8
		Imports	-10.2

Structure of employment

	% of total		% of labour force
Agriculture	5	Unemployed 2003	5.3
Industry	25	Av. ann. rate 1995–2003	4.4
Services	70		

Energy

	m TOE		
Total output	98.1	Net energy imports as %	
Total consumption	516.9	of energy use	8
Consumption per head,			
kg oil equivalent	4,058		

Inflation and finance

Consumer price		av. ann. increase 1998–2003	
inflation 2004	0.0%	Narrow money (M1)	11.1%
Av. ann. inflation 1999–2004	-0.5%	Broad money	2.4%
Money market rate, 2004	0.00%	Household saving rate, 2003	7.4%

Exchange rates

	end 2004		December 2004
¥ per $	104.1	Effective rates	1995 = 100
¥ per SDR	161.7	– nominal	87.4
¥ per €	142.6	– real	78.1

Trade

Principal exports		Principal imports	
	$bn fob		*$bn cif*
Transport equipment	114.4	Machinery & equipment	120.5
Electrical machinery	111.0	Mineral fuels	80.6
Non-electrical machinery	95.1	Food	44.0
Chemicals	39.1	Chemicals	29.8
Metals	29.2	Raw materials	22.8
Total incl. others	**470.5**	Total incl. others	**382.3**

Main export destinations		Main origins of imports	
	% of total		*% of total*
United States	24.6	China	19.7
China	12.2	United States	15.4
South Korea	7.4	South Korea	4.7
Taiwan	6.6	Australia	3.9
Hong Kong	6.3	Taiwan	3.7

Balance of payments, reserves and aid, $bn

Visible exports fob	449.1	Overall balance	187.2
Visible imports fob	-342.7	Change in reserves	203.9
Trade balance	106.4	Level of reserves	
Invisibles inflows	172.8	end Dec.	673.6
Invisibles outflows	-135.5	No. months of import cover	16.9
Net transfers	-7.5	Official gold holdings, m oz	24.6
Current account balance	136.2	Aid given	8.88
– as % of GDP	3.2	– as % of GDP	0.20
Capital balance	67.9		

Health and education

Health spending, % of GDP	7.9	Education spending, % of GDP	3.5
Doctors per 1,000 pop.	2.0	Enrolment, %: primary	101
Hospital beds per 1,000 pop.	17.3	secondary	102
Improved-water source access,		tertiary	49
% of pop.	100		

Society

No. of households	48.1m	Colour TVs per 100 households	99.0
Av. no. per household	2.7	Telephone lines per 100 pop.	47.2
Marriages per 1,000 pop.	5.8	Mobile telephone subscribers	
Divorces per 1,000 pop.	2.3	per 100 pop.	67.9
Cost of living, Dec. 2004		Computers per 100 pop.	38.2
New York = 100	138	Internet hosts per 1,000 pop.	153.0

2001

KENYA

Area	582,646 sq km	Capital	Nairobi
Arable as % of total land	8	Currency	Kenyan shilling (KSh)

People

Population	32.0m	Life expectancy:	men	51.1 yrs
Pop. per sq km	54.9		women	49.4 yrs
Av. ann. growth		Adult literacy		84.3%
in pop. 2000–05	2.20%	Fertility rate (per woman)		5.0
Pop. under 15	42.8%	Urban population		39.4%
Pop. over 60	4.1%			per 1,000 pop.
No. of men per 100 women	100	Crude birth rate		32.5
Human Development Index	48.8	Crude death rate		13.8

The economy

GDP	KSh1,092bn	GDP per head	$450
GDP	$14.4bn	GDP per head in purchasing	
Av. ann. growth in real		power parity (USA=100)	2.7
GDP 1993–2003	1.9%	Economic freedom index	3.28

Origins of GDP		Components of GDP	
	% of total		% of total
Agriculture	25.7	Private consumption	73.8
Industry, of which:	...	Public consumption	17.9
manufacturing	14.0	Investment	12.9
Other	60.3	Exports	24.9
		Imports	-29.5

Structure of employment

	% of total		% of labour force
Agriculture	19	Unemployed 2002	..
Industry	20	Av. ann. rate 1995–2002	..
Services	61		

Energy

	m TOE		
Total output	12.9	Net energy imports as %	
Total consumption	15.3	of energy use	1
Consumption per head,			
kg oil equivalent	489		

Inflation and finance

		av. ann. increase 1998–200	
Consumer price			
inflation 2004	11.6%	Narrow money (M1)	15.6%
Av. ann. inflation 1999–2004	7.8%	Broad money	7.2%
Treasury bill rate, 2004	3.17%		

Exchange rates

	end 2004		December 200
			1995 = 10
KSh per $	77.3	Effective rates	
KSh per SDR	120.1	– nominal	
KSh per €	105.9	– real	

Trade

Principal exports

	$m fob
Tea	435
Horticultural products	351
Coffee	81
Petroleum products	4
Total incl. others	**2,411**

Principal imports

	$m cif
Machinery & transport equip.	969
Crude petroleum	879
Refined petroleum products	591
Manufactured goods	497
Total incl. others	**3,722**

Main export destinations

	% of total
Uganda	19.3
United Kingdom	11.7
Netherlands	7.9
Tanzania	4.0

Main origins of imports

	% of total
United Arab Emirates	12.0
United Kingdom	9.8
Japan	6.5
India	4.4

Balance of payments, reserves and debt, $bn

Visible exports fob	2.4	Change in reserves	0.4
Visible imports fob	-3.6	Level of reserves	
Trade balance	-1.1	end Dec.	1.5
Invisibles inflows	1.2	No. months of import cover	4.1
Invisibles outflows	-0.8	Official gold holdings, m oz	0.0
Net transfers	0.8	Foreign debt	6.8
Current account balance	0.1	– as % of GDP	54
– as % of GDP	0.5	– as % of total exports	206
Capital balance	0.6	Debt service ratio	17
Overall balance	0.4		

Health and education

Health spending, % of GDP	4.9	Education spending, % of GDP	6.2
Doctors per 1,000 pop.	0.1	Enrolment, %: primary	96
Hospital beds per 1,000 pop.	...	secondary	33
Improved-water source access,		tertiary	3
% of pop.	62		

Society

No. of households	7.4m	Colour TVs per 100 households	11.9
Av. no. per household	4.3	Telephone lines per 100 pop.	1.0
Marriages per 1,000 pop.	...	Mobile telephone subscribers	
Divorces per 1,000 pop.	...	per 100 pop.	5.0
Cost of living, Dec. 2004		Computers per 100 pop.	0.7
New York = 100	59	Internet hosts per 1,000 pop.	0.3

LATVIA

Area	63,700 sq km	Capital	Riga
Arable as % of total land	30	Currency	Lats (LVL)

People

Population	2.3m	Life expectancy: men	67.2 yrs
Pop. per sq km	36.1	women	77.8 yrs
Av. ann. growth		Adult literacy[a]	99.7%
in pop. 2000–05	-0.57%	Fertility rate (per woman)	1.3
Pop. under 15	14.7%	Urban population	66.2%
Pop. over 60	22.5%		per 1,000 pop.
No. of men per 100 women	84	Crude birth rate	7.8
Human Development Index	82.3	Crude death rate	13.6

The economy

GDP	LVL6.3bn	GDP per head	$4,770
GDP	$11.1bn	GDP per head in purchasing	
Av. ann. growth in real		power parity (USA=100)	27.0
GDP 1993–2003	4.7%	Economic freedom index	2.31

Origins of GDP

	% of total
Agriculture	4.5
Industry, of which:	24.4
manufacturing	14.9
Services	71.1

Components of GDP

	% of total
Private consumption	63.0
Public consumption	20.8
Investment	28.9
Exports	42.4
Imports	-55.1

Structure of employment

	% of total		% of labour force
Agriculture	15	Unemployed 2003	10.6
Industry	25	Av. ann. rate 1996–2003	14.3
Services	60		

Energy

			m TOE
Total output	1.9	Net energy imports as %	
Total consumption	4.3	of energy use	56
Consumption per head,			
kg oil equivalent	1,825		

Inflation and finance

		av. ann. increase 1998–2003	
Consumer price			
inflation 2004	6.2%	Narrow money (M1)	15.4%
Av. ann. inflation 1999–2004	3.2%	Broad money	19.3%
Money market rate, 2004	3.25%		

Exchange rates

	end 2004		December 2004
			1995 = 100
LVL per $	0.51	Effective rates	
LVL per SDR	0.80	– nominal	..
LVL per €	0.70	– real	..

Trade

Principal exports

	$bn fob
Wood & wood products	1.0
Metals	0.4
Textiles	0.4
Total incl. others	**2.9**

Principal imports

	$bn cif
Machinery & equipment	1.1
Chemicals	0.5
Mineral products	0.5
Transport equipment	0.5
Total incl. others	**5.2**

Main export destinations

	% of total
United Kingdom	15.5
Germany	14.9
Sweden	10.6
Lithuania	8.2
Estonia	6.6
EU15	61.8

Main origins of imports

	% of total
Germany	16.1
Lithuania	9.7
Russia	8.7
Finland	7.4
Sweden	7.2
EU15	51.0

Balance of payments, reserves and debt, $bn

Visible exports fob	3.2	Change in reserves	0.2
Visible imports fob	-5.2	Level of reserves	
Trade balance	-2.0	end Dec.	1.5
Invisibles inflows	1.9	No. months of import cover	2.8
Invisibles outflows	-1.3	Official gold holdings, m oz	0.2
Net transfers	0.5	Foreign debt	8.8
Current account balance	-0.9	– as % of GDP	93
– as % of GDP	-8.3	– as % of total exports	206
Capital balance	1.0	Debt service ratio	22
Overall balance	0.1		

Health and education

Health spending, % of GDP	5.1	Education spending, % of GDP	5.9
Doctors per 1,000 pop.	2.9	Enrolment, %: primary	96
Hospital beds per 1,000 pop.	8.1	secondary	95
Improved-water source access, % of pop.	…	tertiary	69

Society

No. of households	0.8m	Colour TVs per 100 households	72.9
Av. no. per household	3.0	Telephone lines per 100 pop.	28.5
Marriages per 1,000 pop.	3.1	Mobile telephone subscribers	
Divorces per 1,000 pop.	2.5	per 100 pop.	52.6
Cost of living, Dec. 2004		Computers per 100 pop.	18.8
New York = 100	…	Internet hosts per 1,000 pop.	27.5

LITHUANIA

Area	65,200 sq km	Capital	Vilnius
Arable as % of total land	47	Currency	Litas (LTL)

People

Population	3.4m	Life expectancy: men	67.9 yrs
Pop. per sq km	52.1	women	78.6 yrs
Av. ann. growth		Adult literacy	99.6%
in pop. 2000–05	-0.40%	Fertility rate (per woman)	1.3
Pop. under 15	16.7%	Urban population	66.7%
Pop. over 60	20.7%		per 1,000 pop.
No. of men per 100 women	87	Crude birth rate	8.8
Human Development Index	84.2	Crude death rate	12.2

The economy

GDP	LTL55.7bn	GDP per head	$5,360
GDP	$18.2bn	GDP per head in purchasing	
Av. ann. growth in real		power parity (USA=100)	30.2
GDP 1993–2003	3.5%	Economic freedom index	2.18

Origins of GDP

	% of total
Agriculture	6.2
Industry, of which:	30.0
manufacturing and mining	18.4
Services	63.8

Components of GDP

	% of total
Private consumption	64.4
Public consumption	18.9
Investment	21.9
Exports	51.8
Imports	-57.3

Structure of employment

	% of total		% of labour force
Agriculture	16	Unemployed 2003	12.4
Industry	28	Av. ann. rate 1995–2003	15.0
Services	56		

Energy

		m TOE	
Total output	4.9	Net energy imports as %	
Total consumption	8.6	of energy use	43
Consumption per head,			
kg oil equivalent	2,476		

Inflation and finance

		av. ann. increase 1998–200	
Consumer price			
inflation 2004	1.2%	Narrow money (M1)	13.6%
Av. ann. inflation 1999–2004	0.5%	Broad money	16.1%
Money market rate, 2004	1.53%		

Exchange rates

	end 2004		December 200
			1995 = 10
LTL per $	2.53	Effective rates	
LTL per SDR	3.95	– nominal	
LTL per €	3.47	– real	

Trade

Principal exports	$bn fob	Principal imports	$bn cif
Mineral products	1.4	Machinery & equipment	1.8
Transport equipment	1.1	Mineral products	1.8
Textiles	1.0	Transport equipment	1.5
Machinery & equipment	0.8	Chemicals	0.8
Total incl. others	7.0	Total incl. others	9.6

Main export destinations	% of total	Main origins of imports	% of total
Switzerland	12.1	Russia	22.6
Russia	10.5	Germany	16.5
Germany	10.3	Poland	5.3
Latvia	10.0	Italy	4.4
United Kingdom	6.6	France	4.3
EU15	43.5	EU15	45.5

Balance of payments, reserves and debt, $bn

Visible exports fob	7.7	Change in reserves	1.0
Visible imports fob	-9.4	Level of reserves	
Trade balance	-1.7	end Dec.	3.4
Invisibles inflows	2.1	No. months of import cover	3.6
Invisibles outflows	-2.0	Official gold holdings, m oz	0.2
Net transfers	0.3	Foreign debt	8.3
Current account balance	-1.3	– as % of GDP	58
– as % of GDP	-7.0	– as % of total exports	105
Capital balance	1.7	Debt service ratio	84
Overall balance	0.6		

Health and education

Health spending, % of GDP	6.3	Education spending, % of GDP	6.0
Doctors per 1,000 pop.	4.0	Enrolment, %: primary	101
Hospital beds per 1,000 pop.	8.1	secondary	102
Improved-water source access, % of pop.	...	tertiary	64

Society

No. of households	1.4m	Colour TVs per 100 households	75.2
Av. no. per household	2.5	Telephone lines per 100 pop.	23.9
Marriages per 1,000 pop.	4.7	Mobile telephone subscribers	
Divorces per 1,000 pop.	3.3	per 100 pop.	63.0
Cost of living, Dec. 2004		Computers per 100 pop.	11.0
New York = 100	...	Internet hosts per 1,000 pop.	31.3

MALAYSIA

Area	332,665 sq km	Capital	Kuala Lumpur
Arable as % of total land	5	Currency	Malaysian dollar/ringgit (M$)

People

Population	24.4m	Life expectancy: men	71.9 yrs
Pop. per sq km	73.3	women	76.5 yrs
Av. ann. growth		Adult literacy	88.7%
in pop. 2000–05	1.95%	Fertility rate (per woman)	2.9
Pop. under 15	32.4%	Urban population	63.9%
Pop. over 60	7.0%		per 1,000 pop.
No. of men per 100 women	103	Crude birth rate	22.6
Human Development Index	79.3	Crude death rate	4.7

The economy

GDP	M$394bn	GDP per head	$4,250
GDP	$103.7bn	GDP per head in purchasing	
Av. ann. growth in real		power parity (USA=100)	23.8
GDP 1993–2003	5.2%	Economic freedom index	2.96

Origins of GDP		**Components of GDP**	
	% of total		% of total
Agriculture	9.5	Private consumption	43.3
Industry, of which:	45.4	Public consumption	13.7
manufacturing	31.2	Investment	21.4
Services	45.1	Exports	114.9
		Imports	-93.8

Structure of employment

	% of total		% of labour force
Agriculture	15	Unemployed 2003	3.6
Industry	36	Av. ann. rate 1995–2003	3.2
Services	50		

Energy

	m TOE		
Total output	80.2	Net energy imports as %	
Total consumption	51.8	of energy use	-55
Consumption per head,			
kg oil equivalent	2,129		

Inflation and finance

		av. ann. increase 1998–2003	
Consumer price			
inflation 2004	1.5%	Narrow money (M1)	12.5%
Av. ann. inflation 1999–2004	1.5%	Broad money	8.6%
Money market rate, 2004	2.70%		

Exchange rates

	end 2004		December 2004
			1995 = 100
M$ per $	3.80	Effective rates	
M$ per SDR	5.90	– nominal	89.9
M$ per €	5.21	– real	88.8

Trade

Principal exports

	$bn fob
Electronics & electrical mach.	54.5
Petroleum & gas	7.6
Chemicals & products	5.6
Palm oil	5.3
Textiles, clothing & footwear	2.3
Total incl. others	**104.7**

Principal imports

	$bn cif
Intermediate goods	58.8
Consumption goods	49.7
Capital goods & transport equipment	11.2
Total incl. others	**83.3**

Main export destinations

	% of total
United States	18.0
Singapore	16.4
EU15	12.6
Japan	10.9
China	6.4
Hong Kong	6.2

Main origins of imports

	% of total
Japan	17.4
United States	15.2
Singapore	12.0
EU15	11.8
China	8.4
South Korea	5.3

Balance of payments, reserves and debt, $bn

Visible exports fob	105.0	Change in reserves	10.4
Visible imports fob	-79.3	Level of reserves	
Trade balance	25.7	end Dec.	45.0
Invisibles inflows	17.0	No. months of import cover	5.1
Invisibles outflows	-26.9	Official gold holdings, m oz	1.2
Net transfers	-2.4	Foreign debt	49.1
Current account balance	13.4	– as % of GDP	55
– as % of GDP	12.9	– as % of total exports	44
Capital balance	-3.2	Debt service ratio	8
Overall balance	10.2		

Health and education

Health spending, % of GDP	3.8	Education spending, % of GDP	7.9
Doctors per 1,000 pop.	0.7	Enrolment, %: primary	95
Hospital beds per 1,000 pop.	1.4	secondary	70
Improved-water source access, % of pop.	95	tertiary	27

Society

No. of households	5.3m	Colour TVs per 100 households	90.2
Av. no. per household	4.7	Telephone lines per 100 pop.	18.2
Marriages per 1,000 pop.	...	Mobile telephone subscribers	
Divorces per 1,000 pop.	...	per 100 pop.	44.2
Cost of living, Dec. 2004		Computers per 100 pop.	16.7
New York = 100	61	Internet hosts per 1,000 pop.	5.7

MEXICO

Area	1,972,545 sq km	Capital	Mexico city
Arable as % of total land	13	Currency	Mexican peso (PS)

People

Population	103.5m	Life expectancy:	men	73.7 yrs
Pop. per sq km	52.5		women	78.6 yrs
Av. ann. growth		Adult literacy		92.2%
in pop. 2000–05	1.34%	Fertility rate (per woman)		2.4
Pop. under 15	31.0%	Urban population		75.5%
Pop. over 60	7.8%			per 1,000 pop.
No. of men per 100 women	96	Crude birth rate		22.4
Human Development Index	80.2	Crude death rate		4.5

The economy

GDP	6,755bn pesos	GDP per head	$6,050
GDP	$626.1bn	GDP per head in purchasing	
Av. ann. growth in real		power parity (USA=100)	23.8
GDP 1993–2003	2.7%	Economic freedom index	2.89

Origins of GDP		**Components of GDP**	
	% of total		% of total
Agriculture	4.0	Private consumption	69.2
Industry, of which:	26.4	Public consumption	12.7
manufacturing & mining	19.5	Investment	19.8
Services	69.6	Exports	28.4
		Imports	-30.1

Structure of employment

	% of total		% of labour force
Agriculture	18	Unemployed 2003	2.1
Industry	24	Av. ann. rate 1995–2003	2.5
Services	58		

Energy

	m TOE		
Total output	229.9	Net energy imports as %	
Total consumption	157.3	of energy use	-46
Consumption per head,			
kg oil equivalent	1,560		

Inflation and finance

		av. ann. increase 1998–2003	
Consumer price			
inflation 2004	4.7%	Narrow money (M1)	16.0%
Av. ann. inflation 1999–2004	6.0%	Broad money	8.1%
Money market rate, 2004	7.15%		

Exchange rates

	end 2004		December 2004
PS per $	11.26	Effective rates	1995 = 100
PS per SDR	17.49	– nominal	
PS per €	15.43	– real	

Trade

Principal exports

	$bn fob
Manufactured products	160.0
(Maquiladora[a]	*77.5)*
Crude oil & products	20.5
Agricultural products	5.2
Total incl. others	**164.9**

Principal imports

	$bn fob
Intermediate goods	129.2
(Maquiladora[a]	*68.4)*
Consumer goods	21.5
Capital goods	20.2
Total	**170.5**

Main export destinations

	% of total
United States	88.8
Canada	1.7
Spain	0.9
Japan	0.4

Main origins of imports

	% of total
United States	61.8
China	5.5
Japan	4.5
Germany	3.7

Balance of payments, reserves and debt, $bn

Visible exports fob	164.9	Change in reserves	8.4
Visible imports fob	-170.5	Level of reserves	
Trade balance	-5.6	end Dec.	59.0
Invisibles inflows	16.4	No. months of import cover	3.5
Invisibles outflows	-33.6	Official gold holdings, m oz	0.2
Net transfers	13.8	Foreign debt	140.0
Current account balance	-9.0	– as % of GDP	23
– as % of GDP	-1.4	– as % of total exports	74
Capital balance	17.7	Debt service ratio	22
Overall balance	9.8		

Health and education

Health spending, % of GDP	6.1	Education spending, % of GDP	5.1
Doctors per 1,000 pop.	1.6	Enrolment, %: primary	110
Hospital beds per 1,000 pop.	1.0	secondary	79
Improved-water source access,		tertiary	21
% of pop.	91		

Society

No. of households	23.7m	Colour TVs per 100 households	90.0
Av. no. per household	4.3	Telephone lines per 100 pop.	16.0
Marriages per 1,000 pop.	6.6	Mobile telephone subscribers	
Divorces per 1,000 pop.	0.5	per 100 pop.	29.5
Cost of living, Dec. 2004		Computers per 100 pop.	8.3
New York = 100	77	Internet hosts per 1,000 pop.	18.1

a Manufacturing assembly plants near the Mexican-US border where goods for processing may be imported duty-free and all output is exported.

MOROCCO

Area	446,550 sq km	Capital	Rabat
Arable as % of total land	19	Currency	Dirham (Dh)

People

Population	30.6m	Life expectancy: men	68.8 yrs
Pop. per sq km	68.5	women	73.3 yrs
Av. ann. growth		Adult literacy	51.7%
in pop. 2000–05	1.48%	Fertility rate (per woman)	2.8
Pop. under 15	31.1%	Urban population	57.5%
Pop. over 60	6.8%		per 1,000 pop.
No. of men per 100 women	99	Crude birth rate	23.2
Human Development Index	62.0	Crude death rate	5.6

The economy

GDP	Dh419bn	GDP per head	$1,430
GDP	$43.7bn	GDP per head in purchasing	
Av. ann. growth in real		power parity (USA=100)	10.4
GDP 1993–2003	3.6%	Economic freedom index	3.18

Origins of GDP		Components of GDP	
	% of total		% of total
Agriculture	17	Private consumption	61.6
Industry, of which:	30	Public consumption	19.8
manufacturing	17	Investment	22.4
Services	54	Exports	26.3
		Imports	-30.2

Structure of employment

	% of total		% of labour force
Agriculture	6	Unemployed 2003	11.9
Industry	33	Av. ann. rate 1995–2003	15.6
Services	61		

Energy

	m TOE		
Total output	0.6	Net energy imports as %	
Total consumption	10.8	of energy use	9
Consumption per head, kg oil equivalent	363		

Inflation and finance

		av. ann. increase 1998–2003	
Consumer price inflation 2003	1.2%	Narrow money (M1)	10.7%
Av. ann. inflation 1999–2003	1.6%	Broad money	9.5%
Money market rate, 2004	2.39%		

Exchange rates

	end 2004		December 2004
			1995 = 100
Dh per $	8.22	Effective rates	
Dh per SDR	12.76	– nominal	92
Dh per €	11.26	– real	92

Trade

Principal exports

	$bn fob
Textiles	2.0
Electrical components	0.6
Phosphoric acid	0.6
Phosphate rock	0.4
Citrus fruits	0.2
Total incl. others	**8.7**

Principal imports

	$bn cif
Consumer goods	3.5
Semi-finished goods	3.4
Capital goods	3.3
Energy & lubricants	2.3
Food, drink & tobacco	1.3
Total incl. others	**14.2**

Main export destinations

	% of total
France	26.1
Spain	16.4
United Kingdom	7.0
Germany	5.4

Main origins of imports

	% of total
France	21.2
Spain	13.6
Italy	6.7
Germany	6.5

Balance of payments, reserves and debt, $bn

Visible exports fob	8.8	Change in reserves	3.8
Visible imports fob	-13.1	Level of reserves	
Trade balance	-4.3	end Dec.	14.1
Invisibles inflows	5.8	No. months of import cover	9.9
Invisibles outflows	-4.0	Official gold holdings, m oz	0.7
Net transfers	4.1	Foreign debt	18.8
Current account balance	1.6	– as % of GDP	51
– as % of GDP	3.5	– as % of total exports	116
Capital balance	-3.3	Debt service ratio	27
Overall balance	-2.1		

Health and education

Health spending, % of GDP	4.6	Education spending, % of GDP	5.1
Doctors per 1,000 pop.	0.5	Enrolment, %: primary	107
Hospital beds per 1,000 pop.	1.0	secondary	45
Improved-water source access,		tertiary	10
% of pop.	80		

Society

No. of households	5.8m	Colour TVs per 100 households	46.9
Av. no. per household	5.2	Telephone lines per 100 pop.	4.1
Marriages per 1,000 pop.	...	Mobile telephone subscribers	
Divorces per 1,000 pop.	...	per 100 pop.	24.4
Cost of living, Dec. 2004		Computers per 100 pop.	2.0
New York = 100	...	Internet hosts per 1,000 pop.	4.2

NETHERLANDS

Area[a]	41,526 sq km	Capital	Amsterdam
Arable as % of total land	27	Currency	Euro (€)

People

Population	16.1m	Life expectancy: men	76.3 yrs
Pop. per sq km	387.7	women	81.6 yrs
Av. ann. growth		Adult literacy	99.0%
in pop. 2000–05	0.50%	Fertility rate (per woman)	1.7
Pop. under 15	18.2%	Urban population[b]	89.6%
Pop. over 60	19.2%		per 1,000 pop.
No. of men per 100 women	99	Crude birth rate	12.1
Human Development Index	94.2	Crude death rate	9.1

The economy

GDP	€453bn	GDP per head	$31,770
GDP	$511.5bn	GDP per head in purchasing	
Av. ann. growth in real		power parity (USA=100)	75.7
GDP 1993–2003	2.5%	Economic freedom index	1.95

Origins of GDP

	% of total
Agriculture	2.4
Industry, of which:	24.6
manufacturing	...
Services	73.0

Components of GDP

	% of total
Private consumption	49.4
Public consumption	25.4
Investment	20.2
Exports	61.5
Imports	-56.5

Structure of employment

	% of total		% of labour force
Agriculture	4	Unemployed 2003	4.3
Industry	22	Av. ann. rate 1995–2003	4.7
Services	74		

Energy

	m TOE		
Total output	59.9	Net energy imports as %	
Total consumption	77.9	of energy use	23
Consumption per head,			
kg oil equivalent	4,827		

Inflation and finance

		av. ann. increase 1998–2003
Consumer price		
inflation 2004	1.2%	Euro area:
Av. ann. inflation 1999–2004	2.8%	Narrow money (M1) 8.9%
Lending rate, 2004	2.75%	Broad money 6.7%
		Household saving rate, 2003 10.1%

Exchange rates

	end 2004		December 2004
€ per $	0.73	Effective rates	1995 = 100
€ per SDR	1.14	– nominal	109.
		– real	111.

Trade

Principal exports

	$bn fob
Machinery & transport equipment	86.7
Chemicals	43.9
Food, drink & tobacco	39.9
Fuels	21.9
Total incl. others	**264.4**

Principal imports

	$bn cif
Machinery & transport equipment	88.0
Chemicals	28.2
Fuels	24.2
Food, drink & tobacco	23.3
Total incl. others	**233.8**

Main export destinations

	% of total
Germany	24.3
Belgium	11.7
United Kingdom	10.2
France	10.0
EU15	75.8

Main origins of imports

	% of total
Germany	19.9
Belgium	11.4
United States	7.8
United Kingdom	7.3
EU15	56.6

Balance of payments, reserves and aid, $bn

Visible exports fob	252.4	Overall balance	-0.9
Visible imports fob	-225.7	Change in reserves	2.5
Trade balance	26.6	Level of reserves	
Invisibles inflows	113.2	end Dec.	21.4
Invisibles outflows	-74.7	No. months of import cover	0.8
Net transfers	-7.8	Official gold holdings, m oz	25.0
Current account balance	16.4	Aid given	3.98
– as % of GDP	3.2	– as % of GDP	0.80
Capital balance	-25.1		

Health and education

Health spending, % of GDP	8.8	Education spending, % of GDP	5.0
Doctors per 1,000 pop.	3.3	Enrolment, %: primary	108
Hospital beds per 1,000 pop.	10.8	secondary	122
Improved-water source access, % of pop.	100	tertiary	57

Society

No. of households	7.0m	Colour TVs per 100 households	98.5
Av. no. per household	2.3	Telephone lines per 100 pop.	61.4
Marriages per 1,000 pop.	4.9	Mobile telephone subscribers per 100 pop.	76.8
Divorces per 1,000 pop.	2.0	Computers per 100 pop.	46.7
Cost of living, Dec. 2004 New York = 100	103	Internet hosts per 1,000 pop.	400.2

Includes water.
2001

NEW ZEALAND

Area	270,534 sq km	Capital	Wellington
Arable as % of total land	6	Currency	New Zealand dollar (NZ$)

People

Population	3.9m	Life expectancy: men	77.7 yrs
Pop. per sq km	14.4	women	82.0 yrs
Av. ann. growth		Adult literacy	99.0%
in pop. 2000–05	1.07%	Fertility rate (per woman)	2.0
Pop. under 15	21.3%	Urban population	85.9%
Pop. over 60	16.7%		per 1,000 pop.
No. of men per 100 women	97	Crude birth rate	14.0
Human Development Index	92.6	Crude death rate	7.4

The economy

GDP	NZ$137bn	GDP per head	$20,400
GDP	$79.6bn	GDP per head in purchasing	
Av. ann. growth in real		power parity (USA=100)	56.6
GDP 1993–2003	3.3%	Economic freedom index	1.70

Origins of GDP

	% of total
Agriculture & mining	7.4
Manufacturing	15.3
Other	77.3

Components of GDP

	% of total
Private consumption	60.2
Public consumption	17.4
Investment	24.6
Exports	32.1
Imports	-33.9

Structure of employment

	% of total		% of labour force
Agriculture	9	Unemployed 2003	4.7
Industry	23	Av. ann. rate 1995–2003	6.1
Services	68		

Energy

	m TOE		
Total output	14.9	Net energy imports as %	
Total consumption	18.0	of energy use	17
Consumption per head,			
kg oil equivalent	4,573		

Inflation and finance

		av. ann. increase 1998–2003	
Consumer price			
inflation 2004	2.3%	Narrow money (M1)	11.9%
Av. ann. inflation 1999–2004	2.4%	Broad money	6.4%
Money market rate, 2004	5.77%	Household saving rate, 2003	-6.5%

Exchange rates

	end 2004		December 2004
NZ$ per $	1.39	Effective rates	1995 = 100
NZ$ per SDR	2.16	– nominal	129.1
NZ$ per €	1.90	– real	132.5

Trade

Principal exports

	$bn fob
Dairy produce	2.7
Meat	2.4
Forestry products	1.2
Fish	0.6
Total incl. others	**16.5**

Principal imports

	$bn cif
Machinery & electrical equipment	4.1
Transport equipment	2.9
Mineral fuels	1.7
Total incl. others	**18.5**

Main export destinations

	% of total
Australia	21.6
United States	14.5
Japan	11.0
United Kingdom	4.8

Main origins of imports

	% of total
Australia	22.5
Japan	11.7
United States	11.7
China	9.0

Balance of payments, reserves and aid, $bn

Visible exports fob	16.8	Overall balance	0.8
Visible imports fob	-17.3	Change in reserves	1.1
Trade balance	-0.5	Level of reserves	
Invisibles inflows	7.8	end Dec.	4.9
Invisibles outflows	-10.9	No. months of import cover	2.1
Net transfers	0.1	Official gold holdings, m oz	0.0
Current account balance	-3.4	Aid given	0.17
– as % of GDP	-4.2	– as % of GDP	0.23
Capital balance	3.9		

Health and education

Health spending, % of GDP	8.5	Education spending, % of GDP	6.9
Doctors per 1,000 pop.	2.2	Enrolment, %: primary	102
Hospital beds per 1,000 pop.	5.8	secondary	118
Improved-water source access, % of pop.	95	tertiary	74

Society

No. of households	1.5m	Colour TVs per 100 households	97.8
Av. no. per household	2.7	Telephone lines per 100 pop.	44.9
Marriages per 1,000 pop.	4.7	Mobile telephone subscribers	
Divorces per 1,000 pop.	3.3	per 100 pop.	64.8
Cost of living, Dec. 2004		Computers per 100 pop.	41.4
New York = 100	89	Internet hosts per 1,000 pop.	166.9

NIGERIA

Area	923,768 sq km	Capital	Abuja
Arable as % of total land	33	Currency	Naira (N)

People

Population	124.0m	Life expectancy: men		44.1 yrs
Pop. per sq km	134.2	women		44.3 yrs
Av. ann. growth		Adult literacy		68.0%
in pop. 2000–05	2.24%	Fertility rate (per woman)		5.6
Pop. under 15	44.3%	Urban population		46.7%
Pop. over 60	4.8%			per 1,000 pop.
No. of men per 100 women	102	Crude birth rate		39.1
Human Development Index	46.6	Crude death rate		18.4

The economy

GDP	N7,545bn	GDP per head	$470
GDP	$58.4bn	GDP per head in purchasing	
Av. ann. growth in real		power parity (USA=100)	2.4
GDP 1993–2003	3.1%	Economic freedom index	3.95

Origins of GDP		Components of GDP	
	% of total		% of total
Agriculture	34.6	Private consumption	67.6
Manufacturing	4.4	Public consumption	6.2
Other	61.0	Investment	13.6
		Exports	33.2
		Imports	-20.6

Structure of employment

	% of total		% of labour force
Agriculture	70	Unemployed 2001	3.9
Industry	10	Av. ann. rate 1995–2001	3.7
Services	20		

Energy

	m TOE		
Total output	192.7	Net energy imports as %	
Total consumption	95.7	of energy use	-101
Consumption per head,			
kg oil equivalent	718		

Inflation and finance

		av. ann. increase 1998–200.	
Consumer price			
inflation 2004	15.0%	Narrow money (M1)	30.2%
Av. ann. inflation 1999–2004	13.9%	Broad money	30.4%
Treasury bill rate 2004	14.34%		

Exchange rates

	end 2004		December 200
		Effective rates	1995 = 10
N per $	132.4	– nominal	62.
N per SDR	205.5		
N per €	181.3	– real	108.

Trade

Principal exports

	$bn fob
Oil	21.6
Non-oil	0.7
Total incl. others	22.4

Principal imports

	$bn cif
Manufactured goods	4.3
Machinery & transport equipment	3.6
Chemicals	3.2
Agric products & foodstuffs	1.8
Total incl. others	15.1

Main export destinations[a]

	% of total
United States	40.2
Brazil	8.3
Spain	5.3
France	5.0

Main origins of imports[a]

	% of total
China	13.6
United Kingdom	9.3
France	8.0
United States	7.8

Balance of payments[b], reserves and debt, $bn

Visible exports fob	21.4	Change in reserves	-0.2
Visible imports fob	-11.1	Level of reserves	
Trade balance	10.3	end Dec.	7.4
Invisibles inflows	1.1	No. months of import cover[a]	3.7
Invisibles outflows	-8.8	Official gold holdings, m oz	0.7
Net transfers	1.6	Foreign debt	35.0
Current account balance	4.3	– as % of GDP	78
– as % of GDP	2.3	– as % of total exports	153
Capital balance	-4.1	Debt service ratio	7
Overall balance[c]	-3.5		

Health and education

Health spending, % of GDP	4.7	Education spending, % of GDP	2.3
Doctors per 1,000 pop.	0.3	Enrolment, %: primary	96
Hospital beds per 1,000 pop.	...	secondary	36
Improved-water source access, % of pop.	60	tertiary	...

Society

No. of households	25.4m	Colour TVs per 100 households	51.6
Av. no. per household	4.8	Telephone lines per 100 pop.	0.7
Marriages per 1,000 pop.	...	Mobile telephone subscribers	
Divorces per 1,000 pop.	...	per 100 pop.	2.6
Cost of living, Dec. 2004		Computers per 100 pop.	0.7
New York = 100	80	Internet hosts per 1,000 pop.	...

a Estimate.
b 2000
c 1999

NORWAY

| Area | 323,878 sq km | Capital | Oslo |
| Arable as % of total land | 3 | Currency | Norwegian krone (Nkr) |

People

Population	4.5m	Life expectancy: men	77.8 yrs
Pop. per sq km	13.9	women	82.5 yrs
Av. ann. growth		Adult literacy	99.0%
in pop. 2000–05	0.52%	Fertility rate (per woman)	1.8
Pop. under 15	19.6%	Urban population	78.6%
Pop. over 60	20.0%		per 1,000 pop.
No. of men per 100 women	99	Crude birth rate	12.0
Human Development Index	95.6	Crude death rate	9.3

The economy

GDP	Nkr1,564bn	GDP per head	$49,080
GDP	$220.9bn	GDP per head in purchasing	
Av. ann. growth in real		power parity (USA=100)	100.4
GDP 1993–2003	3.1%	Economic freedom index	2.33

Origins of GDP

Components of GDP

	% of total		% of total
Agriculture	1.9	Private consumption	46.0
Industry, of which:	38.9	Public consumption	22.5
manufacturing	...	Investment	18.0
Services	59.2	Exports	41.2
		Imports	-27.6

Structure of employment

	% of total		% of labour force
Agriculture	4	Unemployed 2003	4.5
Industry	22	Av. ann. rate 1995–2003	3.9
Services	74		

Energy

	m TOE		
Total output	232.2	Net energy imports as %	
Total consumption	26.5	of energy use	-776
Consumption per head,			
kg oil equivalent	5,843		

Inflation and finance

		av. ann. increase 1998–2003	
Consumer price			
inflation 2004	0.5%	Narrow money (M1)	8.5%
Av. ann. inflation 1999–2004	2.1%	Broad money	6.0%
Interbank rate, 2004	2.17%	Household saving rate, 2003	9.9%

Exchange rates

	end 2004		December 2004
			1995 = 100
Nkr per $	6.04	Effective rates	
Nkr per SDR	9.38	– nominal	108.3
Nkr per €	8.27	– real	122.7

Trade

Principal exports

	$bn fob
Oil, gas & products	53.3
Manufactured materials	7.6
Machinery & equipment	6.9
Food, drink & tobacco	4.0
Total incl. others	**67.4**

Principal imports

	$bn cif
Machinery & equipment	15.4
Misc. manufactures	6.7
Manufactured materials	6.4
Chemicals	4.0
Total incl. others	**39.4**

Main export destinations

	% of total
United Kingdom	20.3
Germany	13.5
France	9.9
Netherlands	9.3
United States	8.2
Sweden	7.3
EU15	76.3

Main origins of imports

	% of total
Sweden	16.1
Germany	13.3
Denmark	7.9
United Kingdom	7.1
United States	5.2
Netherlands	4.5
EU15	66.9

Balance of payments, reserves and aid, $bn

Visible exports fob	69.1	Overall balance	0.3
Visible imports fob	-40.8	Change in reserves	5.3
Trade balance	28.3	Level of reserves	
Invisibles inflows	32.2	end Dec.	37.7
Invisibles outflows	-29.3	No. months of import cover	6.5
Net transfers	-3.0	Official gold holdings, m oz	1.2
Current account balance	28.3	Aid given	2.04
– as % of GDP	12.8	– as % of GDP	0.92
Capital balance	-18.7		

Health and education

Health spending, % of GDP	9.6	Education spending, % of GDP	7.2
Doctors per 1,000 pop.	3.7	Enrolment, %: primary	101
Hospital beds per 1,000 pop.	14.6	secondary	115
Improved-water source access,		tertiary	74
% of pop.	100		

Society

No. of households	2.0m	Colour TVs per 100 households	93.4
Av. no. per household	2.3	Telephone lines per 100 pop.	71.4
Marriages per 1,000 pop.	5.4	Mobile telephone subscribers	
Divorces per 1,000 pop.	2.4	per 100 pop.	90.9
Cost of living, Dec. 2004		Computers per 100 pop.	52.8
New York = 100	126	Internet hosts per 1,000 pop.	274.9

PAKISTAN

Area	803,940 sq km	Capital	Islamabad
Arable as % of total land	28	Currency	Pakistan rupee (PRs)

People

Population	153.6m	Life expectancy: men	64.6 yrs
Pop. per sq km	191.0	women	64.9 yrs
Av. ann. growth		Adult literacy	41.5%
in pop. 2000–05	2.04%	Fertility rate (per woman)	4.3
Pop. under 15	38.3%	Urban population	34.1%
Pop. over 60	5.8%		per 1,000 pop.
No. of men per 100 women	106	Crude birth rate	35.9
Human Development Index	49.7	Crude death rate	7.5

The economy

GDP	PRs4,821bn	GDP per head	$540
GDP	$82.3bn	GDP per head in purchasing	
Av. ann. growth in real		power parity (USA=100)	5.4
GDP 1993–2003	3.6%	Economic freedom index	3.73

Origins of GDP		Components of GDP[a]	
	% of total		% of total
Agriculture	23	Private consumption	73.1
Industry, of which:	23	Public consumption	9.1
manufacturing	16	Investment	18.1
Other	53	Exports	16.0
		Imports	-16.2

Structure of employment

	% of total		% of labour force
Agriculture	42	Unemployed 2002	8.3
Industry	20	Av. ann. rate 1995–2002	6.4
Services	38		

Energy

	m TOE		
Total output	49.7	Net energy imports as %	
Total consumption	65.8	of energy use	25
Consumption per head,			
kg oil equivalent	454		

Inflation and finance

		av. ann. increase 1998–200.	
Consumer price			
inflation 2004	7.4%	Narrow money (M1)	13.6%
Av. ann. inflation 1999–2004	4.2%	Broad money	12.4%
Money market rate, 2004	2.70%		

Exchange rates

	end 2004		December 200
			1995 = 10
PRs per $	59.12	Effective rates	
PRs per SDR	91.82	– nominal	76.0
PRs per €	80.99	– real	87.2

Trade

Principal exports[b]

	$bn fob
Textile yarn & fabrics	2.5
Ready-made apparel	1.7
Rice	0.4
Total incl. others	**11.9**

Principal imports[b]

	$bn fob
Fuels etc	2.8
Machinery	1.6
Chemicals	1.3
Transport equipment	0.5
Total incl. others	**13.0**

Main export destinations

	% of total
United States	21.2
United Arab Emirates	8.4
United Kingdom	6.7
Germany	5.0

Main origins of imports

	% of total
China	14.2
United Arab Emirates	13.6
Saudi Arabia	12.6
Kuwait	7.7

Balance of payments, reserves and debt, $bn

Visible exports fob	11.9	Change in reserves	3.0
Visible imports fob	-12.0	Level of reserves	
Trade balance	-0.1	end Dec.	11.8
Invisibles inflows	3.1	No. months of import cover	8.0
Invisibles outflows	-5.7	Official gold holdings, m oz	2.1
Net transfers	6.2	Foreign debt	36.3
Current account balance	3.6	– as % of GDP	50
– as % of GDP	4.3	– as % of total exports	232
Capital balance	-0.6	Debt service ratio	19
Overall balance	2.9		

Health and education

Health spending, % of GDP	3.2	Education spending, % of GDP	1.8
Doctors per 1,000 pop.	0.7	Enrolment, %: primary	73
Hospital beds per 1,000 pop.	0.7	secondary	23
Improved-water source access,		tertiary	...
% of pop.	90		

Society

No. of households	21.1m	Colour TVs per 100 households	37.1
Av. no. per household	7.2	Telephone lines per 100 pop.	2.7
Marriages per 1,000 pop.	...	Mobile telephone subscribers	
Divorces per 1,000 pop.	...	per 100 pop.	1.8
Cost of living, Dec. 2004		Computers per 100 pop.	0.4
New York = 100	44	Internet hosts per 1,000 pop.	0.2

Fiscal year ending June 30, 2004.
2002

PERU

Area	1,285,216 sq km	Capital	Lima
Arable as % of total land	3	Currency	Nuevo Sol (New Sol)

People

Population	27.2m	Life expectancy: men	68.7 yrs
Pop. per sq km	21.2	women	73.9 yrs
Av. ann. growth		Adult literacy	85%
in pop. 2000–05	1.50%	Fertility rate (per woman)	2.9
Pop. under 15	32.2%	Urban population	73.9%
Pop. over 60	7.8%		per 1,000 pop.
No. of men per 100 women	101	Crude birth rate	23.3
Human Development Index	75.2	Crude death rate	5.9

The economy

GDP	New Soles 211bn	GDP per head	$2,230
GDP	$60.6bn	GDP per head in purchasing	
Av. ann. growth in real		power parity (USA=100)	13.5
GDP 1993–2003	4.2%	Economic freedom index	2.78

Origins of GDP		Components of GDP	
	% of total		% of total
Agriculture	9.2	Private consumption	71.0
Industry, of which:	26.1	Public consumption	10.1
manufacturing	14.6	Investment	18.8
Services	64.7	Exports	17.7
		Imports	-17.6

Structure of employment

	% of total		% of labour force
Agriculture	9	Unemployed 2003	10.3
Industry	18	Av. ann. rate 1996–2003	8.6
Services	73		

Energy

	m TOE		
Total output	9.2	Net energy imports as %	
Total consumption	12.0	of energy use	2
Consumption per head,			
kg oil equivalent	450		

Inflation and finance

		av. ann. increase 1998–2003	
Consumer price			
inflation 2004	3.7%	Narrow money (M1)	2.2%
Av. ann. inflation 1999–2004	2.4%	Broad money	3.6
Deposit rate, 2004	3.04%		

Exchange rates

	end 2004		December 2004
			1995 = 100
New Soles per $	3.28	Effective rates	
New Soles per SDR	2.10	– nominal	
New Soles per €	4.49	– real	

Trade

Principal exports	$bn fob	Principal imports	$bn fob
Gold	2.0	Intermediate goods	4.3
Copper	1.3	Capital goods	2.0
Fishmeal	0.8	Consumer goods	1.9
Zinc	0.5	Other goods	0.8
Total incl. others	**9.0**	**Total incl. others**	**8.2**

Main export destinations	% of total	Main origins of imports	% of total
United States	25.9	United States	24.1
China	7.9	Chile	6.1
Switzerland	7.9	Brazil	5.5
Japan	4.7	Colombia	5.5

Balance of payments, reserves and debt, $bn

Visible exports fob	9.0	Change in reserves	0.5
Visible imports fob	-8.3	Level of reserves	
Trade balance	0.7	end Dec.	10.2
Invisibles inflows	2.0	No. months of import cover	9.3
Invisibles outflows	-5.0	Official gold holdings, m oz	1.1
Net transfers	1.2	Foreign debt	29.9
Current account balance	-1.1	– as % of GDP	54
– as % of GDP	-3.5	– as % of total exports	279
Capital balance	1.0	Debt service ratio	24
Overall balance	0.6		

Health and education

Health spending, % of GDP	4.4	Education spending, % of GDP	2.9
Doctors per 1,000 pop.	1.0	Enrolment, %: primary	120
Hospital beds per 1,000 pop.	1.6	secondary	90
Improved-water source access,		tertiary	32
% of pop.	81		

Society

No. of households	5.7m	Colour TVs per 100 households	48.5
Av. no. per household	4.8	Telephone lines per 100 pop.	6.7
Marriages per 1,000 pop.	4.0	Mobile telephone subscribers	
Divorces per 1,000 pop.	...	per 100 pop.	10.6
Cost of living, Dec. 2004		Computers per 100 pop.	4.3
New York = 100	62	Internet hosts per 1,000 pop.	6.5

PHILIPPINES

Area	300,000 sq km	Capital	Manila
Arable as % of total land	19	Currency	Philippine peso (P)

People

Population	80.0m	Life expectancy: men	69.5 yrs
Pop. per sq km	266.6	women	73.8 yrs
Av. ann. growth		Adult literacy	92.6%
in pop. 2000–05	1.84%	Fertility rate (per woman)	3.2
Pop. under 15	35.1%	Urban population	61.0%
Pop. over 60	6.1%		per 1,000 pop.
No. of men per 100 women	101	Crude birth rate	25.3
Human Development Index	75.3	Crude death rate	4.8

The economy

GDP	P4,359bn	GDP per head	$1,010
GDP	$80.6bn	GDP per head in purchasing	
Av. ann. growth in real		power parity (USA=100)	12.3
GDP 1993–2003	4.1%	Economic freedom index	3.25

Origins of GDP		Components of GDP	
	% of total		% of total
Agriculture	14.8	Private consumption	69.5
Industry, of which:	31.9	Public consumption	11.0
manufacturing	23.3	Investment	16.6
Services	53.3	Exports	49.1
		Imports	-51.7

Structure of employment

	% of total		% of labour force
Agriculture	36	Unemployed 2002	9.8
Industry	16	Av. ann. rate 1995–2002	9.0
Services	48		

Energy

	m TOE		
Total output	21.9	Net energy imports as %	
Total consumption	42.0	of energy use	48
Consumption per head,			
kg oil equivalent	525		

Inflation and finance

Consumer price		av. ann. increase 1998–2003	
inflation 2004	5.9%	Narrow money (M1)	12.7%
Av. ann. inflation 1999–2004	4.5%	Broad money	8.4%
Money market rate, 2004	7.05%		

Exchange rates

	end 2004		December 2004
			1995 = 100
P per $	56.27	Effective rates	
P per SDR	87.38	– nominal	70.3
P per €	77.09	– real	80.9

Trade

Principal exports		Principal imports	
	$bn fob		*$bn fob*
Electrical & electronic		Semi-processed raw	
equipment	23.7	materials	13.2
Semiconductors	16.7	Telecom & electrical machinery	8.4
Clothing	2.3	Electrical equipment parts	6.4
Coconut products	0.5	Chemicals	2.9
Petroleum products	0.5	Crude petroleum	2.5
Total incl. others	**37.1**	Total incl. others	**37.5**

Main export destinations		Main origins of imports	
	% of total		*% of total*
United States	24.6	Japan	22.2
Japan	17.0	United States	21.4
China	14.0	Singapore	8.4
Hong Kong	9.2	South Korea	8.1
Singapore	7.2	China	8.0
Malaysia	6.0	Hong Kong	5.7

Balance of payments, reserves and debt, $bn

Visible exports fob	34.8	Change in reserves	0.8
Visible imports fob	-36.1	Level of reserves	
Trade balance	-1.3	end Dec.	16.9
Invisibles inflows	11.4	No. months of import cover	4.7
Invisibles outflows	-7.4	Official gold holdings, m oz	8.2
Net transfers	0.6	Foreign debt	62.7
Current account balance	3.3	– as % of GDP	77
– as % of GDP	4.2	– as % of total exports	141
Capital balance	-5.5	Debt service ratio	23
Overall balance	-0.1		

Health and education

Health spending, % of GDP	2.9	Education spending, % of GDP	3.2
Doctors per 1,000 pop.	1.2	Enrolment, %: primary	112
Hospital beds per 1,000 pop.	1.0	secondary	84
Improved-water source access,		tertiary	31
% of pop.	85		

Society

No. of households	16.4m	Colour TVs per 100 households	66.3
Av. no. per household	5.0	Telephone lines per 100 pop.	4.1
Marriages per 1,000 pop.	6.6	Mobile telephone subscribers	
Divorces per 1,000 pop.	...	per 100 pop.	27.0
Cost of living, Dec. 2004		Computers per 100 pop.	2.8
New York = 100	37	Internet hosts per 1,000 pop.	1.2

POLAND

Area	312,683 sq km	Capital	Warsaw
Arable as % of total land	45	Currency	Zloty (Zl)

People

Population	38.6m	Life expectancy: men	71.2 yrs
Pop. per sq km	123.4	women	79.0 yrs
Av. ann. growth		Adult literacy	99.7%
in pop. 2000–05	-0.06%	Fertility rate (per woman)	1.3
Pop. under 15	16.3%	Urban population	61.9%
Pop. over 60	16.8%		per 1,000 pop.
No. of men per 100 women	94	Crude birth rate	9.6
Human Development Index	85.0	Crude death rate	10.1

The economy

GDP	Zl815bn	GDP per head	$5,430
GDP	$209.6bn	GDP per head in purchasing	
Av. ann. growth in real		power parity (USA=100)	29.7
GDP 1993–2003	4.9%	Economic freedom index	2.54

Origins of GDP[a]		Components of GDP	
	% of total		% of total
Agriculture	3.2	Private consumption	66.0
Industry, of which:	30.6	Public consumption	17.8
manufacturing	17.6	Investment	18.7
Services	66.2	Exports	34.5
		Imports	-36.9

Structure of employment

	% of total		% of labour force
Agriculture	16	Unemployed 2003	19.4
Industry	29	Av. ann. rate 1995–2003	15.4
Services	55		

Energy

	m TOE		
Total output	79.6	Net energy imports as %	
Total consumption	89.2	of energy use	1
Consumption per head,			
kg oil equivalent	2,333		

Inflation and finance

		av. ann. increase 1998–2003	
Consumer price			
inflation 2004	3.5%	Narrow money (M1)	13.3%
Av. ann. inflation 1999–2004	4.3%	Broad money	9.5%
Money market rate, 2003	5.8%		

Exchange rates

	end 2004		December 2004
Zl per $	2.99	Effective rates	1995 = 100
Zl per SDR	4.64	– nominal	107
Zl per €	4.10	– real	111

Trade

Principal exports		Principal imports	
	$bn fob		*$bn cif*
Machinery &		Machinery &	
transport equipment	20.2	transport equipment	25.9
Manufactured goods	12.7	Manufactured goods	14.3
Other manufactured goods	9.2	Chemicals	10.0
Agric. products & foodstuffs	4.1	Mineral fuels	6.2
Total incl. others	**53.7**	Total incl. others	**68.2**

Main export destinations		Main origins of imports	
	% of total		*% of total*
Germany	32.3	Germany	24.4
France	6.1	Italy	8.5
Italy	5.7	Russia	7.7
United Kingdom	5.0	France	7.1

Balance of payments, reserves and debt, $bn

Visible exports fob	61.0	Change in reserves	4.2
Visible imports fob	-66.7	Level of reserves	
Trade balance	-5.7	end Dec.	34.0
Invisibles inflows	13.3	No. months of import cover	4.9
Invisibles outflows	-16.4	Official gold holdings, m oz	3.3
Net transfers	4.2	Foreign debt	95.2
Current account balance	-4.6	– as % of GDP	49
– as % of GDP	-2.2	– as % of total exports	150
Capital balance	8.7	Debt service ratio	30
Overall balance	1.2		

Health and education

Health spending, % of GDP	6.1	Education spending, % of GDP	5.6
Doctors per 1,000 pop.	2.2	Enrolment, %: primary	100
Hospital beds per 1,000 pop.	4.9	secondary	105
Improved-water source access, % of pop.	...	tertiary	60

Society

No. of households	13.4m	Colour TVs per 100 households	84.2
Av. no. per household	2.9	Telephone lines per 100 pop.	31.9
Marriages per 1,000 pop.	3.3	Mobile telephone subscribers	
Divorces per 1,000 pop.	1.1	per 100 pop.	45.1
Cost of living, Dec. 2004		Computers per 100 pop.	14.2
New York = 100	70	Internet hosts per 1,000 pop.	64.3

PORTUGAL

Area	88,940 sq km	Capital	Lisbon
Arable as % of total land	22	Currency	Euro (€)

People

Population	10.1m	Life expectancy: men	74.6 yrs
Pop. per sq km	113.6	women	81.2 yrs
Av. ann. growth		Adult literacy	93.3%
in pop. 2000–05	0.52%	Fertility rate (per woman)	1.5
Pop. under 15	15.9%	Urban population	54.6%
Pop. over 60	22.3%		per 1,000 pop.
No. of men per 100 women	94	Crude birth rate	11.0
Human Development Index	89.7	Crude death rate	10.9

The economy

GDP	€131bn	GDP per head	$14,640
GDP	$147.9bn	GDP per head in purchasing	
Av. ann. growth in real		power parity (USA=100)	46.9
GDP 1993–2003	2.6%	Economic freedom index	2.44

Origins of GDP

	% of total
Agriculture	4.0
Industry, of which:	27.9
manufacturing	...
Services	68.1

Components of GDP

	% of total
Private consumption	61.7
Public consumption	21.2
Investment	22.8
Exports	30.8
Imports	-36.4

Structure of employment

	% of total		% of labour force
Agriculture	13	Unemployed 2003	6.3
Industry	35	Av. ann. rate 1995–2003	5.5
Services	52		

Energy

	m TOE		
Total output	3.6	Net energy imports as %	
Total consumption	26.4	of energy use	86
Consumption per head, kg oil equivalent	2,546		

Inflation and finance

			av. ann. increase 1998–2003
Consumer price inflation 2004	2.4%	Euro area:	
Av. ann. inflation 1999–2004	3.3%	Narrow money (M1)	8.9%
Deposit rate, h'holds, 2004	1.97%	Broad money	6.7%
		Household saving rate, 2003	11.4%

Exchange rates

	end 2004		December 2004
€ per $	0.73	Effective rates	1995 = 100
€ per SDR	1.14	– nominal	105.
		– real	111

Trade

Principal exports

	$bn fob
Transport goods	5.9
Machinery	5.3
Clothing	3.6
Shoes	1.8
Total incl. others	**30.6**

Principal imports

	$bn cif
Machinery	9.1
Transport goods	5.9
Chemicals	4.4
Agricultural goods	3.3
Total incl. others	**40.8**

Main export destinations

	% of total
Spain	28.7
Germany	19.2
France	16.3
United Kingdom	13.3
United States	5.8
EU15	79.2

Main origins of imports

	% of total
Spain	27.9
Germany	19.2
France	12.9
Italy	8.3
United Kingdom	3.6
EU15	76.7

Balance of payments, reserves and debt, $bn

Visible exports fob	32.8	Overall balance	-6.5
Visible imports fob	-46.1	Change in reserves	-4.9
Trade balance	-13.4	Level of reserves	
Invisibles inflows	17.4	end Dec.	12.8
Invisibles outflows	-15.9	No. months of import cover	2.5
Net transfers	3.4	Official gold holdings, m oz	16.6
Current account balance	-8.4	Aid given	0.32
– as % of GDP	-5.7	– as % of GDP	0.22
Capital balance	1.9		

Health and education

Health spending, % of GDP	9.3	Education spending, % of GDP	5.9
Doctors per 1,000 pop.	3.2	Enrolment, %: primary	116
Hospital beds per 1,000 pop.	3.6	secondary[a]	113
Improved-water source access, % of pop.	...	tertiary	53

Society

No. of households	3.8m	Colour TVs per 100 households	97.9
Av. no. per household	2.9	Telephone lines per 100 pop.	41.1
Marriages per 1,000 pop.	6.5	Mobile telephone subscribers	
Divorces per 1,000 pop.	1.7	per 100 pop.	89.9
Cost of living, Dec. 2004		Computers per 100 pop.	13.5
New York = 100	80	Internet hosts per 1,000 pop.	60.0

a Includes training for unemployed.

ROMANIA

Area	237,500 sq km	Capital	Bucharest
Arable as % of total land	41	Currency	Leu (L)

People

Population	22.3m	Life expectancy: men	68.7 yrs
Pop. per sq km	93.9	women	75.7 yrs
Av. ann. growth		Adult literacy	97.3%
in pop. 2000–05	-0.37%	Fertility rate (per woman)	1.3
Pop. under 15	15.4%	Urban population	54.2%
Pop. over 60	19.3%		per 1,000 pop.
No. of men per 100 women	95	Crude birth rate	10.4
Human Development Index	77.8	Crude death rate	12.6

The economy

GDP	L1,891trn	GDP per head	$2,550
GDP	$57.0bn	GDP per head in purchasing	
Av. ann. growth in real		power parity (USA=100)	18.9
GDP 1993–2003	2.0%	Economic freedom index	3.58

Origins of GDP

	% of total
Agriculture	13.1
Industry, of which:	38.1
manufacturing	...
Services	48.8

Components of GDP

	% of total
Private consumption	76.
Public consumption	6.
Investment	24.
Exports	36.
Imports	-44.

Structure of employment

	% of total		% of labour force
Agriculture	31	Unemployed 2003	7.
Industry	31	Av. ann. rate 1995–2003	7.
Services	38		

Energy

	m TOE		
Total output	28.4	Net energy imports as %	
Total consumption	37.0	of energy use	2
Consumption per head,			
kg oil equivalent	1,696		

Inflation and finance

		av. ann. increase 1998–200	
Consumer price			
inflation 2004	11.9%	Narrow money (M1)	38.5
Av. ann. inflation 1999–2004	25.4%	Broad money	37.9
Bank rate, 2004	20.3%		

Exchange rates

	end 2004		December 20
L per $	29,067	Effective rates	1995 = 1
L per SDR	45,141	– nominal	58
L per €	39,822	– real	120

Trade

Principal exports	$bn fob	Principal imports	$bn cif
Textiles	4.5	Machinery & equipment	5.8
Machinery & equipment	2.8	Textiles & footwear	3.6
Basic metals & products	2.3	Fuels & minerals	3.0
Minerals & fuels	1.2	Chemicals	1.9
Total incl. others	**17.6**	Total incl. others	**24.0**

Main export destinations	% of total	Main origins of imports	% of total
Italy	24.2	Italy	19.5
Germany	15.7	Germany	14.8
France	7.3	Russia	8.3
EU15	67.7	EU15	57.7

Balance of payments, reserves and debt, $bn

Visible exports fob	17.6	Change in reserves	2.2
Visible imports fob	-22.2	Level of reserves	
Trade balance	-4.5	end Dec.	9.4
Invisibles inflows	3.4	No. months of import cover	4.3
Invisibles outflows	-4.0	Official gold holdings, m oz	3.4
Net transfers	1.9	Foreign debt	21.3
Current account balance	-3.3	– as % of GDP	45
– as % of GDP	-5.8	– as % of total exports	124
Capital balance	4.6	Debt service ratio	21
Overall balance	1.0		

Health and education

Health spending, % of GDP	6.3	Education spending, % of GDP	3.3
Doctors per 1,000 pop.	1.9	Enrolment, %: primary	98
Hospital beds per 1,000 pop.	8.0	secondary	85
Improved-water source access,		tertiary	30
% of pop.	57		

Society

No. of households	7.5m	Colour TVs per 100 households	53.5
Av. no. per household	3.0	Telephone lines per 100 pop.	19.9
Marriages per 1,000 pop.	5.5	Mobile telephone subscribers	
Divorces per 1,000 pop.	2.0	per 100 pop.	32.4
Cost of living, Dec. 2004		Computers per 100 pop.	9.7
New York = 100	54	Internet hosts per 1,000 pop.	12.4

RUSSIA

Area	17,075,400 sq km	Capital	Moscow
Arable as % of total land	7	Currency	Rouble (Rb)

People

Population	143.2m	Life expectancy: men		58.7 yrs
Pop. per sq km	8.4	women		71.8 yrs
Av. ann. growth		Adult literacy		99.6%
in pop. 2000–05	-0.46%	Fertility rate (per woman)		1.3
Pop. under 15	15.3%	Urban population		73.3%
Pop. over 60	17.1%			per 1,000 pop.
No. of men per 100 women	87	Crude birth rate		8.6
Human Development Index	79.5	Crude death rate		16.0

The economy

GDP	Rb13,285bn	GDP per head	$3,020
GDP	$432.9bn	GDP per head in purchasing	
Av. ann. growth in real		power parity (USA=100)	23.7
GDP 1993–2003	0.7%	Economic freedom index	3.56

Origins of GDP		Components of GDPa	
	% of total		% of total
Agriculture	5.2	Private consumption	50.7
Industry, of which:	35.2	Public consumption	17.6
manufacturing	...	Investment	20.5
Services	59.6	Exports	35.3
		Imports	-23.9

Structure of employment

	% of total		% of labour force
Agriculture	12	Unemployed 2002	10.2
Industry	23	Av. ann. rate 1995–2002	10.9
Services	65		

Energy

	m TOE		
Total output	1,034.5	Net energy imports as %	
Total consumption	617.8	of energy use	-6
Consumption per head,			
kg oil equivalent	4,288		

Inflation and finance

		av. ann. increase 1998–2003	
Consumer price			
inflation 2004	10.9%	Narrow money (M1)	44.7%
Av. ann. inflation 1999–2004	16.4%	Broad money	44.3%
Money market rate, 2004	3.33%		

Exchange rates

	end 2004		December 2004
			1995 = 100
Rb per $	27.75	Effective rates	
Rb per SDR	43.09	– nominal	94.4
Rb per 7	38.02	– real	137.7

Trade

Principal exports

	$bn fob
Mineral products	69.3
Metals	17.2
Machinery & equipment	10.6
Chemicals	8.3
Total incl. others	**134.4**

Principal imports

	$bn fob
Machinery & equipment	21.1
Food products	12.1
Chemicals	9.9
Metals	3.9
Total incl. others	**81.7**

Main export destinations

	% of total
Germany	8.2
China	6.2
Italy	6.1
Netherlands	5.8
Ukraine	5.6

Main origins of imports

	% of total
Germany	12.9
Belarus	6.4
Ukraine	5.9
China	4.1
Kazakhstan	3.9

Balance of payments, reserves and debt, $bn

Visible exports fob	135.9	Change in reserves	30.1
Visible imports fob	-76.1	Level of reserves	
Trade balance	59.9	end Dec.	78.4
Invisibles inflows	27.3	No. months of import cover	7.4
Invisibles outflows	-41.4	Official gold holdings, m oz	12.5
Net transfers	-0.4	Foreign debt	175.3
Current account balance	35.4	– as % of GDP	50
– as % of GDP	8.2	– as % of total exports	128
Capital balance	0.6	Debt service ratio	14
Overall balance	27.8		

Health and education

Health spending, % of GDP	6.2	Education spending, % of GDP	3.1
Doctors per 1,000 pop.	4.2	Enrolment, %: primary	114
Hospital beds per 1,000 pop.	14.4	secondary	95
Improved-water source access, % of pop.	96	tertiary	70

Society

No. of households	52.7m	Colour TVs per 100 households	75.8
Av. no. per household	2.7	Telephone lines per 100 pop.	25.3
Marriages per 1,000 pop.	4.7	Mobile telephone subscribers	
Divorces per 1,000 pop.	2.9	per 100 pop.	24.9
Cost of living, Dec. 2004		Computers per 100 pop.	8.9
New York = 100	92	Internet hosts per 1,000 pop.	7.9

Production based.

SAUDI ARABIA

Area	2,200,000 sq km	Capital	Riyadh
Arable as % of total land	2	Currency	Riyal (SR)

People

Population	24.2m	Life expectancy: men	71.1 yrs
Pop. per sq km	11.0	women	75.1 yrs
Av. ann. growth		Adult literacy	77.9%
in pop. 2000–05	2.69%	Fertility rate (per woman)	4.1
Pop. under 15	37.3%	Urban population	87.7%
Pop. over 60	4.6%		per 1,000 pop.
No. of men per 100 women	117	Crude birth rate	31.5
Human Development Index	76.8	Crude death rate	3.7

The economy

GDP	SR804bn	GDP per head	$8,870
GDP	$214.7bn	GDP per head in purchasing	
Av. ann. growth in real		power parity (USA=100)	35.0
GDP 1993–2002	1.8%	Economic freedom index	2.99

Origins of GDP		Components of GDP	
	% of total		% of total
Agriculture	4.6	Private consumption	33.1
Industry, of which:	54.6	Public consumption	24.6
manufacturing	10.3	Investment	19.4
Services	40.8	Exports	46.9
		Imports	-24.1

Structure of employment

	% of total		% of labour force
Agriculture	5	Unemployed 2002	5.2
Industry	26	Av. ann. rate 1995–2002	4.4
Services	69		

Energy

	m TOE		
Total output	462.8	Net energy imports as %	
Total consumption	126.4	of energy use	-26
Consumption per head,			
kg oil equivalent	5,775		

Inflation and finance

Consumer price			av. ann. increase 1998–200
inflation 2004	0.4%	Narrow money (M1)	9.7
Av. ann. inflation 1999–2004	-0.2%	Broad money	7.9
Deposit rate, 2004	1.73%		

Exchange rates

	end 2004		December 200
			1995 = 10
SR per $	3.75	Effective rates	
SR pe0 SDR	5.82	– 3ominal	84
SREper €	5.14	–1real	78

Trade

Principal exports^a

	$bn fob
Crude oil & refined petroleum	62.6
Oil products	12.7
Total incl. others	**93.4**

Principal imports^a

	$bn cif
Machinery & transport equipment	15.9
Foodstuffs	6.0
Total incl. others	**37.0**

Main export destinations

	% of total
United States	20.9
Japan	15.8
South Korea	9.8
China	5.6

Main origins of imports

	% of total
United States	9.5
Japan	8.3
Germany	7.3
United Kingdom	6.2

Balance of payments, reserves and aid, $bn

Visible exports fob	93.4	Overall balance	1.6
Visible imports fob	-33.9	Change in reserves	2.4
Trade balance	59.5	Level of reserves	
Invisibles inflows	8.7	end Dec.	24.5
Invisibles outflows	-26.2	No. months of import cover	5.0
Net transfers	-14.9	Official gold holdings, m oz	4.6
Current account balance	28.1	Aid given	2.39
– as % of GDP	13.1	– as % of GDP	1.11
Capital balance	-26.5		

Health and education

Health spending, % of GDP	4.3	Education spending, % of GDP	8.3
Doctors per 1,000 pop.	1.5	Enrolment, %: primary	67
Hospital beds per 1,000 pop.	0.2	secondary	67
Improved-water source access, % of pop.	95	tertiary	22

Society

No. of households	3.9m	Colour TVs per 100 households	99.1
Av. no. per household	5.9	Telephone lines per 100 pop.	15.5
Marriages per 1,000 pop.	2.9	Mobile telephone subscribers	
Divorces per 1,000 pop.	...	per 100 pop.	32.1
Cost of living, Dec. 2004		Computers per 100 pop.	13.7
New York = 100	69	Internet hosts per 1,000 pop.	0.2

a Estimates.

SINGAPORE

Area	639 sq km	Capital	Singapore
Arable as % of total land	1	Currency	Singapore dollar (S$)

People

Population	4.3m	Life expectancy: men	77.6 yrs
Pop. per sq km	6,729.3	women	81.3 yrs
Av. ann. growth		Adult literacy	92.5%
in pop. 2000–05	1.48%	Fertility rate (per woman)	1.4
Pop. under 15	19.5%	Urban population	100.0%
Pop. over 60	12.2%		per 1,000 pop.
No. of men per 100 women	101	Crude birth rate	10.2
Human Development Index	90.2	Crude death rate	5.5

The economy

GDP	S$159bn	GDP per head	$21,490
GDP	$91.3bn	GDP per head in purchasing	
Av. ann. growth in real		power parity (USA=100)	64.1
GDP 1993–2003	5.2%	Economic freedom index	1.60

Origins of GDP		Components of GDP	
	% of total		% of total
Agriculture	0	Private consumption	43.1
Industry, of which:	35	Public consumption	11.9
manufacturing	28	Investment	13.4
Services	65	Exports	206.4
		Imports	-173.0

Structure of employment

	% of total		% of labour force
Agriculture	0	Unemployed 2003	5.4
Industry	26	Av. ann. rate 1995–2003	3.8
Services	74		

Energy

	m TOE		
Total output	0.06	Net energy imports as %	
Total consumption	25.3	of energy use	10
Consumption per head,			
kg oil equivalent	6,078		

Inflation and finance

		av. ann. increase 1998–2004	
Consumer price			
inflation 2004	1.7%	Narrow money (M1)	7.3%
Av. ann. inflation 1999–2004	0.8%	Broad money	3.9%
Money market rate, 2004	1.04%		

Exchange rates

	end 2004		December 2004
			1995 = 100
S$ per $	1.63	Effective rates	
S$ per SDR	2.54	– nominal	95
S$ per 7	2.23	– real	92

Trade

Principal exports

	$bn fob
Machinery & equipment	90.3
Chemicals	17.4
Mineral fuels	12.2
Manufactured products	5.5
Food	1.7
Total incl. others	**144.1**

Principal imports

	$bn cif
Machinery & equipment	77.4
Manufactured products	8.9
Chemicals	8.7
Petroleum	8.2
Food	3.2
Total incl. others	**127.9**

Main export destinations

	% of total
Malaysia	15.8
United States	13.3
Hong Kong	10.0
China	7.0
Japan	6.7
Taiwan	4.8
Thailand	4.3

Main origins of imports

	% of total
Malaysia	16.8
United States	13.9
Japan	12.0
China	8.7
Taiwan	5.1
Thailand	4.3
Saudi Arabia	3.1

Balance of payments, reserves and debt, $bn

Visible exports fob	157.9	Change in reserves	13.7
Visible imports fob	-128.5	Level of reserves	
Trade balance	29.3	end Dec.	95.7
Invisibles inflows	44.1	No. months of import cover	6.7
Invisibles outflows	-44.1	Official gold holdings, m oz	...
Net transfers	-1.1	Foreign debt	22.2
Current account balance	28.2	– as % of GDP	24.1
– as % of GDP	30.9	– as % of total exports	11.0
Capital balance	-25.2	Debt service ratio	2
Overall balance	6.7		

Health and education

Health spending, % of GDP	4.3	Education spending, % of GDP	3.7
Doctors per 1,000 pop.	1.4	Enrolment, %: primary	92
Hospital beds per 1,000 pop.	3.5	secondary	67
Improved-water source access,		tertiary	39
% of pop.	100		

Society

No. of households	1.0m	Colour TVs per 100 households	98.6
Av. no. per household	3.5	Telephone lines per 100 pop.	45.0
Marriages per 1,000 pop.	6.3	Mobile telephone subscribers	
Divorces per 1,000 pop.	1.8	per 100 pop.	85.3
Cost of living, Dec. 2004		Computers per 100 pop.	62.2
New York = 100	100	Internet hosts per 1,000 pop.	142.0

SLOVAKIA

Area	49,035 sq km	Capital	Bratislava
Arable as % of total land	30	Currency	Koruna (Kc)

People

Population	5.4m	Life expectancy: men		71.1 yrs
Pop. per sq km	110.1	women		78.7 yrs
Av. ann. growth		Adult literacy		99.7%
in pop. 2000–05	0.00%	Fertility rate (per woman)		1.2
Pop. under 15	16.7%	Urban population		57.4%
Pop. over 60	16.2%			per 1,000 pop.
No. of men per 100 women	94	Crude birth rate		10.2
Human Development Index	84.2	Crude death rate		9.8

The economy

GDP	Kc1,196bn	GDP per head	$6,040
GDP	$32.5bn	GDP per head in purchasing	
Av. ann. growth in real		power parity (USA=100)	35.6
GDP 1993–2003	4.3%	Economic freedom index	2.43

Origins of GDP		Components of GDP	
	% of total		% of total
Agriculture	3.7	Private consumption	56.7
Industry, of which:	29.7	Public consumption	20.0
manufacturing	20.0	Investment	25.8
Services	66.6	Exports	78.0
		Imports	-79.5

Structure of employment

	% of total		% of labour force
Agriculture	6	Unemployed 2003	17.5
Industry	38	Av. ann. rate 1995–2003	15.5
Services	56		

Energy

	m TOE		
Total output	6.7	Net energy imports as %	
Total consumption	18.5	of energy use	6
Consumption per head,			
kg oil equivalent	3,448		

Inflation and finance

		av. ann. increase 1998–2004	
Consumer price			
inflation 2004	7.6%	Narrow money (M1)	
Av. ann. inflation 1999–2004	7.7%	Broad money	10.4%
Money market rate, 2004	3.82%	Household saving rate, 2003	6.6%

Exchange rates

	end 2004		December 2004
			1995 = 100
Kc per $	28.50	Effective rates	
Kc per SDR	44.26	– nominal	76.7
Kc per €	39.05	– real	91.8

Trade

Principal exports		Principal imports	
	$bn fob		*$bn fob*
Machinery & transport equipment	10.3	Machinery & transport equipment	9.2
Intermediate manufactured goods	5.2	Intermediate manufactured goods	4.3
Other manufactured goods	2.8	Fuels	2.7
Chemicals	1.1	Other manufactured goods	2.3
Fuels	1.1	Chemicals	2.2
Total incl. others	**21.8**	Total incl. others	**22.5**

Main export destinations		Main origins of imports	
	% of total		*% of total*
Germany	31.1	Germany	25.5
Czech Republic	12.1	Czech Republic	14.3
Austria	9.0	Russia	10.7
Italy	5.0	Italy	4.4
EU15	60.6	EU15	51.4

Balance of payments, reserves and debt, $bn

Visible exports fob	21.9	Change in reserves	3.0
Visible imports fob	-22.6	Level of reserves	
Trade balance	-0.6	end Dec.	12.1
Invisibles inflows	4.2	No. months of import cover	5.5
Invisibles outflows	-4.1	Official gold holdings, m oz	1.1
Net transfers	0.3	Foreign debt	18.4
Current account balance	-0.3	– as % of GDP	72
– as % of GDP	-0.9	– as % of total exports	93
Capital balance	1.8	Debt service ratio	18
Overall balance	1.5		

Health and education

Health spending, % of GDP	5.9	Education spending, % of GDP	4.1
Doctors per 1,000 pop.	3.3	Enrolment, %: primary	101
Hospital beds per 1,000 pop.	5.4	secondary	92
Improved-water source access, % of pop.	100	tertiary	32

Society

No. of households	2.1m	Colour TVs per 100 households	86.1
Av. no. per household	2.6	Telephone lines per 100 pop.	24.1
Marriages per 1,000 pop.	4.8	Mobile telephone subscribers	
Divorces per 1,000 pop.	1.7	per 100 pop.	68.4
Cost of living, Dec. 2004		Computers per 100 pop.	23.6
New York = 100	...	Internet hosts per 1,000 pop.	34.9

SLOVENIA

Area	20,253 sq km	Capital	Ljubljana
Arable as % of total land	8	Currency	Tolars (SIT)

People

Population	2.0m	Life expectancy: men	73.5 yrs
Pop. per sq km	98.8	women	80.7 yrs
Av. ann. growth		Adult literacy	99.7%
in pop. 2000–05	0.00%	Fertility rate (per woman)	1.2
Pop. under 15	13.9%	Urban population	50.8%
Pop. over 60	20.5%		per 1,000 pop.
No. of men per 100 women	95	Crude birth rate	8.3
Human Development Index	89.5	Crude death rate	10.4

The economy

GDP	SIT5,747bn	GDP per head	$14,130
GDP	$27.7bn	GDP per head in purchasing	
Av. ann. growth in real		power parity (USA=100)	50.6
GDP 1993–2003	3.9%	Economic freedom index	2.64

Origins of GDP		Components of GDP	
	% of total		% of total
Agriculture	3.0	Private consumption	54.7
Industry, of which:	37.6	Public consumption	20.4
manufacturing	28.1	Investment	25.3
Services	59.4	Exports	58.1
		Imports	-58.5

Structure of employment

	% of total		% of labour force
Agriculture	6	Unemployed 2003	6.6
Industry	40	Av. ann. rate 1995–2003	6.9
Services	54		

Energy

	m TOE		
Total output	3.4	Net energy imports as %	
Total consumption	7.0	of energy use	5
Consumption per head,			
kg oil equivalent	3,486		

Inflation and finance

		av. ann. increase 1998–200	
Consumer price			
inflation 2004	3.6%	Narrow money (M1)	21.7%
Av. ann. inflation 1999–2004	6.8%	Broad money	16.1%
Money market rate, 2004	4.40%		

Exchange rates

	end 2004		December 200
			1995 = 10
SIT per $	176.2	Effective rates	
SIT per SDR	273.7	– nominal	
SIT per €	241.5	– real	

Trade

Principal exports

	$bn fob
Manufactures	5.5
Machinery & transport equipment	4.7
Chemicals	1.8
Food & live animals	0.3
Total incl. others	12.8

Principal imports

	$bn fob
Machinery & transport equipment	4.8
Manufactures	4.7
Chemicals	1.8
Mineral fuels	1.1
Total incl. others	13.9

Main export destinations

	% of total
Germany	23.1
Italy	13.1
Croatia	8.9
Austria	7.3
France	5.7
EU15	58.4

Main origins of imports

	% of total
Germany	19.3
Italy	18.3
France	10.0
Austria	8.6
Croatia	3.6
EU15	67.3

Balance of payments, reserves and debt, $bn

Visible exports fob	12.9	Change in reserves	1.5
Visible imports fob	-13.5	Level of reserves	
Trade balance	-0.6	end Dec.	8.6
Invisibles inflows	3.4	No. months of import cover	6.2
Invisibles outflows	-3.0	Official gold holdings, m oz	0.2
Net transfers	0.1	Foreign debt	12.5
Current account balance	-0.1	– as % of GDP	45.2
– as % of GDP	-0.4	– as % of total exports	76.7
Capital balance	0.3	Debt service ratio	13
Overall balance	0.3		

Health and education

Health spending, % of GDP	8.3	Education spending, % of GDP	...
Doctors per 1,000 pop.	2.2	Enrolment, %: primary	103
Hospital beds per 1,000 pop.	5.0	secondary	109
Improved-water source access, % of pop.	100	tertiary	66

Society

No. of households	0.7m	Colour TVs per 100 households	92.4
Av. no. per household	2.9	Telephone lines per 100 pop.	40.7
Marriages per 1,000 pop.	3.6	Mobile telephone subscribers	
Divorces per 1,000 pop.	1.0	per 100 pop.	87.1
Cost of living, Dec. 2004		Computers per 100 pop.	32.6
New York = 100	...	Internet hosts per 1,000 pop.	24.0

SOUTH AFRICA

Area	1,225,815 sq km	Capital	Pretoria
Arable as % of total land	12	Currency	Rand (R)

People

Population	45.0m	Life expectancy: men	44.2 yrs
Pop. per sq km	36.7	women	43.8 yrs
Av. ann. growth		Adult literacy	82.4%
in pop. 2000–05	0.78%	Fertility rate (per woman)	2.8
Pop. under 15	32.6%	Urban population	56.9%
Pop. over 60	6.8%		per 1,000 pop.
No. of men per 100 women	96	Crude birth rate	22.6
Human Development Index	66.6	Crude death rate	20.6

The economy

GDP	R1,209bn	GDP per head	$3,550
GDP	$159.9bn	GDP per head in purchasing	
Av. ann. growth in real		power parity (USA=100)	26.8
GDP 1993–2003	2.8%	Economic freedom index	2.78

Origins of GDP

Components of GDP

	% of total		% of total
Agriculture	4	Private consumption	62.8
Industry, of which:	31	Public consumption	19.1
manufacturing	19	Investment	17.2
Services	65	Exports	27.2
		Imports	-25.5

Structure of employment

	% of total		% of labour force
Agriculture	11	Unemployed 2003	29.7
Industry	25	Av. ann. rate 1995–2003	23.8
Services	64		

Energy

	m TOE		
Total output	146.5	Net energy imports as %	
Total consumption	113.5	of energy use	-29
Consumption per head,			
kg oil equivalent	2,502		

Inflation and finance

		av. ann. increase 1998–2003	
Consumer price			
inflation 2004	1.4%	Narrow money (M1)	12.0%
Av. ann. inflation 1999–2004	5.5%	Broad money	13.1%
Money market rate, 2004	7.15%		

Exchange rates

	end 2004		December 2004
			1995 = 100
R per $	5.63	Effective rates	
R per SDR	8.74	– nominal	98.
R per €	7.71	– real	116.5

Trade

Principal exports[a]

	$bn fob
Gold	5.0
Coal	1.5
Diamonds	1.4
Total incl. others	**36.3**

Principal imports[a]

	$bn cif
Crude oil	3.7
Motor vehicles	2.1
Aircraft	1.7
Total incl. others	**40.7**

Main export destinations

	% of total
United Kingdom	12.3
United States	12.0
Japan	8.8
Germany	8.0

Main origins of imports

	% of total
Germany	15.4
United Kingdom	8.1
United States	7.8
China	5.6

Balance of payments, reserves and debt, $bn

Visible exports fob	38.5	Change in reserves	0.3
Visible imports fob	-35.0	Level of reserves	
Trade balance	3.5	end Dec.	8.2
Invisibles inflows	9.4	No. months of import cover	2.0
Invisibles outflows	-13.7	Official gold holdings, m oz	4.0
Net transfers	-0.8	Foreign debt	27.8
Current account balance	-1.6	– as % of GDP	23
– as % of GDP	-1.0	– as % of total exports	67
Capital balance	6.3	Debt service ratio	10
Overall balance	7.6		

Health and education

Health spending, % of GDP	8.7	Education spending, % of GDP	5.7
Doctors per 1,000 pop.	0.3	Enrolment, %: primary	105
Hospital beds per 1,000 pop.	...	secondary	88
Improved-water source access,		tertiary	15
% of pop.	87		

Society

No. of households	11.9m	Colour TVs per 100 households	65.1
Av. no. per household	3.9	Telephone lines per 100 pop.	10.7
Marriages per 1,000 pop.	4.3	Mobile telephone subscribers	
Divorces per 1,000 pop.	0.9	per 100 pop.	36.4
Cost of living, Dec. 2004		Computers per 100 pop.	7.3
New York = 100	70	Internet hosts per 1,000 pop.	10.0

a Estimates.

SOUTH KOREA

Area	99,274 sq km	Capital	Seoul
Arable as % of total land	17	Currency	Won (W)

People

Population	47.7m	Life expectancy: men	74.5 yrs
Pop. per sq km	480.5	women	81.9 yrs
Av. ann. growth		Adult literacy	97.9%
in pop. 2000–05	0.4%	Fertility rate (per woman)	1.2
Pop. under 15	18.6%	Urban population	80.3%
Pop. over 60	13.7%		per 1,000 pop.
No. of men per 100 women	101	Crude birth rate	11.9
Human Development Index	88.8	Crude death rate	6.0

The economy

GDP	W721trn	GDP per head	$12,690
GDP	$605.3bn	GDP per head in purchasing	
Av. ann. growth in real		power parity (USA=100)	47.7
GDP 1993–2003	5.4%	Economic freedom index	2.64

Origins of GDP

	% of total
Agriculture	3
Industry, of which:	35
manufacturing	23
Services	62

Components of GDP

	% of total
Private consumption	52.5
Public consumption	13.5
Investment	29.4
Exports	45.6
Imports	-41.2

Structure of employment

	% of total		% of labour force
Agriculture	8	Unemployed 2003	3.4
Industry	19	Av. ann. rate 1995–2003	3.8
Services	73		

Energy

	m TOE		
Total output	36.2	Net energy imports as %	
Total consumption	203.5	of energy use	82
Consumption per head,			
kg oil equivalent	4,272		

Inflation and finance

Consumer price		av. ann. increase 1998–2003	
inflation 2004	3.6%	Narrow money (M1)	13.0%
Av. ann. inflation 1999–2004	5.5%	Broad money	16.4%
Money market rate, 2004	3.65%	Household saving rate, 2003	3.6%

Exchange rates

	end 2004		December 2004
W per $	1,035	Effective rates	1995 = 100
W per SDR	1,608	– nominal	...
W per €	1,418	– real	...

Trade

Principal exports		Principal imports	
	$bn fob		$bn cif
Electronic products	68.2	Electrical machinery	42.5
Motor vehicles	17.5	Crude petroleum	23.1
Machinery	16.0	Machinery & equipment	21.7
Chemicals	14.8	Chemicals	14.4
Metal goods	13.1	Consumer durables	9.9
Total incl. others	**193.8**	Total incl. others	**178.8**

Main export destinations		Main origins of imports	
	% of total		% of total
China	18.1	Japan	20.3
United States	17.7	United States	13.9
Japan	8.9	China	12.3
Hong Kong	7.6	Saudi Arabia	5.2
Taiwan	3.6	Australia	3.8

Balance of payments, reserves and debt, $bn

Visible exports fob	197.6	Change in reserves	34.0
Visible imports fob	-175.5	Level of reserves	
Trade balance	22.2	end Dec.	155.5
Invisibles inflows	39.8	No. months of import cover	8.4
Invisibles outflows	-46.8	Official gold holdings, m oz	0.4
Net transfers	-2.8	Foreign debt	132.6
Current account balance	12.3	– as % of GDP	22
– as % of GDP	2.0	– as % of total exports	56
Capital balance	13.1	Debt service ratio	6
Overall balance	25.8		

Health and education

Health spending, % of GDP	5.0	Education spending, % of GDP	4.9
Doctors per 1,000 pop.	1.8	Enrolment, %: primary	104
Hospital beds per 1,000 pop.	5.7	secondary	91
Improved-water source access,		tertiary	85
% of pop.	92		

Society

No. of households	16.8m	Colour TVs per 100 households	93.3
Av. no. per household	2.8	Telephone lines per 100 pop.	53.8
Marriages per 1,000 pop.	6.4	Mobile telephone subscribers	
Divorces per 1,000 pop.	3.1	per 100 pop.	70.1
Cost of living, Dec. 2004		Computers per 100 pop.	55.8
New York = 100	97	Internet hosts per 1,000 pop.	4.5

SPAIN

Area	504,782 sq km	Capital	Madrid
Arable as % of total land	28	Currency	Euro (€)

People

Population	41.1m	Life expectancy: men	76.5 yrs
Pop. per sq km	81.4	women	83.8 yrs
Av. ann. growth		Adult literacy	97.9%
in pop. 2000–05	1.12%	Fertility rate (per woman)	1.3
Pop. under 15	14.3%	Urban population	76.5%
Pop. over 60	21.4%		per 1,000 pop.
No. of men per 100 women	96	Crude birth rate	9.3
Human Development Index	92.2	Crude death rate	9.1

The economy

GDP	€743bn	GDP per head	$20,400
GDP	$838.7bn	GDP per head in purchasing	
Av. ann. growth in real		power parity (USA=100)	58.7
GDP 1993–2003	3.1%	Economic freedom index	2.34

Origins of GDP		**Components of GDP**	
	% of total		% of total
Agriculture	3.6	Private consumption	57.9
Industry, of which:	28.6	Public consumption	17.9
manufacturing	...	Investment	26.0
Services	67.8	Exports	27.9
		Imports	-29.7

Structure of employment

	% of total		% of labour force
Agriculture	5	Unemployed 2003	11.3
Industry	30	Av. ann. rate 1995–2003	16.8
Services	65		

Energy

	m TOE		
Total output	31.7	Net energy imports as %	
Total consumption	131.6	of energy use	76
Consumption per head,			
kg oil equivalent	3,215		

Inflation and finance

Consumer price		av. ann. increase 1998–2003	
inflation 2004	3.0%	Euro area:	
Av. ann. inflation 1999–2004	3.2%	Narrow money (M1)	8.9%
Money market rate, 2004	2.04%	Broad money	6.7%
		Household saving rate, 2003	10.6%

Exchange rates

	end 2004		December 2004
€ per $	0.73	Effective rates	1995 = 100
€ per SDR	1.14	– nominal	106.4
		– real	113.7

Trade

Principal exports

	$bn fob
Raw materials & intermediate products	68.0
Consumer goods	64.0
Capital goods	19.1
Energy products	4.6
Total incl. others	**155.7**

Principal imports

	$bn cif
Consumer goods	70.1
Raw materials & intermediate products (excl. fuels)	68.0
Capital goods	29.0
Energy products	21.6
Total incl. others	**208.0**

Main export destinations

	% of total
France	19.2
Germany	12.0
United Kingdom	9.9
Italy	9.7
United States	4.1
EU15	71.8

Main origins of imports

	% of total
Germany	16.3
France	16.1
Italy	9.1
United Kingdom	6.4
United States	3.7
EU15	64.0

Balance of payments, reserves and aid, $bn

Visible exports fob	159.5	Overall balance	-15.5
Visible imports fob	-202.5	Change in reserves	-13.5
Trade balance	-42.9	Level of reserves	
Invisibles inflows	101.5	end Dec.	26.8
Invisibles outflows	-82.5	No. months of import cover	1.1
Net transfers	0.3	Official gold holdings, m oz	16.8
Current account balance	-23.7	Aid given	1.96
– as % of GDP	-2.8	– as % of GDP	0.23
Capital balance	14.4		

Health and education

Health spending, % of GDP	7.6	Education spending, % of GDP	4.4
Doctors per 1,000 pop.	3.3	Enrolment, %: primary	107
Hospital beds per 1,000 pop.	3.6	secondary	117
Improved-water source access, % of pop.	...	tertiary	59

Society

No. of households	14.8m	Colour TVs per 100 households	98.5
Av. no. per household	2.7	Telephone lines per 100 pop.	42.9
Marriages per 1,000 pop.	5.1	Mobile telephone subscribers	
Divorces per 1,000 pop.	0.8	per 100 pop.	91.6
Cost of living, Dec. 2004		Computers per 100 pop.	19.6
New York = 100	91	Internet hosts per 1,000 pop.	31.7

SWEDEN

Area	449,964 sq km	Capital	Stockholm
Arable as % of total land	7	Currency	Swedish krona (Skr)

People

Population	8.9m	Life expectancy: men	78.6 yrs
Pop. per sq km	19.8	women	83.0 yrs
Av. ann. growth		Adult literacy	99.0%
in pop. 2000–05	0.37%	Fertility rate (per woman)	1.6
Pop. under 15	17.5%	Urban population	83.4%
Pop. over 60	23.4%		per 1,000 pop.
No. of men per 100 women	98	Crude birth rate	10.3
Human Development Index	94.6	Crude death rate	10.1

The economy

GDP	Skr2,439bn	GDP per head	$33,890
GDP	$301.6bn	GDP per head in purchasing	
Av. ann. growth in real		power parity (USA=100)	70.8
GDP 1993–2003	2.9%	Economic freedom index	1.89

Origins of GDP

	% of total
Agriculture	2
Industry, of which:	28
manufacturing	21
Services	70

Components of GDP

	% of total
Private consumption	49.0
Public consumption	28.3
Investment	16.0
Exports	43.7
Imports	-37.1

Structure of employment

	% of total		% of labour force
Agriculture	2	Unemployed 2003	4.9
Industry	24	Av. ann. rate 1995–2003	5.9
Services	74		

Energy

	m TOE		
Total output	32.4	Net energy imports as %	
Total consumption	51.0	of energy use	37
Consumption per head,			
kg oil equivalent	5,718		

Inflation and finance

		av. ann. increase 1998–2003	
Consumer price			
inflation 2004	0.4%	Narrow money (M0)	...
Av. ann. inflation 1999–2004	1.6%	Broad money	7.6%
Repurchase rate, end-2004	2.00%	Household saving rate, 2003	8.6%

Exchange rates

	end 2004		December 2004
			1995 = 100
Skr per $	6.61	Effective rates	
Skr per SDR	10.27	– nominal	102.8
Skr per €	9.06	– real	104.9

Trade

Principal exports		**Principal imports**	
	$bn fob		*$bn cif*
Machinery & transport		Machinery & transport	
equipment	51.6	equipment	38.5
Wood & paper products	13.5	Miscellaneous manufactures	17.1
Chemicals	12.9	Chemicals	10.3
Manufactured goods	11.5	Mineral fuels	7.8
Total incl. others	**100.9**	Total incl. others	**82.5**

Main export destinations		**Main origins of imports**	
	% of total		*% of total*
United States	11.5	Germany	18.7
Germany	10.1	Denmark	9.0
Norway	8.4	Norway	8.0
United Kingdom	7.8	United Kingdom	8.0
Denmark	6.4	Netherlands	6.8
EU15	54.2	EU15	66.9

Balance of payments, reserves and aid, $bn

Visible exports fob	102.1	Overall balance	2.1
Visible imports fob	-83.1	Change in reserves	3.0
Trade balance	18.9	Level of reserves	
Invisibles inflows	53.6	end Dec.	22.2
Invisibles outflows	-51.4	No. months of import cover	2.0
Net transfers	1.7	Official gold holdings, m oz	6.0
Current account balance	22.8	Aid given	2.40
– as % of GDP	7.6	– as % of GDP	0.79
Capital balance	-20.2		

Health and education

Health spending, % of GDP	9.2	Education spending, % of GDP	7.6
Doctors per 1,000 pop.	2.9	Enrolment, %: primary	110
Hospital beds per 1,000 pop.	4.0	secondary	139
Improved-water source access,		tertiary	76
% of pop.	100		

Society

No. of households	4.2m	Colour TVs per 100 households	97.3
Av. no. per household	2.1	Telephone lines per 100 pop.	73.6
Marriages per 1,000 pop.	4.3	Mobile telephone subscribers	
Divorces per 1,000 pop.	2.1	per 100 pop.	98.1
Cost of living, Dec. 2004		Computers per 100 pop.	62.1
New York = 100	103	Internet hosts per 1,000 pop.	299.9

SWITZERLAND

Area	41,293 sq km	Capital	Berne
Arable as % of total land	10	Currency	Swiss franc (SFr)

People

Population	7.2m	Life expectancy: men		78.2 yrs
Pop. per sq km	174.4	women		83.8 yrs
Av. ann. growth		Adult literacy		99.0%
in pop. 2000–05	0.24%	Fertility rate (per woman)		1.4
Pop. under 15	16.5%	Urban population		67.5%
Pop. over 60	21.8%			per 1,000 pop.
No. of men per 100 women	94	Crude birth rate		8.7
Human Development Index	93.6	Crude death rate		8.8

The economy

GDP	SFr431bn	GDP per head	$44,460
GDP	$320.1bn	GDP per head in purchasing	
Av. ann. growth in real		power parity (USA=100)	85.4
GDP 1993–2003	1.1%	Economic freedom index	1.85

Origins of GDP[a]		Components of GDP	
	% of total		% of total
Agriculture	1.2	Private consumption	60.7
Industry, of which:	26.7	Public consumption	12.0
manufacturing	...	Investment	20.0
Services	72.1	Exports	44.1
		Imports	-37.0

Structure of employment

	% of total		% of labour force
Agriculture	4	Unemployed 2003	4.1
Industry	26	Av. ann. rate 1995–2003	3.3
Services	70		

Energy

	m TOE		
Total output	11.9	Net energy imports as %	
Total consumption	27.1	of energy use	56
Consumption per head,			
kg oil equivalent	3,723		

Inflation and finance

Consumer price		av. ann. increase 1998–2003	
inflation 2004	0.8%	Narrow money (M1)	9.7%
Av. ann. inflation 1999–2004	0.9%	Broad money	2.3%
Money market rate, 2004	0.55%	Household saving rate, 2003	8.3%

Exchange rates

	end 2004		December 2004
SFr per $	1.13	Effective rates	1995 = 100
SFr per SDR	1.76	– nominal	110.5
SFr per €	1.55	– real	118.1

Trade

Principal exports

	$bn
Chemicals	33.6
Machinery	23.0
Watches & jewellery	7.6
Metals & metal manufactures	7.4
Precision instruments	7.2
Total incl. others	**97.0**

Principal imports

	$bn
Chemicals	20.3
Machinery	19.1
Motor vehicles	10.0
Textiles	6.4
Precision instruments	5.6
Total incl. others	**91.9**

Main export destinations

	% of total
Germany	21.2
United States	10.6
France	8.8
Italy	8.4
United Kingdom	4.8
Japan	3.9
EU15	60.2

Main origins of imports

	% of total
Germany	33.3
France	11.1
Italy	11.1
Netherlands	5.2
United States	4.4
United Kingdom	4.0
EU15	81.7

Balance of payments, reserves and aid, $bn

Visible exports fob	115.4	Overall balance	3.4
Visible imports fob	-108.5	Change in reserves	8.3
Trade balance	7.0	Level of reserves	
Invisibles inflows	98.2	end Dec.	69.6
Invisibles outflows	-56.3	No. months of import cover	5.1
Net transfers	-5.2	Official gold holdings, m oz	52.5
Current account balance	43.6	Aid given	1.30
– as % of GDP	13.6	– as % of GDP	0.39
Capital balance	-25.4		

Health and education

Health spending, % of GDP	11.2	Education spending, % of GDP	5.6
Doctors per 1,000 pop.	3.5	Enrolment, %: primary	107
Hospital beds per 1,000 pop.	17.9	secondary	98
Improved-water source access,		tertiary	44
% of pop.	100		

Society

No. of households	3.3m	Colour TVs per 100 households	97.1
Av. no. per household	2.2	Telephone lines per 100 pop.	72.8
Marriages per 1,000 pop.	4.9	Mobile telephone subscribers	
Divorces per 1,000 pop.	2.8	per 100 pop.	84.3
Cost of living, Dec. 2004		Computers per 100 pop.	70.9
New York = 100	114	Internet hosts per 1,000 pop.	247.9

2000

TAIWAN

Area	36,179 sq km	Capital	Taipei
Arable as % of total land	25	Currency	Taiwan dollar (T$)

People

Population	22.6m	Life expectancy:[a] men		74.5 yrs
Pop. per sq km	624.7		women	80.3 yrs
Av. ann. growth		Adult literacy		96.1
in pop. 2000–05	0.60%	Fertility rate (per woman)		1.6
Pop. under 15	21.0%	Urban population		...
Pop. over 60	12.1%			per 1,000 pop.
No. of men per 100 women	104	Crude birth rate		13
Human Development Index	...	Crude death rate[a]		6.4

The economy

GDP	T$9,848bn	GDP per head	$12,670
GDP	$286.2bn	GDP per head in purchasing	
Av. ann. growth in real		power parity (USA=100)	65.3
GDP 1993–2003	4.6%	Economic freedom index	2.29

Origins of GDP		Components of GDP	
	% of total		% of total
Agriculture	1.8	Private consumption	62.7
Industry, of which:	30.4	Public consumption	12.8
manufacturing	25.5	Investment	16.7
Services	67.8	Exports	58.3
		Imports	-50.6

Structure of employment

	% of total		% of labour force
Agriculture	8	Unemployed 2003	5.0
Industry	36	Av. ann. rate 1995–2003	3.2
Services	56		

Energy

	m TOE		
Total output	...	Net energy imports as %	
Total consumption	...	of energy use	...
Consumption per head,			
kg oil equivalent	...		

Inflation and finance

Consumer price		av. ann. increase 1998–2003	
inflation 2004	1.6%	Narrow money (M1)	11.2%
Av. ann. inflation 1999–2004	0.5%	Broad money	5.5%
Money market rate, 2004	1.14%		

Exchange rates

	end 2004		December 2004
			1995 = 100
T$ per $	31.98	Effective rates	
T$ per SDR	49.97	– nominal	...
T$ per €	43.81	– real	...

Trade

Principal exports		Principal imports	
	$bn fob		*$bn cif*
Machinery & electrical		Machinery & electrical	
equipment	75.4	equipment	52.9
Base metals & manufactures	14.3	Minerals	16.3
Textiles & clothing	11.9	Chemicals	13.5
Plastics and rubber products	10.0	Metals	11.3
Vehicles, aircraft & ships	5.7	Precision instruments, clocks	
		& watches	8.6
Total incl. others	**144.2**	Total incl. others	**127.2**

Main export destinations		Main origins of imports	
	% of total		*% of total*
Hong Kong	19.7	Japan	25.6
United States	18.0	United States	13.2
China	14.9	China	8.6
Japan	8.3	South Korea	6.8

Balance of payments, reserves and debt, $bn

Visible exports fob	143.4	Change in reserves	44.9
Visible imports fob	-118.5	Level of reserves	
Trade balance	24.9	end Dec.	206.6
Invisibles inflows	36.1	No. months of import cover	16.8
Invisibles outflows	-29.1	Official gold holdings, m oz	0.0
Net transfers	-2.7	Foreign debt	60.8
Current account balance	29.2	– as % of GDP	21
– as % of GDP	10.2	– as % of total exports	34
Capital balance	6.7	Debt service ratio	3
Overall balance	37.1		

Health and education

Health spending, % of GDP	...	Education spending, % of GDP	...
Doctors per 1,000 pop.	...	Enrolment, %: primary	100
Hospital beds per 1,000 pop.	4.9	secondary[b]	59
Improved-water source access,		tertiary[b]	21
% of pop.	...		

Society

No. of households	6.9m	Colour TVs per 100 households	99.3
Av. no. per household	3.3	Telephone lines per 100 pop.	59.1
Marriages per 1,000 pop.	7.3	Mobile telephone subscribers	
Divorces per 1,000 pop.	1.9	per 100 pop.	114.1
Cost of living, Dec. 2004		Computers per 100 pop.	47.1
New York = 100	85	Internet hosts per 1,000 pop.	155.6

2002 estimate.
1997

THAILAND

Area	513,115 sq km	Capital	Bangkok
Arable as % of total land	31	Currency	Baht (Bt)

People

Population	62.8m	Life expectancy: men	68.5 yrs
Pop. per sq km	122.4	women	75.0 yrs
Av. ann. growth		Adult literacy	92.6%
in pop. 2000–05	0.89%	Fertility rate (per woman)	1.9
Pop. under 15	23.8%	Urban population	31.9%
Pop. over 60	10.5%		per 1,000 pop.
No. of men per 100 women	96	Crude birth rate	17.3
Human Development Index	76.8	Crude death rate	7.2

The economy

GDP	Bt5,930bn	GDP per head	$2,280
GDP	$143.0bn	GDP per head in purchasing	
Av. ann. growth in real		power parity (USA=100)	19.7
GDP 1993–2003	3.4%	Economic freedom index	2.98

Origins of GDP		Components of GDP	
	% of total		% of total
Agriculture	10.0	Private consumption	56.7
Industry, of which:	46.4	Public consumption	10.6
manufacturing	35.2	Investment	25.0
Services	43.6	Exports	65.5
		Imports	-58.8

Structure of employment

	% of total		% of labour force
Agriculture	46	Unemployed 2003	1.5
Industry	21	Av. ann. rate 1995–2003	2.0
Services	33		

Energy

	m TOE		
Total output	45.3	Net energy imports as %	
Total consumption	83.3	of energy use	46
Consumption per head,			
kg oil equivalent	1,353		

Inflation and finance

		av. ann. increase 1998–2003	
Consumer price			
inflation 2004	2.8%	Narrow money (M1)	14.0%
Av. ann. inflation 1999–2004	1.7%	Broad money	3.8%
Money market rate, 2004	1.23%		

Exchange rates

	end 2004		December 2004
Bt per $	39.06	Effective rates	1995 = 100
Bt per SDR	60.66	– nominal	...
Bt per €	53.51	– real	...

Trade

Principal exports		Principal imports	
	$bn fob		*$bn cif*
Integrated circuits	10.6	Capital goods	33.9
Machinery & mech. appliances	10.6	Raw materials & intermediates	20.0
Computer parts	8.0	Petroleum & products	8.5
Electrical appliances	6.4	Consumer goods	7.7
Total incl. others	**80.2**	**Total incl. others**	**75.6**

Main export destinations		Main origins of imports	
	% of total		*% of total*
United States	17.0	Japan	24.1
Japan	14.2	United States	9.5
Singapore	7.3	China	8.0
China	7.1	Malaysia	6.0
Hong Kong	5.4	Singapore	4.3

Balance of payments, reserves and debt, $bn

Visible exports fob	78.1	Change in reserves	3.3
Visible imports fob	-66.9	Level of reserves	
Trade balance	11.2	end Dec.	42.2
Invisibles inflows	18.8	No. months of import cover	5.6
Invisibles outflows	-23.0	Official gold holdings, m oz	2.6
Net transfers	0.9	Foreign debt	51.8
Current account balance	8.0	– as % of GDP	41
– as % of GDP	5.6	– as % of total exports	59
Capital balance	-8.1	Debt service ratio	17
Overall balance	0.5		

Health and education

Health spending, % of GDP	4.4	Education spending, % of GDP	5.2
Doctors per 1,000 pop.	0.3	Enrolment, %: primary	98
Hospital beds per 1,000 pop.	7.4	secondary	77
Improved-water source access,		tertiary	37
% of pop.	85		

Society

No. of households	16.6m	Colour TVs per 100 households	83.2
Av. no. per household	3.7	Telephone lines per 100 pop.	10.5
Marriages per 1,000 pop.	6.6	Mobile telephone subscribers	
Divorces per 1,000 pop.	1.0	per 100 pop.	39.4
Cost of living, Dec. 2004		Computers per 100 pop.	4.0
New York = 100	59	Internet hosts per 1,000 pop.	8.2

TURKEY

Area	779,452 sq km	Capital	Ankara
Arable as % of total land	34	Currency	Turkish Lira (L)[a]

People

Population	71.3m	Life expectancy: men	67.5 yrs
Pop. per sq km	91.5	women	72.1 yrs
Av. ann. growth		Adult literacy	86.5%
in pop. 2000–05	1.40%	Fertility rate (per woman)	2.5
Pop. under 15	29.2%	Urban population	66.3%
Pop. over 60	8.0%		per 1,000 pop.
No. of men per 100 women	102	Crude birth rate	20.9
Human Development Index	75.1	Crude death rate	6.6

The economy

GDP	L359,763trn	GDP per head	$3,370
GDP	$240.4bn	GDP per head in purchasing	
Av. ann. growth in real		power parity (USA=100)	17.8
GDP 1993–2003	2.7%	Economic freedom index	3.46

Origins of GDP		**Components of GDP**	
	% of total		% of total
Agriculture	11.8	Private consumption	66.6
Industry, of which:	30.3	Public consumption	13.6
manufacturing	...	Investment	22.8
Services	57.9	Exports	27.4
		Imports	-30.7

Structure of employment

	% of total		% of labour force
Agriculture	36	Unemployed 2003	10.5
Industry	23	Av. ann. rate 1995–2003	7.9
Services	41		

Energy

	m TOE		
Total output	24.4	Net energy imports as %	
Total consumption	75.4	of energy use	68
Consumption per head,			
kg oil equivalent	1,083		

Inflation and finance

		av. ann. increase 1998–2003	
Consumer price			
inflation 2004	8.6%	Narrow money (M1)	54.2%
Av. ann. inflation 1999–2004	36.4%	Broad money	50.6%
Money market rate, 2004	21.57%		

Exchange rates[a]

	end 2004		December 2004
L per $	1,339,500	Effective rates	1995 = 100
L per SDR	2,080,257	– nominal	..
L per €	1,835,115	– real	..

Trade

Principal exports		**Principal imports**	
	$bn fob		*$bn cif*
Textiles	14.3	Machinery & transport equip.	15.8
Motor vehicles & parts	5.2	Fuels	11.4
Metals	5.1	Metals	6.8
Agricultural products	4.0	Chemicals & manufactured	
Food	1.8	goods	5.5
Total incl. others	**46.6**	Total incl. others	**65.6**

Main export destinations		**Main origins of imports**	
	% of total		*% of total*
Germany	15.9	Germany	13.7
United States	8.0	Italy	7.9
United Kingdom	7.8	Russia	7.9
Italy	6.8	France	6.0
France	6.0	United States	5.0
EU15	51.9	EU15	45.8

Balance of payments, reserves and debt, $bn

Visible exports fob	51.2	Change in reserves	7.2
Visible imports fob	-65.2	Level of reserves	
Trade balance	-14.0	end Dec.	35.5
Invisibles inflows	21.3	No. months of import cover	5.2
Invisibles outflows	-16.3	Official gold holdings, m oz	3.7
Net transfers	1.0	Foreign debt	145.7
Current account balance	-7.9	– as % of GDP	77
– as % of GDP	-3.3	– as % of total exports	232
Capital balance	7.0	Debt service ratio	45
Overall balance	4.1		

Health and education

Health spending, % of GDP	6.5	Education spending, % of GDP	3.7
Doctors per 1,000 pop.	1.2	Enrolment, %: primary	94
Hospital beds per 1,000 pop.	2.1	secondary[a]	79
Improved-water source access,		tertiary[a]	25
% of pop.	93		

Society

No. of households	14.9m	Colour TVs per 100 households	67.8
Av. no. per household	4.8	Telephone lines per 100 pop.	26.8
Marriages per 1,000 pop.	8.4	Mobile telephone subscribers	
Divorces per 1,000 pop.	0.6	per 100 pop.	39.4
Cost of living, Dec. 2004		Computers per 100 pop.	4.3
New York = 100	77	Internet hosts per 1,000 pop.	8.0

On January 1 2005 the currency dropped six noughts; L1,000,000 = YTL 1.

UKRAINE

Area	603,700 sq km	Capital	Kiev
Arable as % of total land	56	Currency	Hryvnya (UAH)

People

Population	48.5m	Life expectancy: men	60.7 yrs
Pop. per sq km	80.3	women	72.5 yrs
Av. ann. growth		Adult literacy	99.6%
in pop. 2000–05	-1.10%	Fertility rate (per woman)	1.1
Pop. under 15	14.9%	Urban population	67.2%
Pop. over 60	20.9%		per 1,000 pop.
No. of men per 100 women	85	Crude birth rate	8.4
Human Development Index	77.7	Crude death rate	16.9

The economy

GDP	UAH264bn	GDP per head	$1,020
GDP	$49.5bn	GDP per head in purchasing	
Av. ann. growth in real		power parity (USA=100)	14.4
GDP 1993–2003	-2.6%	Economic freedom index	3.21

Origins of GDP

	% of total
Agriculture	14
Industry, of which:	40
manufacturing	25
Services	46

Components of GDP

	% of total
Private consumption	69.3
Public consumption	7.9
Investment	20.0
Exports	58.7
Imports	-56.0

Structure of employment

	% of total		% of labour force
Agriculture	20	Unemployed 2003	9.1
Industry	31	Av. ann. rate 1995–2003	9.7
Services	49		

Energy

	m TOE		
Total output	71.5	Net energy imports as %	
Total consumption	130.7	of energy use	45
Consumption per head,			
kg oil equivalent	2,684		

Inflation and finance

		av. ann. increase 1998–2003	
Consumer price			
inflation 2004	9.0%	Narrow money (M1)	38.6%
Av. ann. inflation 1999–2004	10.7%	Broad money	43.4%
Money market rate, 2004	6.34%		

Exchange rates

	end 2004		December 2004
UAH per $	5.30	Effective rates	1995 = 100
UAH per SDR	8.20	– nominal	96.7
UAH per €	7.26	– real	81.4

Trade

Principal exports		Principal imports	
	$bn fob		*$bn cif*
Metals	8.5	Fuels, mineral products	8.3
Machinery & equipment	3.6	Machinery & equipment	5.7
Fuels & mineral products	3.3	Food & agricultural produce	2.2
Food & agricultural produce	2.7	Chemicals	1.8
Chemicals	1.9		
Total incl. others	**23.1**	Total incl. others	**23.0**

Main export destinations		Main origins of imports	
	% of total		*% of total*
Russia	18.7	Russia	34.0
Germany	6.2	Germany	12.9
Italy	5.5	Turkmenistan	9.9
Turkey	3.9	Italy	4.7

Balance of payments, reserves and debt, $bn

Visible exports fob	23.7	Change in reserves	2.5
Visible imports fob	-24.0	Level of reserves	
Trade balance	-0.3	end Dec.	6.9
Invisibles inflows	5.5	No. months of import cover	2.9
Invisibles outflows	-4.5	Official gold holdings, m oz	0.5
Net transfers	2.2	Foreign debt	16.3
Current account balance	2.9	– as % of GDP	38
– as % of GDP	5.8	– as % of total exports	66
Capital balance	0.2	Debt service ratio	15
Overall balance	2.2		

Health and education

Health spending, % of GDP	4.7	Education spending, % of GDP	4.2
Doctors per 1,000 pop.	3.0	Enrolment, %: primary	117
Hospital beds per 1,000 pop.	9.4	secondary	97
Improved-water source access,		tertiary	58
% of pop.	98		

Society

No. of households	19.7m	Colour TVs per 100 households	75.7
Av. no. per household	2.4	Telephone lines per 100 pop.	23.3
Marriages per 1,000 pop.	5.8	Mobile telephone subscribers	
Divorces per 1,000 pop.	3.3	per 100 pop.	13.6
Cost of living, Dec. 2004		Computers per 100 pop.	2.0
New York = 100	64	Internet hosts per 1,000 pop.	3.1

UNITED ARAB EMIRATES

Area	83,600 sq km	Capital	Abu Dhabi
Arable as % of total land	1	Currency	Dirham (AED)

People

Population	3.0m	Life expectancy: men		77.4 yrs
Pop. per sq km	35.6	women		82.2 yrs
Av. ann. growth		Adult literacy		77.3%
in pop. 2000–05	6.51%	Fertility rate (per woman)		2.5
Pop. under 15	22.0%	Urban population		85.1%
Pop. over 60	1.6%			per 1,000 pop.
No. of men per 100 women	214	Crude birth rate		16.7
Human Development Index	82.4	Crude death rate		1.3

The economy

GDP[a]	AED261bn	GDP per head	$23,650
GDP[a]	$71.0bn	GDP per head in purchasing	
Av. ann. growth in real		power parity (USA=100)	55.4
GDP 1993–2002	4.8%	Economic freedom index	2.68

Origins of GDP		Components of GDP	
	% of total		% of total
Crude oil	32	Private consumption	49.5
Manufacturing	14	Public consumption	21.5
Other	54	Investment	15.0
		Exports	86.0
		Imports	-72.1

Structure of employment

	% of total		% of labour force
Agriculture	8	Unemployed 2001	2.3
Industry	33	Av. ann. rate 1995–2001	2.1
Services	59		

Energy

			m TOE
Total output	142.1	Net energy imports as %	
Total consumption	36.1	of energy use	-294
Consumption per head,			
kg oil equivalent	9,609		

Inflation and finance

		av. ann. increase 1998–2003	
Consumer price			
inflation 2004	3.6%	Narrow money (M1)	16.0%
Av. ann. inflation 1999–2004	2.7%	Broad money	15.2%

Exchange rates

	end 2004		December 2004
AED per $	...	Effective rates	1995 = 100
AED per SDR	...	– nominal	...
AED per €	...	– real	...

Trade

Principal exports		Principal imports[b]	
	$bn fob		$bn cif
Re-exports	22.3	Consumer goods	15.2
Crude oil	22.1	Capital goods	12.6
		Intermediate goods	5.3
Total incl. others	**50.0**	**Total incl. others**	**38.1**

Main export destinations		Main origins of imports	
	% of total		% of total
Japan	27.0	China	11.4
South Korea	9.6	United States	8.0
Iran	3.9	France	7.9
Thailand	3.8	Germany	7.4

Balance of payments, reserves and debt, $bn

Visible exports fob	60.8	Change in reserves	-0.3
Visible imports fob	-41.7	Level of reserves	
Trade balance	19.1	end Dec.	15.1
Invisibles inflows	5.1	No. months of import cover	3.3
Invisibles outflows	-12.7	Official gold holdings, m oz	0.0
Net transfers	-4.7	Foreign debt	22.2
Current account balance	6.8	– as % of GDP	24.1
– as % of GDP	9.6	– as % of total exports	11.0
Capital balance[c]	-9.5	Debt service ratio	2
Overall balance[c]	0.5		

Health and education

Health spending, % of GDP	3.1	Education spending, % of GDP	1.9
Doctors per 1,000 pop.	1.8	Enrolment, %: primary	92
Hospital beds per 1,000 pop.	0.8	secondary	79
Improved-water source access,		tertiary	10
% of pop.	...		

Society

No. of households	0.6m	Colour TVs per 100 households	96.6
Av. no. per household	6.4	Telephone lines per 100 pop.	28.1
Marriages per 1,000 pop.	3.2	Mobile telephone subscribers	
Divorces per 1,000 pop.	1.1	per 100 pop.	73.6
Cost of living, Dec. 2004		Computers per 100 pop.	12.0
New York = 100	70	Internet hosts per 1,000 pop.	39.1

2002
2000
1999

UNITED KINGDOM

Area	242,534 sq km	Capital	London
Arable as % of total land	24	Currency	Pound (£)

People

Population	59.3m	Life expectancy: men		76.7 yrs
Pop. per sq km	244.5	women		81.2 yrs
Av. ann. growth		Adult literacy		99.0%
in pop. 2000–05	0.34%	Fertility rate (per woman)		1.7
Pop. under 15	17.9%	Urban population		89.1%
Pop. over 60	21.2%			per 1,000 pop.
No. of men per 100 women	96	Crude birth rate		11.0
Human Development Index	93.6	Crude death rate		10.2

The economy

GDP	£1,099bn	GDP per head	$30,280
GDP	$1,795bn	GDP per head in purchasing	
Av. ann. growth in real		power parity (USA=100)	73.4
GDP 1993–2003	2.8%	Economic freedom index	1.75

Origins of GDP		Components of GDP	
	% of total		% of total
		Private consumption	65.9
Agriculture	1.0	Private consumption	65.9
Industry, of which:	26.3	Public consumption	20.9
manufacturing	15.7	Investment	16.5
Services	72.7	Exports	25.2
		Imports	-28.2

Structure of employment

	% of total		% of labour force
Agriculture	2	Unemployed 2003	4.8
Industry	19	Av. ann. rate 1995–2003	6.2
Services	79		

Energy

	m TOE		
Total output	257.5	Net energy imports as %	
Total consumption	226.5	of energy use	-14
Consumption per head,			
kg oil equivalent	3,824		

Inflation and finance

Consumer price		av. ann. increase 1998–200	
inflation 2004	3.0%	Narrow money (M0)	7.6%
Av. ann. inflation 1999–2004	2.4%	Broad money (M4)	6.7%
Money market rate, 2004	4.29%	Household saving rate, 2003	5.8%

Exchange rates

	end 2004		December 200
			1995 = 10
£ per $	0.52	Effective rates	
£ per SDR	0.80	– nominal	96.
£ per €	0.71	– real	103.

Trade

Principal exports		Principal imports	
	$bn fob		*$bn fob*
Finished manufactured		Finished manufactured	
products	166.3	products	226.6
Semi-manufactured products	88.5	Semi-manufactured products	91.1
Fuels	26.9	Food, beverages & tobacco	34.4
Food, beverages & tobacco	17.6	Fuels	18.6
Basic materials	5.4	Basic materials	9.9
Total incl. others	**304.3**	Total incl. others	**380.6**

Main export destinations		Main origins of imports	
	% of total		*% of total*
United States	15.4	Germany	14.1
Germany	11.0	United States	9.7
France	10.0	France	8.5
Netherlands	7.2	Netherlands	6.7
Ireland	6.5		
EU15	56.0	EU15	55.0

Balance of payments, reserves and aid, $bn

Visible exports fob	308.3	Overall balance	-2.6
Visible imports fob	-385.8	Change in reserves	3.2
Trade balance	-77.5	Level of reserves	
Invisibles inflows	355.0	end Dec.	46.1
Invisibles outflows	-291.8	No. months of import cover	0.8
Net transfers	-16.1	Official gold holdings, m oz	10.1
Current account balance	-30.5	Aid given	6.28
– as % of GDP	-1.7	– as % of GDP	0.34
Capital balance	24.8		

Health and education

Health spending, % of GDP	7.7	Education spending, % of GDP	4.8
Doctors per 1,000 pop.	1.6	Enrolment, %: primary	100
Hospital beds per 1,000 pop.	3.9	secondary	179
Improved-water source access,		tertiary	64
% of pop.	100		

Society

No. of households	25.1m	Colour TVs per 100 households	98.8
Av. no. per household	2.4	Telephone lines per 100 pop.	59.1
Marriages per 1,000 pop.	5.2	Mobile telephone subscribers	
Divorces per 1,000 pop.	3.0	per 100 pop.	91.2
Cost of living, Dec. 2004		Computers per 100 pop.	40.6
New York = 100	119	Internet hosts per 1,000 pop.	75.0

UNITED STATES

Area	9,372,610 sq km	Capital	Washington DC
Arable as % of total land	19	Currency	US dollar ($)

People

Population	294.0m	Life expectancy: men	75.2 yrs
Pop. per sq km	31.4	women	80.6 yrs
Av. ann. growth		Adult literacy	99.0%
in pop. 2000–05	0.97%	Fertility rate (per woman)	2.0
Pop. under 15	20.8%	Urban population	80.1%
Pop. over 60	16.7%		per 1,000 pop.
No. of men per 100 women	97	Crude birth rate	14.5
Human Development Index	93.9	Crude death rate	8.4

The economy

GDP	$10,949bn	GDP per head	$37,240
Av. ann. growth in real		GDP per head in purchasing	
GDP 1993–2003	3.3%	power parity (USA=100)	100
		Economic freedom index	1.85

Origins of GDP		**Components of GDP**	
	% of total		% of total
Agriculture	1.0	Private consumption	70.5
Industry, of which:	18.2	Public consumption	15.6
manufacturing	12.7	Non-government investment	18.4
Services[a]	80.8	Exports	9.5
		Imports	-14.0

Structure of employment

	% of total		% of labour force
Agriculture	1	Unemployed 2003	6.0
Industry	23	Av. ann. rate 1995–2003	6.2
Services	76		

Energy

	m TOE		
Total output	1,666.1	Net energy imports as %	
Total consumption	2,290.4	of energy use	2
Consumption per head,			
kg oil equivalent	7,943		

Inflation and finance

		av. ann. increase 1998–2003	
Consumer price			
inflation 2004	2.7%	Narrow money (M1)	6.1%
Av. ann. inflation 1999–2004	2.5%	Broad money	7.0%
Money market rate, 2004	1.35%	Household saving rate, 2003	1.4%

Exchange rates

	end 2004		December 2004
$ per SDR	1.55	Effective rates	1995 = 100
$ per €	1.40	– nominal	78
		– real	81

Trade

Principal exports

	$bn fob
Capital goods, excl. vehicles	293.0
Industrial supplies	172.9
Consumer goods, excl. vehicles	89.9
Vehicles & products	80.1
Food & beverages	55.1
Total incl. others	**724.8**

Principal imports

	$bn fob
Consumer goods, excl. vehicles	333.8
Industrial supplies	316.5
Capital goods, excl. vehicles	295.7
Vehicles & products	210.4
Food & beverages	55.8
Total incl. others	**1,257.1**

Main export destinations

	% of total
Canada	23.4
Mexico	13.5
Japan	7.2
United Kingdom	4.7
Germany	4.0
EU15	20.8

Main origins of imports

	% of total
Canada	17.8
China	12.1
Mexico	11.0
Japan	9.4
Germany	5.4
EU15	19.4

Balance of payments, reserves and aid, $bn

Visible exports fob	716.4	Overall balance	-1.5
Visible imports fob	-1,260.7	Change in reserves	26.3
Trade balance	-544.3	Level of reserves	
Invisibles inflows	598.5	end Dec.	184.0
Invisibles outflows	-517.4	No. months of import cover	1.2
Net transfers	-67.4	Official gold holdings, m oz	261.6
Current account balance	-530.7	Aid given	16.25
– as % of GDP	-4.8	– as % of GDP	0.15
Capital balance	541.2		

Health and education

Health spending, % of GDP	14.6	Education spending, % of GDP	5.7
Doctors per 1,000 pop.	2.8	Enrolment, %: primary	98
Hospital beds per 1,000 pop.	3.0	secondary	94
Improved-water source access,		tertiary	81
% of pop.	100		

Society

No. of households	109.3m	Colour TVs per 100 households	99.5
Av. no. per household	2.6	Telephone lines per 100 pop.	62.4
Marriages per 1,000 pop.	8.3	Mobile telephone subscribers	
Divorces per 1,000 pop.	4.8	per 100 pop.	54.6
Cost of living, Dec. 2004		Computers per 100 pop.	66.0
New York = 100	100	Internet hosts per 1,000 pop.[b]	680.4

---

a Including utilities.
b Includes all hosts ending ".com", ".net" and ".org" which exaggerates the numbers.

VENEZUELA

Area	912,050 sq km	Capital	Caracas
Arable as % of total land	3	Currency	Bolivar (Bs)

People

Population	25.7m	Life expectancy:	men	70.9 yrs
Pop. per sq km	28.2		women	76.8 yrs
Av. ann. growth		Adult literacy		93.0%
in pop. 2000–05	1.82%	Fertility rate (per woman)		2.7
Pop. under 15	31.2%	Urban population		87.7%
Pop. over 60	7.6%			per 1,000 pop.
No. of men per 100 women	101	Crude birth rate		22.8
Human Development Index	77.8	Crude death rate		5.0

The economy

GDP	Bs137,368bn	GDP per head	$3,320
GDP	$85.4bn	GDP per head in purchasing	
Av. ann. growth in real		power parity (USA=100)	12.6
GDP 1993–2003	-1.2%	Economic freedom index	4.09

Origins of GDP		Components of GDP	
	% of total		% of total
Agriculture	5.7	Private consumption	67.8
Industry, of which:	47.1	Public consumption	7.5
manufacturing	16.2	Investment	9.2
Services	47.2	Exports	30.6
		Imports	-15.0

Structure of employment[b]

	% of total		% of labour force
Agriculture	10	Unemployed 2002	15.8
Industry	22	Av. ann. rate 1995–2002	12.8
Services	68		

Energy

	m TOE		
Total output	210.2	Net energy imports as %	
Total consumption	54.0	of energy use	-289
Consumption per head,			
kg oil equivalent	2,141		

Inflation and finance

Consumer price		av. ann. increase 1998–2003	
inflation 2004	21.8%	Narrow money (M1)	29.9%
Av. ann. inflation 1999–2004	20.6%	Broad money	25.6%
Money market rate, 2004	4.38%		

Exchange rates

	end 2004		December 2004
Bs per $	1,918	Effective rates	1995 = 100
Bs per SDR	2,979	– nominal	31.0
Bs per €	2,628	– real	66.0

Trade

Principal exports		Principal imports	
	$bn fob		*$bn fob*
Oil	20.8	Non-oil	8.8
Non-oil	2.8	Oil	1.5
Total incl. others	**24.0**	Total incl. others	**14.8**

Main export destinations		Main origins of imports	
	% of total		*% of total*
United States	69.6	United States	33.7
Dominican Rep	3.9	Colombia	12.8
Colombia	3.8	Brazil	10.0
Brazil	2.8	Mexico	7.0

Balance of payments, reserves and debt, $bn

Visible exports fob	27.2	Change in reserves	8.7
Visible imports fob	-10.7	Level of reserves	
Trade balance	16.5	end Dec.	20.8
Invisibles inflows	2.6	No. months of import cover	13.6
Invisibles outflows	-7.7	Official gold holdings, m oz	11.5
Net transfers	0.0	Foreign debt	34.8
Current account balance	11.4	– as % of GDP	35
– as % of GDP	13.4	– as % of total exports	117
Capital balance	-4.9	Debt service ratio	30
Overall balance	5.5		

Health and education

Health spending, % of GDP	4.9	Education spending, % of GDP	...
Doctors per 1,000 pop.	2.0	Enrolment, %: primary	106
Hospital beds per 1,000 pop.	1.9	secondary	70
Improved-water source access,		tertiary	27
% of pop.	83		

Society

No. of households	5.5m	Colour TVs per 100 households	93.9
Av. no. per household	4.6	Telephone lines per 100 pop.	11.1
Marriages per 1,000 pop.	4.1	Mobile telephone subscribers	
Divorces per 1,000 pop.	0.9	per 100 pop.	27.3
Cost of living, Dec. 2004		Computers per 100 pop.	6.1
New York = 100	53	Internet hosts per 1,000 pop.	1.7

VIETNAM

Area	331,114 sq km	Capital	Hanoi
Arable as % of total land	21	Currency	Dong (D)

People

Population	81.4m	Life expectancy: men	69.9 yrs
Pop. per sq km	245.8	women	73.9 yrs
Av. ann. growth		Adult literacy	90.3%
in pop. 2000–05	1.37%	Fertility rate (per woman)	2.3
Pop. under 15	29.5%	Urban population	25.7%
Pop. over 60	7.5%		per 1,000 pop.
No. of men per 100 women	100	Crude birth rate	20.2
Human Development Index	69.1	Crude death rate	5.8

The economy

GDP	D606trn	GDP per head	$480
GDP	$39.2bn	GDP per head in purchasing	
Av. ann. growth in real		power parity (USA=100)	6.6
GDP 1993–2003	7.4%	Economic freedom index	3.83

Origins of GDP		Components of GDP	
	% of total		% of total
Agriculture	21.8	Private consumption	64.8
Industry, of which:	38.5	Public consumption	6.9
manufacturing	21.0	Investment	35.1
Services	39.7	Exports	59.1
		Imports	68.0

Structure of employment

	% of total		% of labour force
Agriculture	63	Unemployed 2003	2.3
Industry	16	Av. ann. rate 1995–2003	...
Services	21		

Energy

	m TOE		
Total output	53.4	Net energy imports as %	
Total consumption	42.6	of energy use	-25
Consumption per head,			
kg oil equivalent	530		

Inflation and finance

		av. ann. increase 1998–2003	
Consumer price			
inflation 2004	7.8%	Narrow money (M1)	28.3
Av. ann. inflation 1999–2004	2.5%	Broad money	34.0
Treasury bill rate, Oct 2004	5.85%		

Exchange rates

	end 2004		December 2004
D per $	15,788	Effective rates	1995 = 100
D per SDR	24,669	– nominal	...
D per €	21,630	– real	...

Trade

Principal exports		Principal imports	
	$bn fob		*$bn cif*
Crude oil	3.8	Machinery & spare parts	5.3
Textiles & garments	3.6	Petroleum products	2.4
Footwear	2.3	Textiles	2.0
Fisheries products	2.2	Steel	1.6
Rice	0.7	Electronic goods	1.0
Total incl. others	20.2	Total incl. others	24.9

Main export destinations		Main origins of imports	
	% of total		*% of total*
United States	22.1	China	14.1
Japan	14.5	South Korea	12.0
Australia	7.7	Japan	11.4
China	6.6	Singapore	10.7
Germany	6.0	United States	5.9
Singapore	4.6	Thailand	5.6
United Kingdom	4.5	Hong Kong	4.3

Balance of payments[a], reserves and debt, $bn

Visible exports fob	16.7	Change in reserves	2.1
Visible imports fob	-17.8	Level of reserves	
Trade balance	-1.1	end Dec.	6.4
Invisibles inflows	3.1	No. months of import cover	2.6
Invisibles outflows	-4.6	Official gold holdings, m oz	0.0
Net transfers	1.9	Foreign debt	15.8
Current account balance[b]	-0.6	– as % of GDP	45
– as % of GDP[b]	-1.5	– as % of total exports	77
Capital balance	2.1	Debt service ratio	4
Overall balance	0.4		

Health and education

Health spending, % of GDP	5.2	Education spending, % of GDP	...
Doctors per 1,000 pop.	0.5	Enrolment, %: primary	103
Hospital beds per 1,000 pop.	2.8	secondary	72
Improved-water source access,		tertiary	10
% of pop.	73		

Society

No. of households	23.8m	Colour TVs per 100 households	40.0
Av. no. per household	3.4	Telephone lines per 100 pop.	5.4
Marriages per 1,000 pop.	12.1	Mobile telephone subscribers	
Divorces per 1,000 pop.	0.5	per 100 pop.	3.4
Cost of living, Dec. 2004		Computers per 100 pop.	1.0
New York = 100	65	Internet hosts per 1,000 pop.	...

a 2002
b 2003

ZIMBABWE

Area	390,759 sq km	Capital	Harare
Arable as % of total land	8	Currency	Zimbabwe dollar (Z$)

People

Population	12.9m	Life expectancy: men		38.2 yrs
Pop. per sq km	33.0		women	36.3 yrs
Av. ann. growth		Adult literacy		90%
in pop. 2000–05	0.65%	Fertility rate (per woman)		3.6
Pop. under 15	40.0%	Urban population		34.9%
Pop. over 60	5.4%			per 1,000 pop.
No. of men per 100 women	98	Crude birth rate		32.1
Human Development Index	49.1	Crude death rate		23.0

The economy

GDPª	Z$977bn	GDP per head	$1,380
GDPª	$17.8bn	GDP per head in purchasing	
Av. ann. growth in real		power parity (USA=100)	5.8
GDP 1993–2002	0.5%	Economic freedom index	4.36

Origins of GDPª		**Components of GDPᵇ**	
	% of total		% of total
Agriculture	17.3	Private consumption	71.7
Industry, of which:	29.0	Public consumption	15.4
manufacturing	18.3	Investment	13.5
Services	53.7	Net exports	-0.6

Structure of employment

	% of total		% of labour force
Agriculture	...	Unemployed 1999	6
Industry	...	Av. ann. rate 1995–99	6.5
Services	...		

Energy

	m TOE		
Total output	8.5	Net energy imports as %	
Total consumption	9.8	of energy use	13
Consumption per head,			
kg oil equivalent	751		

Inflation and finance

Consumer price		av. ann. increase 1998–2003	
inflation 2002	140.1%	Narrow money (M1)	139.8%
Av. ann. inflation 1999–2002	87.7%	Broad money	140.9%
Money market rate, 2004	130.4%		

Exchange rates

	end 2004		December 2004
Z$ per $	5,609	Effective rates	1995 = 100
Z$ per SDR	8,764	– nominal	..
Z$ per €	7,684	– real	...

Trade

Principal exports[c]		**Principal imports**[c]	
	$m fob		*$m cif*
Tobacco	321	Machinery & transport	
Gold	137	equipment	342
Horticulture	118	Chemicals	329
Ferro-alloys	105	Food	281
Nickel	78	Manufactured products	220
Total incl. others	**1,225**	Total incl. others	**1,627**

Main export destinations		**Main origins of imports**	
	% of total		*% of total*
South Africa	12.2	South Africa	51.1
China	10.6	Congo	6.1
Germany	10.0	Germany	2.9
Japan	8.6	United Kingdom	2.6
Netherlands	7.4	Mozambique	2.3

Balance of payments[c], reserves and debt, $bn

Visible exports fob	1.3	Change in reserves[a]	0.0
Visible imports fob	-1.6	Level of reserves[a]	
Trade balance	-0.3	end Dec.	0.1
Net invisibles outflows	-0.5	No. months of import cover[a]	0.6
Net transfers	0.5	Official gold holdings, m oz[a]	0.1
Current account balance	-0.3	Foreign debt	4.4
– as % of GDP	-1.7	– as % of GDP	50
Capital balance[d]	-0.4	– as % of total exports	274
Overall balance[d]	-0.4	Debt service ratio	3

Health and education

Health spending, % of GDP	8.5	Education spending, % of GDP	4.7
Doctors per 1,000 pop.	0.1	Enrolment, %: primary	94
Hospital beds per 1,000 pop.	...	secondary	36
Improved-water source access,		tertiary	4
% of pop.	83		

Society

No. of households	3.2m	Colour TVs per 100 households	2.1
Av. no. per household	4.1	Telephone lines per 100 pop.	2.6
Marriages per 1,000 pop.	...	Mobile telephone subscribers	
Divorces per 1,000 pop.	...	per 100 pop.	3.2
Cost of living, Dec. 2004		Computers per 100 pop.	5.3
New York = 100	...	Internet hosts per 1,000 pop.	0.5

a 2002
b 2000
c Estimates.
d 2001 estimates.

EURO AREA[a]

Area	2,497,000 sq km	Capital	–
Arable as % of total land	26	Currency	Euro (€)

People

Population	306.4m	Life expectancy: men	76.6 yrs
Pop. per sq km	122.7	women	82.8 yrs
Av. ann. growth		Adult literacy	98.3%
in pop. 2000–05	0.4%	Fertility rate (per woman)	1.5
Pop. under 15	16.2%	Urban population	78.0%
Pop. over 60	21.9%		per 1,000 pop.
No. of men per 100 women	96	Crude birth rate	9.9
Human Development Index	92.5	Crude death rate[b]	10.1

The economy

GDP	€7,243bn	GDP per head	$26,750
GDP	$8,175bn	GDP per head in purchasing	
Av. ann. growth in real		power parity (USA=100)	69.8
GDP 1993–2003	2.1%	Economic freedom index	2.26

Origins of GDP

	% of total
Agriculture	2
Industry, of which:	28
manufacturing	20
Services	70

Components of GDP

	% of total
Private consumption	57.3
Public consumption	20.7
Investment	19.9
Exports	35.7
Imports	-33.6

Structure of employment

	% of total		% of labour force
Agriculture	4.5	Unemployed 2003	8.9
Industry	29.6	Av. ann. rate 1995–2002	9.5
Services	65.9		

Energy

	m TOE		
Total output	466.9	Net energy imports as %	
Total consumption	1,192.1	of energy use	63
Consumption per head,			
kg oil equivalent	3,895		

Inflation and finance

			av. ann. increase 1998–2003
Consumer price			
inflation 2004	2.1%	Narrow money (M1)	8.9%
Av. ann. inflation 1999–2004	2.2%	Broad money	6.7%
Interbank rate, 2004	2.11%	Household saving rate, 2003	11.0%

Exchange rates

	end 2004		December 2004
€ per $	0.73	Effective rates	1995 = 100
€ per SDR	1.14	– nominal	121.2
		– real	115.4

Trade[b]

Principal exports

	$bn fob
Machinery & transport equip.	450
Manufactures	260
Chemicals	160
Food, drink & tobacco	55
Energy and raw materials	46
Total incl. others	**998**

Principal imports

	$bn cif
Machinery & transport equip.	368
Manufactures	279
Energy	219
Chemicals	90
Food, drink & tobacco	64
Total incl. others	**801**

Main export destinations

	% of total
United States	26.0
Switzerland	8.1
Japan	4.7
Poland	4.7
China	3.9
Russia	3.3

Main origins of imports

	% of total
United States	17.3
Japan	11.0
China	7.6
Switzerland	6.4
Russia	6.0
Norway	5.6

Balance of payments, reserves and aid, $bn

Visible exports fob	1,176.6	Overall balance	-35.1
Visible imports fob	-1,056.9	Change in reserves	3.2
Trade balance	119.7	Level of reserves	
Invisibles inflows	629.7	end Dec.	386.9
Invisibles outflows	-659.7	No. months of import cover	2.7
Net transfers	-64.3	Official gold holdings, m oz	393.5
Current account balance	25.5	Aid given	26.70
– as % of GDP	0.3	– as % of GDP	0.40
Capital balance	-39.6		

Health and education

Health spending, % of GDP	9.4	Education spending, % of GDP	4.81
Doctors per 1,000 pop.	3.5	Enrolment, %: primary	104
Hospital beds per 1,000 pop.	8.0	secondary	106
Improved-water source access, % of pop.	...	tertiary	54

Society

No. of households	127.4m	Colour TVs per 100 households	95.3
Av. no. per household	2.41	Telephone lines per 100 pop.	51.9
Marriages per 1,000 pop.	4.8	Mobile telephone subscribers	
Divorces per 1,000 pop.	1.7	per 100 pop.	81.4
Cost of living, Dec. 2004		Computers per 100 pop.	38.7
New York = 100	...	Internet hosts per 1,000 pop.	106.5

Data refer to the 12 EU members that have adopted the euro.
EU25 data.

WORLD

Area	148,698,382 sq km	Capital	..
Arable as % of total land	10.8	Currency	..

People

Population	6,301.5m	Life expectancy: men	64.3 yrs
Pop. per sq km	42.4	women	68.7 yrs
Av. ann. growth		Adult literacy	79.0%
in pop. 2000–05	1.21%	Fertility rate (per woman)	2.7
Pop. under 15	28.2%	Urban population	48.0%
Pop. over 60	10.4%		per 1,000 pop.
No. of men per 100 women	101	Crude birth rate	21.3
Human Development Index	72.9	Crude death rate	8.9

The economy

GDP	$36.3trn	GDP per head	$5,760
Av. ann. growth in real		GDP per head in purchasing	
GDP 1993–2003	3.6%	power parity (USA=100)	21.
		Economic freedom index	3.2

Origins of GDP		Components of GDP	
	% of total		% of total
Agriculture	4	Private consumption	6
Industry, of which:	28	Public consumption	1
manufacturing	18	Investment	2
Services	68	Exports	2
		Imports	-2

Structure of employment[a]

	% of total		% of labour force
Agriculture	4	Unemployed 2003	7.
Industry	26	Av. ann. rate 1995–2003	6.
Services	70		

Energy

	m TOE		
Total output	10,274.6	Net energy imports as %	
Total consumption	10,196.8	of energy use	-
Consumption per head,			
kg oil equivalent	1,699		

Inflation and finance[a]

		av. ann. increase 1998–200	
Consumer price			
inflation 2004	3.5%	Narrow money (M0)	6.1
Av. ann. inflation 1999–2004	3.8%	Broad money	9.1
LIBOR $ rate, 3-month, 2004	1.62%	Household saving rate, 2003	5.7

Trade

World exports

	$bn fob		$bn fob
Manufactures	5,836	Ores & metals	227
Food	606	Agricultural raw materials	152
Fuels	531	Total incl. others	**7,579**

Main export destinations

	% of total
United States	16.3
Germany	7.9
France	5.2
United Kingdom	5.2
Japan	4.6

Main origins of imports

	% of total
United States	10.0
Germany	9.5
China	7.9
Japan	6.7
France	4.7

Balance of payments, reserves and aid, $bn

Visible exports fob	7,443	Overall balance	0
Visible imports fob	-7,377	Change in reserves	694
Trade balance	67	Level of reserves	
Invisibles inflows	3,282	end Dec.	3,537
Invisibles outflows	-3,353	No. months of import cover	4
Net transfers	-32	Official gold holdings, m oz	913.1
Current account balance	-37	Aid given[b]	72.4
– as % of GDP	-0.1	– as % of GDP[b]	0.25
Capital balance	29		

Health and education

Health spending, % of GDP	10.6	Education spending, % of GDP	4.5
Doctors per 1,000 pop.	...	Enrolment, %: primary	103
Hospital beds per 1,000 pop.	...	secondary	70
Improved-water source access, % of pop.	82	tertiary	24

Society

No. of households	...	TVs per 100 households	...
Av. no. per household	...	Telephone lines per 100 pop.	18.7
Marriages per 1,000 pop.	...	Mobile telephone subscribers	
Divorces per 1,000 pop.	...	per 100 pop.	22.9
Cost of living, Dec. 2004		Computers per 100 pop.	10.1
New York = 100	...	Internet hosts per 1,000 pop.	50.3

OECD countries.
OECD and Middle East countries.

Glossary

Balance of payments The record of a country's transactions with the rest of the world. The **current account** of the balance of payments consists of: visible trade (goods); "invisible" trade (services and income); private transfer payments (eg, remittances from those working abroad); official transfers (eg, payments to international organisations, famine relief). Visible imports and exports are normally compiled on rather different definitions to those used in the trade statistics (shown in principal imports and exports) and therefore the statistics do not match. The **capital account** consists of long- and short-term transactions relating to a country's assets and liabilities (eg, loans and borrowings). The current account and the capital account, plus an errors and omissions item, make up the **overall balance**. In the country pages of this book this item is included in the overall balance. **Changes in reserves** include gold at market prices and are shown without the practice often followed in balance of payments presentations of reversing the sign.

Body-mass index A measure for assessing obesity – weight in kilograms divided by height in metres squared. An index of 30 or more is regarded as an indicator of obesity; 25 to 29.9 as over-weight. Guidelines vary for men and for women and may be adjusted for age.

CFA Communauté Financière Africaine. Its members, most of the francophone African nations, share a common currency, the CFA franc, which used to be pegged to the French franc but is now pegged to the euro.

Cif/fob Measures of the value of merchandise trade. Imports include the cost of "carriage, insurance and freight" (cif) from the exporting country to the importing. The value of exports does not include these elements and is recorded "free on board" (fob). Balance of payments statistics are generally adjusted so that both exports and imports are shown fob; the cif elements are included in invisibles.

Commonwealth of Independent States All former Soviet Union Republics, excluding Estonia, Latvia and Lithuania. It was established January 1 1992; Azerbaijan joined in September 1993 and Georgia in December 1993.

Crude birth rate The number of live births in a year per 1,000 population. The crude birth rate will automatically be relatively high if a large proportion of the population is of childbearing age.

Crude death rate The number of deaths in a year per 1,000 population. Also affected by the population's age structure.

Debt, foreign Financial obligations owed by a country to the rest of the world and repayable in foreign currency. **The debt service ratio** is debt service (principal repayments plus interest payments) expressed as a percentage of the country's earnings from exports of goods and services.

EU European Union. Members are: Austria, Belgium, Denmark, Finland, France, Germany, Greece, Ireland, Italy, Luxembourg, Netherlands, Portugal, Spain, Sweden and the United Kingdom and, as of May 1 2004, Cyprus, Czech Republic, Estonia, Hungary, Latvia, Lithuania, Malta, Poland, Slovakia and Slovenia.

Effective exchange rate The nominal index measures a currency's depreciation (figures below 100) or appreciation (figures over 100) from a base date against a trade-weighted basket of the currencies of the country's main trading partners. The real effective exchange rate reflects adjustments for relative movements in prices or costs.

Euro area The 12 euro area members of the EU are Austria, Belgium, Finland, France, Germany, Greece, Ireland, Italy,

Luxembourg, Netherlands, Portugal and Sweden. Their common currency is the euro, which came into circulation on January 1 2002.

Fertility rate The average number of children born to a woman who completes her childbearing years.

GDP Gross domestic product. The sum of all output produced by economic activity within a country. GNP (gross national product) and GNI (gross national income) include net income from abroad eg, rent, profits.

Household saving rate Household savings as % of disposable household income.

Import cover The number of months of imports covered by reserves, ie reserves ÷ $1/12$ annual imports (visibles and invisibles).

Inflation The annual rate at which prices are increasing. The most common measure and the one shown here is the increase in the consumer price index.

Internet hosts Websites and other computers that sit permanently on the internet.

Life expectancy The average length of time a baby born today can expect to live.

Literacy is defined by UNESCO as the ability to read and write a simple sentence, but definitions can vary from country to country.

Median age Divides the age distribution into two halves. Half of the population is above and half below the median age.

Money supply A measure of the "money" available to buy goods and services. Various definitions exist. The measures shown here are based on definitions used by the IMF and may differ from measures used nationally. Narrow money (M1)

consists of cash in circulation and demand deposits (bank deposits that can be withdrawn on demand). "Quasi-money" (time, savings and foreign currency deposits) is added to this to create broad money.

OECD Organisation for Economic Co-operation and Development. The "rich countries" club was established in 1961 to promote economic growth and the expansion of world trade. It is based in Paris and now has 30 members.

Opec Organisation of Petroleum Exporting Countries. Set up in 1960 and based in Vienna, Opec is mainly concerned with oil pricing and production issues. Members are; Algeria, Indonesia, Iran, Iraq, Kuwait, Libya, Nigeria, Qatar, Saudi Arabia, United Arab Emirates and Venezuela.

PPP Purchasing power parity. PPP statistics adjust for cost of living differences by replacing normal exchange rates with rates designed to equalise the prices of a standard "basket"of goods and services. These are used to obtain PPP estimates of GDP per head. PPP estimates are shown on an index, taking the United States as 100.

Real terms Figures adjusted to exclude the effect of inflation.

Reserves The stock of gold and foreign currency held by a country to finance any calls that may be made for the settlement of foreign debt.

SDR Special drawing right. The reserve currency, introduced by the IMF in 1970, was intended to replace gold and national currencies in settling international transactions. The IMF uses SDRs for book-keeping purposes and issues them to member countries. Their value is based on a basket of the US dollar (with a weight of 45%), the euro (29%), the Japanese yen (15%) and the pound sterling (11%).

List of countries

Whenever data is available, the world rankings consider 182
countries: all those which had (in 2003) or have recently had a
population of at least 1m or a GDP of at least $1bn. Here is a list of
them.

	Population	GDP	GDP per head	Area	Median age
	m	$bn	$PPP	'000 sq km	years
Afghanistan	23.9	4.7	800[a]	652	16.7
Albania	3.2	6.1	4,710	29	28.3
Algeria	31.8	66.0	5,930	2,382	24.0
Andorra	0.1	1.3[ab]	18790[a]	0.4	37.0
Angola	13.6	13.2	1,910	1,247	16.6
Argentina	38.4	129.7	11,410	2,767	28.9
Armenia	3.1	2.8	3,790	30	31.7
Aruba	0.1	1.9[b]	28,000[a]	0.2	34.0
Australia	19.7	518.4	28,780	7,682	36.6
Austria	8.1	251.5	29,740	84	40.6
Azerbaijan	8.4	7.1	3,390	87	27.5
Bahamas	0.3	5.3	16,140[b]	14	27.6
Bahrain	0.7	7.7[b]	16,180[b]	1	29.8
Bangladesh	146.7	51.9	1,870	144	22.1
Barbados	0.3	2.6	15,060	0.4	34.7
Belarus	9.9	17.5	6,050	208	37.8
Belgium	10.3	302.2	28,920	31	40.6
Benin	6.7	3.5	1,110	113	17.6
Bermuda	0.1	2.3[a]	35,940[a]	1	36.0
Bhutan	2.3	0.6	630[a]	47	20.1
Bolivia	8.8	8.0	2,490	1,099	20.8
Bosnia	4.2	7.0	6,250	51	38.0
Botswana	1.8	7.4	8,370	581	19.9
Brazil	178.5	492.3	7,510	8,512	26.8
Brunei	0.4	6.5[ab]	18,160[ab]	6	26.2
Bulgaria	7.9	19.9	7,540	111	40.6
Burkina Faso	13.0	4.2	1,170	274	16.2
Burundi	6.8	0.7	630	28	17.0
Cambodia	14.1	4.3	2,000	181	20.3
Cameroon	16.0	12.4	1,990	475	18.8
Canada	31.5	834.4	30,040	9,971	38.6
Cayman Islands	0.0[d]	1.3[a]	30,950[a]	0.3	34.0
Central African Rep	3.9	1.2	1,080	622	18.1
Chad	8.6	2.6	1,080	1,284	16.3
Channel Islands	0.1	3.5[ab]	23,300[ab]	0.2	39.7
Chile	15.8	72.4	9,810	757	30.6
China	1,304.2	1,409.9	4,980	9,561	32.6
Colombia	44.2	77.6	6,410	1,142	25.4
Congo-Kinshasa	52.8	5.6	660	2,345	16.3
Congo-Brazzaville	3.7	3.5	730	342	16.3

	Population	GDP	GDP per head	Area	Median age
	m	$bn	$PPP	'000 sq km	years
Costa Rica	4.2	17.5	9,140	51	26.1
Côte d'Ivoire	16.6	13.7	1,400	322	18.5
Croatia	4.4	28.3	10,610	57	40.6
Cuba	11.3	33.9ab	3,000 a	111	35.6
Cyprus	0.8	11.4	19,600	9	35.3
Czech Republic	10.2	85.4	15,600	79	39.0
Denmark	5.4	212.4	31,050	43	39.5
Dominican Republic	8.7	15.9	6,310	48	23.3
Ecuador	13.0	26.9	3,440	272	24.0
Egypt	71.9	82.4	3,940	1,000	22.8
El Salvador	6.5	14.4	4,910	21	23.3
Equatorial Guinea	0.5	2.9	5,100b	28	17.6
Eritrea	4.1	0.7	1,020	117	17.4
Estonia	1.3	8.4	12,680	45	38.9
Ethiopia	70.7	6.6	710	1,134	17.5
Faroe Islands	0.0d	1.0ab	21,600a	1	34.0
Fiji	0.8	2.3	5,650	18	24.5
Finland	5.2	161.5	27,460	338	40.9
France	60.1	1,748.0c	27,640c	544	39.3
French Polynesia	0.2	3.4b	24,620b	3	26.9
Gabon	1.3	5.6	5,500	268	19.4
Gambia, The	1.4	0.4	1,740	11	19.8
Georgia	5.1	3.9	2,610	70	35.5
Germany	82.5	2,400.7	27,610	358	42.1
Ghana	20.9	7.7	2,190	239	19.8
Greece	11.0	173.0	19,900	132	39.7
Greenland	0.1	1.1ab	19,640ab	2,176	31.0
Guadeloupe	0.4	3.5a	7,960a	2	34.1
Guam	0.2	3.2ab	19,750ac	1	28.1
Guatemala	12.3	24.7	4,090	109	18.1
Guinea	8.5	3.6	2,080	246	18.0
Guinea-Bissau	1.5	0.2	680	36	16.2
Haiti	8.3	2.7	1,730	28	20.0
Honduras	6.9	7.0	2,590	112	19.8
Hong Kong	7.0	158.6	28,680	1	38.9
Hungary	9.9	82.8	13,840	93	38.8
Iceland	0.3	10.5	30,570	103	34.1
India	1,065.5	599.0	2,880	3,287	24.3
Indonesia	219.9	208.3	3,210	1,904	26.5
Iran	68.9	136.8	7,000	1,648	23.4
Iraq	25.2	19.9a	2,230a	438	19.1

	Population	GDP	GDP per head	Area	Median age
	m	$bn	$PPP	'000 sq km	years
Ireland	4.0	148.6	30,910	70	34.2
Israel	6.4	110.2	19,440	21	28.9
Italy	57.4	1,465.9	26,830	301	42.3
Jamaica	2.7	7.8	3,790	11	24.9
Japan	127.7	4,326.4	28,450	378	42.9
Jordan	5.5	9.9	4,290	89	21.3
Kazakhstan	15.4	29.7	6,280	2,717	29.4
Kenya	32.0	13.8	1,030	583	17.9
Kirgizstan	5.1	1.7	1,690	583	23.8
Kuwait	2.5	41.7	19,480	18	29.5
Laos	5.7	2.0	1,730	237	19.1
Latvia	2.3	9.7	10,210	64	39.5
Lebanon	3.7	19.0	4,840	10	26.8
Lesotho	1.8	1.1	3,100	30	19.2
Liberia	3.4	0.4	900[a]	111	16.3
Libya	5.6	19.1[b]	9,910[a]	1,760	23.9
Lithuania	3.4	18.2	11,390	65	37.8
Luxembourg	0.5	26.2	55,500	3	38.1
Macau	0.4	7.9	21,950[b]	0.02	36.6
Macedonia	2.1	4.7	6,750	26	34.2
Madagascar	17.4	5.5	800	587	17.8
Malawi	12.1	1.8	590	118	16.3
Malaysia	24.4	103.2	8,970	333	24.7
Mali	13.0	4.3	960	1,240	15.8
Malta	0.4	4.8	17,780	0.3	38.1
Martinique	0.4	6.1[a]	15,570[a]	1	36.4
Mauritania	2.9	1.1	1,870	1,031	18.4
Mauritius	1.2	5.2	11,280	2	30.4
Mexico	103.5	626.1	8,980	1,973	25.0
Moldova	4.3	2.0	1,760	34	33.0
Mongolia	2.6	1.2	1,820	1,565	23.7
Morocco	30.6	44.5	3,940	447	24.2
Mozambique	18.9	4.3	1,060	799	17.7
Myanmar	49.5	74.5[a]	700[a]	677	25.5
Namibia	2.0	4.7	6,660	824	18.6
Nepal	25.2	5.8	1,420	147	20.1
Netherlands	16.1	511.6	28,560	42	39.3
Netherlands Antilles	0.2	2.5[a]	11,140[a]	1	36.2
New Caledonia	0.2	2.7[b]	22,190[b]	19	28.4
New Zealand	3.9	76.3	21,350	271	35.8
Nicaragua	5.5	4.1	3,180	130	19.7
Niger	12.0	2.7	830	1,267	15.5

	Population	GDP	GDP per head	Area	Median age
	m	$bn	$PPP	'000 sq km	years
Nigeria	124.0	50.2	900	924	17.5
North Korea	22.7	29.6[a]	1,300[a]	121	31.1
Norway	4.5	221.6	37,910	324	38.2
Oman	2.9	21.7	13,000[b]	310	22.3
Pakistan	153.6	68.8	2,040	804	20.0
Panama	3.1	12.9	6,420	77	26.1
Papua New Guinea	5.7	3.4	2,250	463	19.7
Paraguay	5.9	5.8	4,690	407	20.8
Peru	27.2	61.0	5,080	1,285	24.2
Philippines	80.0	80.6	4,640	300	22.2
Poland	38.6	209.6	11,210	313	36.5
Portugal	10.1	149.5	17,710	89	39.5
Puerto Rico	3.9	67.9[b]	16,210[b]	9	33.3
Qatar	0.6	17.5[b]	23,200[a]	11	30.9
Réunion	0.8	4.3[a]	5,750[a]	3	29.3
Romania	22.3	60.4	7,140	238	36.7
Russia	143.2	433.5	8,950	17,075	37.3
Rwanda	8.4	1.6	1,290	26	17.5
Saudi Arabia	24.2	214.7	13,230	2,200	21.6
Senegal	10.1	6.5	1,620	197	18.2
Serbia & Montenegro	10.5	19.2	1,910[a]	102	36.5
Sierra Leone	5.0	0.8	530	72	18.4
Singapore	4.3	91.3	24,180	1	37.5
Slovakia	5.4	31.9	13,440	49	35.6
Slovenia	2.0	26.3	19,100	20	40.2
Somalia	9.9	4.4[a]	440[a]	638	17.9
South Africa	45.0	159.9	10,130	1,226	23.5
South Korea	47.7	605.3	18,000	99	35.1
Spain	41.1	836.1	22,150	505	38.6
Sri Lanka	19.1	18.5	3,740	66	29.6
Sudan	33.6	17.8	1,760	2,506	20.1
Suriname	0.4	1.0	2,280[a]	164	25.1
Swaziland	1.1	1.8	4,850	17	18.1
Sweden	8.9	300.8	26,710	450	40.1
Switzerland	7.2	309.5	32,220	41	40.8
Syria	17.8	21.5	3,430	185	20.6
Taiwan	22.6	286.2	24,650[a]	36	31.0
Tajikistan	6.2	1.3	1,040	143	19.3
Tanzania	37.0	9.9	620	945	18.2
Thailand	62.8	143.2	7,450	513	30.5
Togo	4.9	1.8	1,640	57	17.9

	Population	GDP	GDP per head	Area	Median age
	m	*$bn*	*$PPP*	*'000 sq km*	*years*
Trinidad & Tobago	1.3	10.2	10,390	5	29.4
Tunisia	9.8	24.3	6,850	164	26.8
Turkey	71.3	238.0	6,710	779	26.3
Turkmenistan	4.9	6.0	5,860	488	23.3
Uganda	25.8	6.2	1,430	241	14.8
Ukraine	48.5	49.5	5,430	604	39.0
United Arab Emirates	3.0	71.0[b]	20,920[b]	84	29.0
United Kingdom	59.3	1,794.9	27,690	243	39.0
United States	294.0	10,881.6	37,750	9,373	36.1
Uruguay	3.4	11.2	7,980	176	32.1
Uzbekistan	26.1	9.9	1,720	447	22.6
Venezuela	25.7	84.8	4,750	912	24.7
Vietnam	81.4	39.2	2,490	331	24.9
Virgin Islands	0.1	2.5[ab]	17,200[ab]	0.4	35.0
West Bank and Gaza	3.6	3.5	1,110[a]	6	17.1
Yemen	20.0	10.8	820	528	16.5
Zambia	10.8	4.3	850	753	16.7
Zimbabwe	12.9	17.8[b]	2,180[b]	391	18.7
Euro area (12)	306.4	8,174.7	26,370	2,497	40.6
World	6,464.0	36,330.0	8,220	148,698	28.1

a Estimate.
b Latest available year.
c Including French Guiana, Guadeloupe, Martinique and Réunion.
d Populations less than 50,000.

Sources

Airports Council International, *Worldwide Airport Traffic Report*

BP, *Statistical Review of World Energy*

British Mountaineering Council

CB Richard Ellis, *Global Market Rents*

Central Intelligence Agency, *The World Factbook*

Centre for International Earth Science Information Network, Columbia University

Commission for Distilled Spirits, *World Drink Trends*

Confederation of Swedish Enterprise

Corporate Resources Group, *Quality of Living Report*

Council of Europe

Economist Intelligence Unit, *Cost of Living Survey; Country Forecasts; Country Reports; Global Outlook – Business Environment Rankings; Quality of Life index*

ERC Statistics International, *World Cigarette Report*

Euromonitor, *International Marketing Data and Statistics; European Marketing Data and Statistics*

Europa Publications, *The Europa World Yearbook*

Eurostat, *Statistics in Focus*

FAO, *FAOSTAT database; State of the World's Forests*

Financial Times Business Information, *The Banker*

The Heritage Foundation, *Index of Economic Freedom*

IMD, *World Competitiveness Yearbook*

IMF, *Direction of Trade; International Financial Statistics; World Economic Outlook*

International Cocoa Organisation, *Quarterly Bulletin of Cocoa Statistics*

International Coffee Organisation

International Cotton Advisory Committee, *Bulletin*

International Road Federation, *World Road Statistics*

International Rubber Study Group, *Rubber Statistical Bulletin*

International Federation of the Phonographic Industry

International Grains Council, *The Grain Market Report*

International Obesity Task Force

International Sugar Organisation, *Sugar Yearbook*

International Tea Committee, *Annual Bulletin of Statistics*

International Telecommunication Union, *ITU Indicators*

ISTA Mielke, *Oil World*

Johnson Matthey

Lloyd's Register, *World Fleet Statistics*

Mercer Human Resource Consulting

National statistics offices

Network Wizards
Nobel Foundation
NOP World Culture Score Media
   Habits Index

OECD, *Development Assistance
   Committee Report;
   Environmental Data; Main
   Economic Indicators*

Space.com
Standard & Poor's *Emerging
   Stock Markets Factbook*
Swiss Re, *sigma*

Taiwan Statistical Data Book
The Times, *Atlas of the World*
Time Inc Magazines, *Fortune
   International*
Transparency International

UN, *Demographic Yearbook;
   Global Refugee Trends; State
   of World Population Report;
   Statistical Chart on World
   Families; Survey on Crime
   Trends; World Contraceptive
   Use; World Population; World
   Population Prospects; World
   Urbanisation Prospects*
UNCTAD, *World Investment
   Report*
UN Development Programme,
   Human Development Report
UNESCO, website: unescostat.
   unesco.org
Union Internationale des
   Chemins de Fer, *Statistiques
   Internationales des Chemins
   de Fer*

US Census Bureau
US Department of Agriculture,
   Rice Report
University of Michigan,
   Windows to the Universe
   website

WHO, *Health Behaviour in
   School-aged Children;
   Mortality Database; Weekly
   Epidemiological Record;
   World Health Statistics
   Annual; World Report on
   Violence and Health*
The Woolmark Company
World Bank, *Doing Business;
   Global Development Finance;
   World Development
   Indicators; World
   Development Report*
World Bureau of Metal
   Statistics, *World Metal
   Statistics*
World Economic
   Forum/Harvard University,
   *Global Competitiveness
   Yearbook*
World Resources Institute,
   World Resources
World Tourist Organisation,
   Yearbook of Tourism Statistics
World Trade Organisation,
   Annual Report
World Water Council
World Wide Fund for Nature